LOUVRE

LOUVRE

the collections

Réunion
des Musées
Nationaux

Texts by:
Daniel Alcouffe
Pierre Amiet
François Baratte
Sophie Baratte
Lizzie Boubli
Geneviève Bresc-Bautier
Annie Caubet
Maguy Charritat
Dominique Cordellier
Anne Dion
Jannic Durand
Pierre Ennes
Jacques Foucart
Elisabeth Foucart-Walter
Danielle Gaborit-Chopin
Pierrette Jean-Richard
Michel Laclotte
Amaury Lefébure
Jean-François Méjanes
Régis Michel
Alain Pasquier
Geneviève Pierrat
Marie-Hélène Rutschowskaya
Marie-Catherine Sahut
Arlette Sérullaz
Emmanuel Starcky
Hélène Toussaint
Françoise Viatte

Co-ordination:
Geneviève Bresc-Bautier

Layout: *Grapus 89.*
Pierre Bernard,
Anne-Marie Latrémolière

Translation:
Bridget Strevens Romer

ISBN : 2-7118-2489-6 (English edition)
© Editions de la Réunion des musées nationaux, 1991
49, rue Etienne-Marcel, 75001 Paris

Contents

6   Preface

8   History of the Louvre

32   Oriental Antiquities

86   Egyptian Antiquities

144   Greek Etruscan and Roman Antiquities

210   Decorative Arts

280   Sculpture

348   Painting

446   Drawing

471   Index of artists

476   List of contributors

There are many ways of visiting the Louvre.
Those with little time to spare are anxious not to
miss the major landmarks, the "star" works
known from imitations and reproductions all over
the world; the *Mona Lisa* first and foremost, along
with the *Vénus de Milo* and the *Victory of
Samothrace,* as well as a few other works such as
Michelangelo's *Slaves*, the *Consecration of Napoleon*
by David, *Liberty leading the People* by Delacroix
and the Egyptian *Scribe*. It is quite another matter
for anyone studying a particular period, artist or
technique; much time has to be spent in front of
the works and many visits are required. Between
the tourist pressed for time at the one extreme and
the indefatigable specialist at the other, there is
room for every kind of attentive visitor, the visitor
who is curious or enthusiastic; the artist, art lover,
or simple sightseer keen to familiarize themselves
with how our building works so as to get the most
out of visits made at their leisure. This book is
designed with them in mind. For their benefit, the
most significant works in each of the seven
departments have been selected from thousands
more which they may discover for themselves and
may quite possibly prefer.
There is a good reason why this is not a room-by-
room guide like others of its kind. The Louvre is
currently undergoing long-term and thorough
reorganisation. The decision to incorporate the
north wing of the Louvre buildings into the
museum and to create a spacious entrance under
the *Cour Napoleon* marked by the pyramid has
made the complete transformation of the museum
possible, with general redistribution of the
collections across the whole palace. The advantages
are obvious. The public will be given a better
reception, there will be a more logical progression
to the tour of rooms and lastly, most important
of all, works of art will be displayed more
advantageously. Certain sections can already be
seen in their definitive state: the medieval castle of
the Louvre, the ground floor rooms of Greek,

Etruscan and Roman Antiquities (Denon), certain rooms housing French Painting on the second floor of the *Cour Carrée* (Sully) and the galleries exhibiting large paintings from David to Delacroix on the first floor (Denon). Exhibition space was doubled in 1993, bicentenary year for the museum, with the opening of the Richelieu wing, the former Ministry of Finance. It houses the Arts of Islam and part of the Oriental Antiquities section — around the courtyard devoted to the Assyrian Palace of Khorsabad — French sculpture, Decorative Arts (from the Middle Ages to the 17th century), painting from the Northern schools (Flanders, Holland, Germany and England) and the beginning of the French painting circuit that extends into the rooms around the *Cour Carrée*. The sumptuous reception rooms of Napoleon III's former Ministry of State may also be visited. The plans for modernisation and total redistribution of the collections are thus gradually taking shape. The new rooms for European sculpture outside France will soon be opened in the Denon wing, followed by those dedicated to Egyptian Antiquities and Ancient Greece, while preparations are underway for a revised presentation of Italian painting, Greek ceramics, the continuation of the Oriental Antiquities section and 18th century Decorative Arts. A scheme for grouping together late works from the three departments of Antiquities is being studied. The transformation of the Louvre is thus advancing stage by stage.

Michel Laclotte

Director of the Musée du Louvre

History the Louvre

From Fortress to Museum

The reputation of the Louvre as one of the greatest museums tends to obscure the fact that it is also the largest palace in the world; its evolution from medieval times bears the mark of every epoch of French history. Originally a fortress (the word *Louvre* derives from the Saxon term *lowar* which means fortified castle), it was a royal residence, then a museum which also housed state offices, and now at last it is wholly given over to displaying the French national collections.

It was at the close of the 12th century that Philippe Auguste decided to erect fortifications alongside the Paris ramparts in accordance with the latest principles of military architecture: a dungeon flanked by towers which was called the Louvre. For two centuries it served not only as a stronghold but as an arsenal and prison. When, in the 14th century, the erudite and ostentatious Charles V established a royal residence there, sumptuous apartments were installed which housed the Court sovereign's treasures and magnificent library. After he died, the Court abandoned the Louvre to its original role as a fortress until the time of François I. Much taken with novelty, the latter set about its demolition, building a Renaissance-style palace in its place. From then on, as years went by, successive monarchs made their contribution to the building that we know today.

All the stages of this evolution are visible. Recent excavations revealed the foundations of the old medieval fortress. We can see the style of the Renaissance in the West façades of the *Cour Carrée* and the long gallery which follows the river, planned by Catherine de Médicis to link her palace of the Tuileries, and built under Henri IV. The last medieval vestiges disappeared under Louis XIII and building according to the principles of the *Cour Carrée* was continued and completed under Louis XIV who decided to build the monumental state colonnade on the other side of its Eastern façade.

Succeeding governments never completely

neglected the Louvre, and each one left its mark. Yet it was not until the Second Empire that work on a large scale began again and the "great plan" of former monarchs was finally realized. The wings bordered by the rue de Rivoli completed the *Cour Napoléon* which took on, with its heavy ornamentation, the appearance it retains today. Napoléon III also carried out some important changes to the interior of the palace, and in particular extended the gallery space of the museum. The latter came into being under the Revolution; the *Museum* of 1793 was its embryonic form, but it was Bonaparte, as founder of the *Musée Napoléon*, who set things in motion; the spoils of war from his Italian campaigns were housed alongside the old royal collections. For two centuries thereafter the fame of the museum never ceased to grow.

Our own times have made their mark, further increasing the prestige of the Louvre with the "recreation" of the *Cour Napoléon* dominated by the Pyramid surrounded by fountains. The museum is now benefitting from a sizeable extension into those parts of the palace vacated by the Ministry of Finance.

But illustrations can give a better idea of the long and rich elaboration across the centuries of what is now known as the Grand Louvre.

The Medieval Castle of Philippe Auguste and Charles V

12th to 14th century

The excavations carried out in 1983 constituted a cultural event of major importance in uncovering the foundations of the old dungeon - 32 metres high - and its walls, built by Philippe Auguste shortly after 1190, as well as residential buildings constructed around it two hundred years later by Charles V. They cover a surface area equivalent to a quarter that of the *Cour Carrée*, the new floor of which preserves them in a crypt. A walk along the old moat will give the visitor ample evidence of the sturdy construction of these buildings: 7 metres of the original wall remain standing. In 1528, François I razed the great central tower; the last vestiges of the Old Louvre were finally lost to view at the beginning of the reign of Louis XIV in 1660.

detail

MASTER OF
SAINT-GERMAIN-DES-PRÉS
Active in Paris around 1500

Saint-Germain-des-Prés Pietá

Around 1500

Wood Panel. H 0.97 m; W 1.98 m

Seized in the Revolution; entered the Louvre

in 1845. INV 8561

The realistic and detailed landscape in the background of this *Pietá* offers a perfect general view of the entire medieval Louvre as it was in its final days. The development of buildings along the Seine is visible. The two twin towers in the centre

locate the great royal entrance built under
Charles V.

Pierre LESCOT *1510-1571*
Jean GOUJON *Around 1510-1566*

**South-West wing of the
*Cour Carrée***

1548-1553

François I's intention was to gain the support of
the Parisians by living in their midst. He very
quickly modernized the Gothic apartments of the
Louvre, and on the eve of his death, in 1545, was
planning the building of a new palace in the
Italian style. Lescot, the architect, provided plans
for the project which was taken up by Henri II. It
is to him that we owe the core of the present
Louvre. In 1548, Jean Goujon, who already had an
established reputation and was closely associated
with Lescot, undertook the sculpted décor of the
façade. He decorated it with allegories whose
sinuous figures and flying draperies provide one of
the finest examples of the Renaissance style in Paris.

Jean GOUJON
Around 1510-1566

Gallery of the Cariatids

1550

In 1550, Goujon was commissioned by Lescot to build a musicians' gallery in the great hall on the ground floor of the new Henri II wing, known as the "bathroom". The markedly Athenian character of the caryatids holding it up is the subject of some speculation. It is said that Lescot gave the sculptor a plaster model, which has prompted the suggestion that it derived from a classical statue, but there is no formal proof of this. Much restored in the course of time, the gallery underwent certain modifications; the balustrade on top of it now dates from the First Empire.

detail

Louis MÉTEZEAU
1559-1610

Eastern Section of the riverside Gallery

1595-1607

Reviving Catherine de Médicis's original project to build a gallery along the Seine, to lead to her *Palais des Tuileries*, Henri IV commissioned the architect Métézeau to build a first section leading to what is now the entrance of the *Carrousel* opened by Napoléon III. The second section, to the West, was built by Jacques II Androuet du Cerceau. The remaining original section of the *Galerie du bord de l'eau* was partially decorated with sculpture by the Lheureux brothers and heavily restored under the direction of Duban between 1848 and 1850.

Jacques LEMERCIER
c. 1585-1654
Jacques SARAZIN 1592-1660

Pavillon of the "Cour Carrée"
known as the **Sully Pavillon**
Cour Carrée façade

1640

Louis XIII undertook what had possibly been the dream of his predecessors, the squaring of the courtyard around the medieval remains whose destruction he continued. In 1640 Lemercier was put in charge of the site. He built a pavilion which dominated one end of Lescot's palace. Its function was to serve as a link with a symmetrical wing conceived in the same style. Then he added a semi-wing squaring the north side. The *Cour Carrée* was thus begun. The so-called *Pavillon de l'Horloge* was surmounted with a dome similar to that built by Philibert Delorme on the Tuileries palace. It served as a model for the many others which rise above the roofs of the Louvre. The superimposition of pediments held up by twin caryatids sculpted by Sarazin and his team was not generally considered overdone.

Giovanni Francesco ROMANELLI
1610-1662
Michel ANGUIER
1612-1686

Judith and Holophernes

1655-1656
Fresco and stucco.
Decoration commissioned by Anne of Austria; at present forms the ceiling of Salle 5 in Roman Antiquities. INV 20350

Anne of Austria, Queen Regent, installed her summer quarters on the ground floor of the *Petite Galerie*, at right angles to the Seine. The building, erected in 1566, was originally decorated in 1602 by Henri IV. This suite of salons, reorganized under the Consulate to house the collection of Antiquities, retain their splendid frescoed vaulting by the Italian painter Romanelli, which was in keeping with the great vogue for Roman palaces at the time. The sculptor Michel Anguier, assisted by the stucco worker Pietro Sasso, placed their tall figures in gilt stucco between the paintings. Mazarin himself personally supervised the completion of this group designed for the greater glorification of the young Louis XIV, flattering the queen's admiration for the "great women" of history.

Gilles GUERIN
1606-1678

Ceiling of the King's Bedchamber

1654
Ormolu on oak.

In 1654, when his new apartments were being installed in the Louvre, the young Louis XIV commissioned this ceiling for his bedchamber (now the *Salle des sept cheminées*). Over woodwork assembled by Louis Barrois, the sculptor Guérin, assisted by Girardon (1628-1715) at the start of his career, designed this sumptuous décor of honours and trophies in response to the much celebrated ceiling of Henri II's State Room (1556). These two ceilings, which were taken down in 1817, were put up again by Fontaine in 1829, in the galleries of the museum behind the Perrault colonnade.

Charles LE BRUN
1619-1690

Apollo Gallery

Decoration begun in 1661

The long room on the first floor of the *Petite Galerie* underwent many changes, and the uniformity of its sumptuous ornamentation belies the fact that it was carried out over a span of nearly two centuries. Destroyed by a fire in 1661, rebuilt by Le Vau, the king entrusted Le Brun with the supervision of its decoration. The latter began the ceiling paintings, assisted by Monnoyer in the ornamental areas, and by the Marsy brothers and Girardon for the stucco. In 1678, Louis XIV left Paris for Versailles and work was interrupted until the Academy of Painting moved into the building and continued the painting (Taraval, Renou, Lagrenée...) The central section of the vault remained unfinished. It was left to the Second Republic to commission from Delacroix his great painting of *Apollo* (p. 25). The gallery is now given over to the display of treasures, gold and silver plate, jewels and precious stones from the Louvre collection.

Claude PERRAULT *1613-1688*
Louis LE VAU *1612-1670*
Charles LE BRUN *1619-1690*

The Colonnade

Begun in 1667

Louis XIV was responsible for the completion of the eastern wings which closed the *Cour Carrée*. On the other side a ceremonial façade was envisaged alongside a royal square that was never realized. Bernini, who came from Italy, submitted a project that was not accepted. It was Perrault, Le Vau and Le Brun who won the commission with their somewhat austere colonnade; it was a novelty much imitated thereafter. Most of it was built under Louis XIV, but the building was not

completed until 1812. In more recent times André Malraux, as Minister of Culture, wanted a ditch dug the length of the façade and round the pavilions at each end, following Perrault's plan to expose the base of the edifice.

Noel COYPEL
1628-1707

Apollo Crowned by Minerva

1667

Canvas. H 2.14 m; W 1.03 m

Louis XIV Collection. INV 3460

This painting and its counterpart, *Apollo Crowned by Victory,* which fortunately escaped damage in the Tuileries fire in 1871, come from the Louis XIV cabinets in the Tuileries Palace. In their choice of courtly theme, grand composition and rigorous treatment, these works testify to Le Brun's influence over artists, as First Painter to the king.

Hubert ROBERT
1733-1808

Imaginary projection for the Grande Galerie

1796

Canvas. H 1.12 m; W 1.43 m

Acq. 1975. RF 1975-10

In 1776, the Superintendant of Buildings to Louis XVI, Count d'Angiviller, envisaged opening galleries of art works in the Louvre to the public. He very soon involved Robert in his project, calling him "guard" of paintings (we would say curator). When the Central Museum of Arts was founded in 1793 by the Convention, Robert retained this position until 1803, barring a slight eclipse during the Terror. It is scarcely surprising that the interior design of what was to become such a great museum should have obsessed him. With this in mind he turned his elegant brush to painting numerous views of the Louvre, some of them realist *(La salle des Saisons),* some imaginary, like this *Grande Galerie,* in which he reflected, as a technician, on questions of lighting and the distribution of hanging space.

Hubert ROBERT

1733-1808

The *Salle des Saisons*

1802-1803

Canvas. H 0.38 m; W 0.46 m

Acq. 1964. RF 1964-35

An examination of the statues shown in the painting, and of the inventories, shows that this painting was executed in 1802-1803, when the new Museum of Antiquities opened.

Alexandre Evariste FRAGONARD

1780-1850

Boissy d'Anglas bowing to the head of Deputy Féraud (sketch)

1830

Canvas. H 0.71 m; W 1.04 m

Acq. 1984. RF 1984-19

The Tuileries Palace was also the theatre of some of the most notorious scenes of the Revolution of 1789, even though we possess few images of them. This painting, executed in 1830, records a striking episode: the assassination of Deputy Féraud by the rioters of Prairial Year III (20 May 1795), who presented his head on the end of a spear to Boissy d'Anglas, President of the National Convention, which held sessions in a room of the Tuileries Palace.

Percier and Fontaine Rooms

At the request of Napoleon, the architects Percier and Fontaine enlarged the staircase to the first floor of the Museum which had been built by Soufflot. The architects took particular care over the design and embellishment of the landing, a long hall leading into the *Salon Carré*; the columns are of marble, and goldwork surrounds ceiling frescoes by Charles Meynier (1768-1832). The inauguration of the ensemble took place at the opening of the 1812 Salon. When the staircase was suppressed, under the Second Empire, to make way for the Daru staircase (p. 28), the old landing, retaining its decoration, became the Percier and Fontaine rooms.

Lorenzo BARTOLINI
1778-1850

Monumental Bust of Napoleon I

1805

Bronze. H 1.55 m; W 0.91 m; D 0.76 m

State Commission. MR 3327

In 1803 the *Musée Napoléon* was opened, so named in honour of the First Consul. But it was only in 1805 that its majestic entrance, now suppressed, was crowned by this monumental bust of Bonaparte as Emperor. He is laurelled in the Roman style. The work is one of the masterpieces of the Florentine sculptor Bartolini, who returned to his native country soon after executing this bronze.

Charles PERCIER *1764-1868*
Pierre FONTAINE *1762-1853*

Triumphal Arch of the Carrousel

1806-1808

The architects Percier and Fontaine built the arch as a grand entrance to the Cour du Carrousel leading to the Tuileries Palace. It is decorated with statues by diverse hands, featuring eight soldiers of the *Grande Armée*, and reliefs depicting Napoleonic victories. In 1809, it served as a pedestal for the famous horses of Saint Mark - spoils from the Italian campaigns - which were given back to Venice under the Restoration. Bosio provided a substitute Quadriga. The arch is shown here in a painting by Bellangé (1862).

François HEIM
1787-1865

Charles X awarding prizes to artists at the 1824 Salon

1827 Salon

Canvas. H 1.73 m; W 2.56 m

State Commission, 1825. INV 5313

The first Academy Salons were held in the Louvre in the 17th century at irregular intervals and to

23

mixed fortune. In the next century the exhibition grew considerably to become by the 19th century an event of major cultural importance. The painting shows King Charles X congratulating the artists of the 1824 Salon which took place in the *Salon Carré* and was memorable because it marked the emergence of Romanticism in France with, notably, *The Massacre of Chios* by Delacroix.

Pierre FONTAINE
1762-1833

Musée Charles X

Opened in 1827

New rooms known as the *Musée Charles X* located on the first floor of the Southern wing of the *Cour Carrée* were opened to coincide with the Salon. Fontaine the architect decorated the museum sumptuously using pink marbles, white stucco and gold for the pilaster capitals. Nine ceilings were commissioned from different painters, the most famous being *The Apotheosis of Homer* by Ingres. The eighth room is shown here (Salle H) with a ceiling by François Heim (1787-1868). Today, the *Musée Charles X* houses the Egyptian collections.

François BIARD
1798-1882

Four o'clock at the Salon "Closing time"

1847 Salon

Canvas. H 0.57 m; L 0.67 m

Gift of Mortimer Schiff, 1921. RF 2347

In this light-hearted painting Biard depicts one of the last Salons to be held in the Louvre, that of 1847.

Felix DUBAN
1797-1870
Pierre Charles SIMART
1806-1858

Vault of the *Salon Carré*

1850-1851
Stucco

On taking up his post - after the 1848 Revolution - as the New Director of Museums, Jeanron undertook some major building restoration in the Louvre. The vault of the *Salon Carré* was urgently in need of repair. Duban, architect at the Louvre, entrusted Simart with the execution of stuccoes, picked out in gold, of allegorical subjects treated in a taste which heralds the composite style of the Second Empire. The monogram RF - for the Second Republic appeared for the first time in a Louvre decoration. The room was opened in June 1851 by the Prince-President.

Eugène DELACROIX
1798-1863

Apollo Slayer of Python, the Serpent

1850-1851
Canvas mounted on the vault. H 8 m; W 7.50 m
State Commission, 1848. INV 3818

In 1848, Jeanron, who was the appointed director of the Louvre under the new régime, asked Delacroix to decorate the central section of the ceiling of the *Petite Galerie* which had remained unfinished. Earlier, Le Brun had proposed a subject treating Apollo, and Delacroix adopted the idea, producing one of his most brilliant compositions in a dazzle of colour inspired by Rubens.

Ange TISSIER
1814-1876

The Architect Visconti
presenting the Plans
for the New Louvre
to Napoleon III
and the Empress Eugenie

1866 Salon

Canvas. H 1.78 m; W 2.30 m

Acq. 1866. MV 5435

The "Grand Design" of earlier kings finally came
to fruition under the Second Empire. Napoleon III
swept away the last of the private houses which
cluttered the space between the Louvre and the
Tuileries Palace, now entirely closed off by the
construction of the wing which later became the
Ministry of Finance. The architect Visconti
constructed large museum buildings parallel to the
Galerie du Bord de l'Eau - The Denon, Daru and
Mollien Rooms. Lefuel carried on the work of
Visconti, redoing Androuet's section of the *Grande
Galerie* in addition to the *Pavillon de Flore* which
was in danger of collapsing. The picture shows
Visconti explaining his plans to Napoléon and
Eugénie.

Jean-Baptiste CARPEAUX
1827-1875

The Triumph of Flora

1864

Terracotta. H 1.37 m; W 1.80 m; D 0.79 m

Gift of Dollfuss 1912. RF 1543

Having rebuilt the *Pavillon de Flore*, Lefuel
commissioned a sculpture from Carpeaux for the
pediment facing the Seine. The artist chose Flora,
thereby illustrating the name of the building. It is

difficult to admire this work today - which Théophile Gautier described as "more alive than life itself" - because of its awkward position. Fortunately, preparatory sketches and models exist *(Musée d'Orsay)* which are more accessible.

View of the Duc de Morny's Apartments

The Count, later Duke, of Morny (1811-1865), illegitimate son of Queen Hortense and thus the half-brother of Napoléon III, became a figure of considerable importance during the latter's reign. He was honoured with an apartment in the Louvre, in the newly built north wing. Some of the rooms, which fortunately survived the Commune fire, provide a remarkable example of décor and furnishings in the Second Empire style. These rooms, which for a long time were part of the Ministry of Finance, will be one of the major attractions of the *Musée du Grand Louvre* when it occupies the entire palace.

Giuseppe DE NITTIS
1846-1884

**The Carrousel
Ruins of the Tuileries**

1882

Wood. H 0.45 m; W 0.60 m

Acq. 1883. RF 372

The ruins of the Tuileries, burned during the revolutionary days of the Commune in 1871, remained standing for a long time. They were finally cleared at the end of the century when the restoration of the *Pavillons Flore* and *Marsan* was begun in preparation for the Universal Exhibition of 1900. This painting by De Nittis shows the *Carrousel* as it was before restoration work was begun.

Stairs of the Winged Victory of Samothrace

Napoléon III asked Hector Lefuel to design a monumental stairway leading to the rooms in the new wing by Visconti parallel to the *Grande Galerie*. The work was still unfinished in 1870, and remained so until 1883 when the idea of installing the *Winged Victory of Samothrace*, recently brought from Greece, was conceived in a attempt to complete the project. Several schemes for the decoration were put forward - mosaics, frescoes - and were begun and dropped to general dissatisfaction. The decision was finally taken to remove all this heterogeneous ornamentation, and in 1934 the stairway took on its present form.

Georges BRAQUE
1882-1963

The Birds
1953
Canvas. H 3.47 m; L 5.01 m
State Commission, 1953. INV 20378

The so-called Etruscan Room - formerly Henri II's antechamber - still has the carved Renaissance ceiling he commissioned. Three medallions were left as spaces for paintings. Under the Restoration, Joseph-Merry Blondel provided three canvasses for them, of no great merit. In 1953, they were replaced with three works commissioned from Braque. They are the only contribution by a 20th century master to the interior decoration of the Louvre.

Ieoh Ming PEI
born in 1917

The *Cour Napoléon* Pyramid

In 1984, the American architect of Chinese origin,
Ieoh Ming Peï, submitted his plan for a *Grand
Louvre* which would occupy the entire palace. This
has entailed a complete reorganization, not only
of the collections themselves but of their allocation
and the means of access to them. But the most
spectacular aspect is the transformation of the
great courtyard. In the centre of it a glass and
metal pyramid was officially opened in
October 1988. Thanks to many careful calculations,
its structure fits in harmoniously with the
surrounding architecture.

Mesopotamia

Iran

Levant

Islam

Oriental Antiquities

Introduction

The ancient Orient covered a vast geographical area, united only once under the Persian Empire and stretching from the Indus to the Mediterranean. For a long time the only knowledge of the Near and Middle East came from Biblical accounts and Greek and Latin travellers and historians. Having fallen into almost complete oblivion, their civilization was brought to light during the 19th century thanks to archeological research carried out by Europeans anxious to learn about the roots of their own civilization. This research was begun in 1842, when Paul-Emile Botta, French Consul in Mosul - now in Northern Iraq - determined to unearth what were supposed to be the vestiges of ancient Nineveh. Thus it was at Khorsabad, in March 1843, that the palace of Sargon II of Assyria was discovered, decorated with colossal sculptures. A selection of these was immediately sent to France and housed in the Louvre in the "Department of Antiquities". Thirty years later another diplomat, Ernest de Sarzec, discovered in southern Mesopotamia, on the site of Tello, traces of the much older civilization of Sumer, the very name of which had been forgotten.This discovery prompted the creation of the Department of Oriental Antiquities in 1881, which functioned from then on as an institution closely linked to archeological research and in consequence exhibited not just the works of art but all the remnants that form the archeological context of ancient civilizations. At the same time, other scholars explored the countries of the Levant in search of "Judaic" antiquities, and in 1860 Napoléon III appointed Ernest Renan to head an archeological expedition there. In this way the first collection with Phoenician elements came into being. 1884 saw the start of excavation work on the palace of Darius at Susa, originally located by an English expedition. The site, which was the capital of the kingdom of Elam, before being that of the Persians, is in western Iran. Exploration of this site, from 1896 down to our own times, yielded up a unique series of masterpieces from the Babylonian civilization, brought home as spoils of war by the Elamites in the 12th century BC. These prestigious antiquities were found alongside remnants of the Elamite civilisation, and were exhibited at the Louvre in their entirety, thanks to a special treaty ceding them to France.

After 1918, France was granted a mandate by the League of Nations over the states of the Levant, Syria and Lebanon; it organized the research and conservation of antiquities which was shared between the Louvre and local museums. Two large sites in particular - both still being worked - have yielded collections of primary importance; Ras Shamra, formerly Ugarit, (Schaeffer Expedition) from 1929, and Mari (Parrot Expedition) from 1933. From the start, acquisitions and gifts have complemented the series assembled from regular digs. Since the Second World War, the Department of Oriental Antiquities has been enriched mainly in this way, with collections made in the past by enlightened amateurs such as Louis De Clercq and, more recently, David-Weill. Antiquities that had once been dispersed were thus saved for the purposes of research to which the department is devoted.

Since its reorganisation by André Parrot in 1947, the collections are divided between three great cultural and geographical unities: Mesopotamia, of great historical significance since it was from there that writing was first and most broadly disseminated; Iran and the Levant. The periods which follow the Islamic conquest of these regions are presented in a special section of the department devoted to the arts of Islam.

Mesopotamia

The rich plain of modern-day Iraq, irrigated by the Tigris and the Euphrates, saw the development of the oldest urban civilizations following a long period when the principle of irrigation was steadily mastered in agriculture. The Sumerians created their civilization, characterized by the invention of writing, within the framework of City-States governed by Priest-Kings. Emerging during the fourth millennium, this civilization developed throughout the long period of archaic dynasties during the third. We know about the Lagash dynasty from antiquities discovered at Tello, the ancient town of Girsu. The same civilization is represented at Mari, a Semite city of the Middle Euphrates. Around 2340, King Sargon, of the Semite dynasty of Akkad, founded an expansionist empire which annexed the old cities of Sumerian style. He sponsored an art glorifying royalty and royal victory; the masterpiece in this genre is the stele of his grandson Narâm-Sin [10].

After the fall of this empire, the Sumerian prince Gudea of Lagash was patron of the so-called neo-Sumerian renaissance, illustrated by the series of statues discovered at Tello from 1877 on [11,12]. The kings of Ur were next to develop this renaissance creating in their turn a great empire. The destruction of the latter, around 2000 BC, practically marks the end of the Sumerian people; their archaic language was maintained from then on only for religious and esoteric purposes.

The Amorites, Semite nomads from the west, invaded the country and adopted its civilization, founding a series of kingdoms. Babylon was one of them, and it re-unified Mesopotamia under the great Hammurabi in the eighteenth century BC. Another Amorite dynasty transformed Assyria into a great commercial power.

The First Babylonian dynasty, destroyed at the beginning of the sixteenth century BC, was replaced by that of the Kassites from Iran, over a long period which is often obscure. The Kassites were conquered by the kings of Elam who razed

Babylonia and carried away the immense spoils discovered at Susa by the *Delegation to Persia*. After a dark age marked by the invasions of Aramaean nomads, the Assyrians arose again and subjugated the entire Orient from the 9th to the end of the 7th centuries. Finally, the Chaldean kings of Babylon conquered the Assyrians and were patrons to a latter-day renaissance: Nebuchadnezzar II restored Babylon in grandiose style, with glazed-brick decoration, and completed the famous Tower of Babel, the ancient description of which is in the Louvre.

¹ **Neolithic Statuette**

Tell es-Sawwan (Middle Tigris)
Beginning of the 6th Millenium BC

Alabaster. H 5.4 cm

Loan from the Museum of Baghdad, 1981. DAO 33

This example from the oldest Mesopotamian statuary was found by Iraqi archeologists in a tomb that antedates the use of clay pottery. It comes from a village whose inhabitants had just mastered the principle of irrigation.
The forms in general and especially the face are deliberately simplified, reflecting a fear of human realism which characterizes the Neolithic civilizations in the Orient.

2 Sumerian Priest-King

Southern Mesopotamia
Uruk period around 3300 BC
Statuette, calcareous. H 0.25 m
Early Bequest. AO 5718

The creation of the first properly administered states, which preceded the historical states of Sumer, stimulated the creation of writing in the metropolis of Uruk which gave its name to the corresponding period. This epoch was marked by a cultural "revolution" which led to the elaboration of the classic forms of Oriental art; sculpture in the round, bas-relief, etc., and archaic forms of art such as highly stylized vase painting were abandoned. The new art had realism, crude enough in the beginning, as its ideal. The priest-kings of each city-state, recognisable from their headbands and beards, are the ancestors of the historical Sumerian kings who were called upon to play the role of gods to whom human form was attributed.

3 Prince Ginak

Mesopotamia
Early phase of the Early
Dynastic period
Around 2700 BC
Gypsum. H 0.260 m; W 0.108 m
Gift of Friends of the Louvre, 1951. AO 20146

The period of the first semi-legendary dynasties recorded in Sumerian literature, saw the development of a new art, and particularly of votive statuettes designed to perpetuate the ritual prayers offered by all classes of men and women, on an egalitarian basis, in the temples. To begin with, this art affected an angular, geometric stylization deliberately removed from realism, with a striking idealization of human forms. The figure of Ginak, prince (in Sumerian: *ensi*) from an unknown city-state, is representative of this archaic art.

4 War-Mace of Mesalim

Tello, formerly Girsu
Around 2600 BC

Limestone. H 0.19 m; ⌀ 0.16 m

Gift of Sultan Abd-ul Hamid, 1986. AO 2349

Like the antiquities which follow, this one was found by Ernest de Sarzec at Tello.It is a votive weapon bearing a Sumerian inscription which puts it among the most ancient of historical documents. It was dedicated by Mesalim, king of the Semite town of Kish to the north of Sumer, and presented later as the arbiter of wars between the Sumerian states. The mace is decorated in an archaic style with the "arms" of the Sumerian state of Lagash.There is a lion-headed eagle, personifying the thunder-cloud, dominating other lions which form a circle around the mace. The eagle, called Anzu, personified the realm of the thundercloud god, Ningirsu, the patron divinity of Lagash.

5 Urnanshe Relief
King of Lagash

Tello, formerly Girsu
Around 2500 BC

Limestone. H 0.40 m; W 0.47 m

E de Sarzec Excavations, 1888. AO 2344

Founder of the dynasty which reigned for nearly two centuries over Lagash, King Urnanshe liked to commemorate his constructions. He had himself portrayed as a simple bricklayer, carrying the brick basket in front of his family, then seated at table. He wears the fur skirt - the so-called *kaunakès* - with its traditional, angular tongue-shaped hangings. The inscription names each member of his family, then lists the main temples built under his supervision.

side A

⁶ The Stele of the Vultures

Tello, formerly Girsu
Around 2450 BC

Limestone. H 1.80 m; W 1.30 m

E de Sarzec Excavations. AO 50, 2346, 2347, 2348, 16109

This badly damaged stele carries a long Sumerian text which is the oldest known page of history, relating the struggles between the state of Lagash and its neighbours during the reign of Eannatum, grandson of Urnanshe and his predecessors. His victories are illustrated on both sides, in register form.

Side A

The king in the role of his god Ningirsu has captured his enemies in a great net; the same symbolism is found in the Bible (Ezekiel, 12, 13; Luke, 21, 35).
The king renders thanks for his victory to his goddess, of whom nothing remains but her head, recognizable by her horned tiara.

Side B

At the top, the vultures which tear at the bodies of the enemy gave the stele its name. Below, wearing the warrior's wig-headress, the king leads the heavy infantry which tramples the enemy corpses. Next, in his chariot, he leads his light infantry in the charge. Finally, at the bottom of the stele, the burial of the dead and a funerary sacrifice are depicted.

side B

7 Vase of Entemena
Prince of Lagash

Tello, formerly Girsu
Around 2400 BC

Silver and Copper. H 0.35 m; W 0.18 m

E de Sarzec Excavations. Gift of the Sultan Abd-ul

Hamid, 1896. AO 2674

Entemena, nephew and second successor to
Eannatum, bore only the title "prince" or
"governor", *ensi* instead of king. He dedicated this
vase as part of Ningirsu's "table service", patron-
god of Lagash. The engraving depicts the lion-
headed eagle, repeated four times, dominating
various animals. Entemena was patron to a major
literary flowering. One of his historical texts treats
of the *liberty* given to his people; another, of the
fraternity, which refers to the alliance he struck
with the king of Uruk.

Mesopotamia   **Oriental Antiquities**

8 Ebih-Il, the Superintendent of Mari

Mari, (Middle Euphrates): Temple
of Ishtar
Around 2400 BC

Statuette, alabaster. H 0.52 m

A Parrot Excavations, 1933-1934. AO 17551

Civilization of the Sumerian type dominated the
whole of Semite Mesopotamia, particularly Mari,
modern day Tell Hariri in Syria, explored from
1934 onwards by André Parrot, and in our own
time by Jean Margueron. Here, statuary developed
rapidly from the middle of the third millennium,
and with a marked originality in comparison with
the South. A cheerful optimism distinguishes it
sharply from the severe expressions connected to
the angular stylization of the preceding epoch,
illustrated by the statuette of Ginak $_3$. The
"superintendent" was in fact more the equivalent
of a Minister of Finance. He had himself
portrayed in the fur skirt which is rendered with

41

remarkable realism revealing the *kaunakès* in the style shown for example on the Urnanshe relief [5].

9 The Mari "Standard" (detail)

Mari (Middle Euphrates),
Temple of Ishtar
Around 2400 BC
Shell and Mosaic.
A Parrot Excavations. AO 19820

This picture was assembled from scattered fragments found in the temple of Ishtar and reconstituted by comparing it with one found intact at Ur. Traditionally known as the "standard", it depicts a victory in a style both freer and more refined than that of the Stele of the Vultures [6]. The conquering dignitaries are protected by large scarves worn over the shoulder and they carry battle-axes. The defeated enemy was driven before them.

10 Victory Stele of Naram-Sin

Susa
Akkad period, around 2230 BC
Pink Sandstone. H 2 m; W 1.05 m
J de Morgan Excavations, 1898. Sb 4

Originally this stele was erected in the town of Sippar, centre of the cult of the Sun god, to the north of Babylon. It was taken as booty to Susa by an Elamite king in the 12th century BC. It illustrates the victory over the mountain people of western Iran by Naram-Sin, 4th king of the Semite dynasty of Akkad, who claimed to be the universal monarch and was deified during his lifetime. He had himself depicted climbing the mountain at the head of his troops. His helmet bears the horns emblematic of divine power. Although it is worn, his face is expressive of the ideal human conqueror, a convention imposed on artists by the monarchy. The king tramples on the

bodies of his enemies at the foot of a peak; above
it the solar disk figures several times, and the king
pays homage to it for his victory.

¹¹ Gudea, Prince of Lagash

South Mesopotamian
Neo-Sumerian period
Around 2150 BC

Statue, diorite. H 0.705 m; W 0.224 m

Acq. 1987. AO 29155

After the fall of the Akkadian Empire, Gudea,
prince of Lagash, instigated a Sumerian

renaissance marked by a literary flowering that corresponded to Sumerian classicism, and also by a courtly art devoted to exalting an ideal of serene piety and of a kind of humanism. This independent prince, who was never king, wears the turban-like headpiece of sovereignty. His youthful face may indicate that the statue was executed at the beginning of his reign.

12 Gudea, Prince of Lagash

Tello, formerly Girsu
Neo-Sumerian period
Around 2150 BC

Head, diorite. H 0.23 m; W 0.11 m

E de Sarzec Excavations, 1881. AO 13

This head, with the prince's headpiece, wrongly taken to be a "turban", was found at Tello at the same time as the votive headless statues inscribed with the name of Gudea and placed in the temples the prince had constructed. These statues were designed to perpetuate the prayers he offered up in them. The expression of confident piety is characteristic of the human ideal that inspired the neo-Sumerian princes at the end of the third millennium.

13 Lady from Tello

Tello, formerly Girsu
Neo-Sumerian period
Around 2150 BC

Statuette, chlorite. H 17 cm; W 9 cm

E de Sarzec Excavations, 1881. AO 295

There is every likelihood that this statuette, dating from an epoch when art was at the service of the monarchy, portrays a princess of Gudea's family. Léon Heuzey, a Hellenist and the first curator of the Department of Oriental Antiquities observed its "resemblance to the Greek type" and added: "There is no doubt that, from this epoch onwards, the progress of taste alone would have brought Chaldean sculpture, by the gradual attenuation of a national type, to a conception very close to that of the Hellenic profile."

¹⁴ Bull with a Man's Head

Tello, formerly Girsu
Neo-Sumerian period
Around 2150 BC
Soapstone. H 0.10 m, W 0.14 m
Acq. 1898. AO 2752

For temple decoration, Gudea and his son commissioned a series of statuettes of the bull with a human head which was designed to hold a little vase of offering. The androcephalus bull was called a *lama*, or "protector god". It personified the Eastern Mountain, from where the sun rises in the morning; as such, it was considered to be the animal-attribute of the sun. The neo-Sumerian artist has succeeded in giving this monster, which personifies a primal entity, a serene expression in keeping with the humanism which animated the whole civilization of that period.

¹⁵ Stele of Gudea

Tello, formerly Girsu
Neo-Sumerian period
Around 2150 BC
Limestone. H 1.25 m; W 0.63 m
E de Sarzec Excavations, 1881. AO 52

In the temples that he built, Gudea erected a series of steles commemorating the ceremonies of the cult, but they were shattered in antiquity. The largest fragment depicts a musician playing a great lyre; its sounding board is supposed to represent a bull, because a text by Gudea explains that the sounds obtained were compared poetically to its bellow.

16 Sacrificial Scene

Mari (Middle Euphrates)
Palace of Zimrilim
First half of the 18 century BC
Wall Painting on dried mud plaster.
H 0.76 m; W 1.325 m
A Parrot Excavations, 1935-1936. AO 19825

The palace that king Zimrilim completed before its destruction by Hammurabi of Babylon was decorated with paintings of ceremonial inspiration. This painting shows a very important person, perhaps the king, dressed in the rich fringed costume, leading the lesser priests who are presenting the bull prepared for the sacrifice. This painting is a good illustration of how Mari belonged as much to the world of the Levant as to Mesopotamia.

17 Temple Guardian Lion

Mari, Temple of Dagan
19th century BC
Bronze with inlay. H 0.38 m; W 0.70 m
A Parrot Excavations, 1936-1937. AO 19824

Dagan was the great god of the Semite Amorites; his temple was built at Mari next to the royal palace by the prince or independent "governor" Ishtup-Ilum. Two lions (the second is in the Museum of Aleppo) stood guard over his door to terrify potential enemies. They are made of bronze plaques nailed originally onto a wooden beam which has since disappeared. Eyes of the same proportions, larger than lifesize, were found nearby and suggest that a "pack" of other wild animals accompanied the two which alone remained in place.

18 Law-Codex of Hammurabi

Susa
First half of the 18th century BC

Basalt. H 2.25 m

J de Morgan Excavations, 1901-1902. Sb 8

Like a series of other remarkable works from the Mesopotamian civilization, this tall stele originally stood in a town of Babylon and was taken as spoil to Susa by the Elamites in the 12th century. It was discovered by the de Morgan expedition and its text was translated in six months by Father Vincent Scheil. Hammurabi was the 6th king of the first Babylonian dynasty, and he was first to establish the supremacy of his city which had been of modest standing only. What he had engraved on this stele is not so much a "code" as a collection of exemplary royal pronouncements in keeping with a tradition established by the Sumerians. The bas-relief at the top is a sober representation of the meeting of king and god. The king wears the royal headpiece like Gudea; he holds his hand before his face in the act of prayer. The sun-god Shamash, patron of justice, is recognizable from the flames flaring on his shoulders. His crown, with its four pairs of horns symbolic of divinity, is indicative of his high rank in the hierarchy of the gods. He holds out but does not offer to the king the rod and the ring, also denoting divine power.

19 Royal Head

Susa
First Babylonian Dynasty:
19th-18th centuries BC
Diorite. H 0.150 m; W 0.125 m
J de Morgan Excavations. Sb 95

Like the stele of the "Code", this head was taken to Susa from a Babylonian city. Often thought to represent Hammurabi, it remains anonymous, although it certainly belonged to a statue of the same epoch, and is stylized according to the ideal image of the king-lawmaker, as opposed to that of the devout prince in the time of Gudea or of the sovereign of the universe in the Akkadian period. This is not therefore a personal portrait but an idealized effigy of the king.

20 Worshipper of Larsa

Larsa (Babylonia)
First half of the 18th century BC
Statuette, bronze and Gold. H 0.19 m; W 0.15 m
Acq. 1932. AO 15704

A dignitary named Awil-Nanna, from the ancient Sumerian city of Larsa, dedicated this little bronze "for the life of Hammurabi", king of Babylon, his sovereign. The dedication to the god Amurru, chief of the Amorite nomads who had adopted

Sumerian civilization, means that the bronze must have been housed in the temple of this god. It is possible that the kneeling figure wearing the royal headpiece is Hammurabi himself. He is depicted in bas-relief on the base, praying to the god in front of whom this object would thus have been placed; his prayer could be perpetuated thanks to an offering placed in the little basin in front.

21 Kudurru of Melishipak

Taken from Babylonia to Susa
Beginning of the 12th century BC
Grey Limestone. H 0.65 m; W 0.30 m
J de Morgan Excavations, 1898-1899. Sb 22

The kings of Babylon from the Kassite dynasty made generous gifts to their vassals. Record of this was, in principle, kept on the boundary posts, the *kudurru* of the lands that had been made over. In actual fact it was inscribed on great slabs, or standing stones, kept in the temples. These lists of donations were placed under the protection of the greatest possible number of gods, most often represented in their symbolic form and arranged according to the hierarchy of the pantheon. However, at the top, are symbols of the three heavenly gods; Sin (moon), Shamash (sun) and Ishtar (Venus), in order of their position in the heavens, rather than their importance. They were surpassed by the supreme triad: Anu (sky), Enlil (air) symbolized by their horned crowns and Ea (fresh water from the abyss), symbolized by a kind of sceptre carried by a goat-fish. Below we find the emblems of several other gods; that of Marduk, patron-god of Babylon, is identifiable as a pointed hoe placed on a stand and the serpent-dragon which guards the underworld of the god. The same dragon carries the scribe's stylet, which is the emblem of Nabu, Marduk's son. These emblems were difficult to interpret, even for the ancients who sometimes inscribed the name of the gods symbolized next to the symbols themselves.

22 Neo-Babylonian Kudurru

Uruk (Southern Babylonia)
Middle of the 9th century BC
Limestone. H 0.32 m; W 0.15 m
Acq. 1914. AO 6694

King Marduk-Zakir-Shumi of Babylon, who benefited from Assyrian protection, gave land and eight houses in the second year of his reign (850 BC) to Ibni-Ishtar, a scribe and priest in the temple of the great goddess Ishtar. This high-ranking dignitary is depicted greeting the king who holds a small bouquet and is smelling its scent. Round about are the symbols of gods, guarantors of the donation. There is the great pointed hoe of Marduk, patron-god of Babylon, the double lightning of Adad the storm god, the ram-headed sceptre of Ea, god of the freshwater deep, and the lamp of Nusku, god of fire.

23 Dragon Head

Babylonia, neo-Babylonian Epoch
First half of the 1st millennium BC
Bronze. H 0.15 m
Acq. 1903. AO 4106

This dragon head belonged to the cult of Marduk, patron-god of Babylon, who was originally a minor god in the pantheon. The monster is linked to the formidable horned serpent which symbolized the underworld from which it emerged. For this reason it was also associated with vegetation, and that is why the god also has a pointed hoe for an emblem.

24 Winged Assyrian Bull

*Khorsabad, palace of Sargon II
of Assyria, 721-705 BC*

Gypsum. H 4.20 m; W 4.36 m

P-E Botta Excavations, 1834-1844. AO 19857

King Sargon II built his palace in the citadel of the
new city he founded near Nineveh, which Paul-
Emile Botta unearthed in 1843. The doors were

guarded by pairs of androcephalus bulls. These bening spirits, known as *lamassu*, guarded the foundations of the world. They performed the same service for the palace. The new presentation in the museum courtyard, known as the Khorsabad courtyard, recalls the monumentality of the Assyrian palaces. It is complemented by a reproduction of a bull, cast from the original preserved in Chicago, the only survivor of its kind. The inscription between its hooves reads: *"Palace of Sargon, great King, powerful king, king of the universe, king of Assyria, razed Urartu... subjugated Samaria, captured Hanon king of Gaza..."* It goes on to relate the building of the town, known as Dur-Sharrukin of Fort-Sargon.

25 Medean Tribute-Bearers

Khorsabad (Assyria)
Palace of Sargon II
721-702 BC
Relief, gypsum. H 1.62 m; W 3.66 m
P-E Botta Excavations, 1843-1844.
AO 19887

The reliefs decorating the interior of the palace of Sargon were smaller than the colossal ones on the outside facades. They were arranged in two columns separated by an inscription describing the king's campaigns. This one shows the Medes in their national costume, surrendering their fortress symbolized by a model, and leading their magnificent horses as tribute. The sculptor is as gifted in rendering animals as he is ethnologically exact.

26 Ashurbanipal in a Chariot

Nineveh, palace of Ashurbanipal
668-630 BC
Relief, gypsum. H 1.62 m; W 0.77 m
Gift of Rawlinson to the Place Expedition.
Entered the Louvre in 1856. AO 19904

Ashurbanipal was the last of the great Assyrian kings; he patronized Assyrian palatial art at its apogee. In its upper columns the relief shown illustrates the deportation of the Elamites after the sack of Susa in 646. Below, the king advances in his chariot. He is sheltered by a parasol, wears the royal tiara and, like the king of Babylon ₂₂, holds a little bouquet which he is sniffing. Behind him, servants wave fly-swats and officials bear the king's arms.

front view   back view

27 Exorcism Plate

Assyria
End of 8th-7th centuries BC
Bronze. H 0.135 m ; W 0.085 m
Gift of H de Boisgelin, 1967. AO 22205

This plate illustrates the rites of exorcism; an explanatory text has come down to us with variants. The doctor's role was to expel demons held to be the cause of diseases. The plate hung above the patient by means of the two rings at the top. It is presided over by the demon Pazuzu, charged with putting the other demons to flight. The decoration is divided into columns: at the top are the symbols of the gods invoked for the cure. Next come the Seven Formidable demons. Below there is the patient on his bed, watched over by two fish-genii - the "Sages" of the Ea retinue, god of wisdom and the deep. Finally, at the bottom, appears the evil goddess Lamashtu who torments the patient. She is carried by a donkey whose duty is to take her back into the desert; the donkey stands on a boat floating on the river of hell. Next to her are jewels and other gifts offered to the goddess to entice her back into the underworld.

Iran

Dominating Eastern Mesopotamia, Iran covers a vast mountainous area, divided into several regions that for a long time remained lost in prehistory, except to the South-west where the kingdom of Elam was an organised, historical entity contemporary with those of Sumer and Babylon. Elam was a dual State consisting of the plain of Susa to the West, and the plateau of present day Fars, with the city of Anshan to the East. Susa was founded around 4000 BC by a population linked to those of the plateau, as its magnificent painted ceramics indicate. They compare with those from Tepe Sialk in the centre of the plateau. Susa was then integrated into Sumerian Mesopotamia during the age of the "urban revolution" and of the first States. The first financial accounts and a refined sculpture make their appearance at this time. Then Susa reintegrated the peoples of the plateau, and the proto-elamite culture was created around 3000 BC. Its writing spread as far as Tepe Sialk and Seistan.

In the third millennium, Susa was again annexed by Mesopotamia and left statues comparable to those in Mari, designed to perpetuate the prayers of the devout in the temples. At the same time, cultures of nomad-artisans developed in the Luristan, to the North of Susiana, with the first decorative bronzes, and to the East, in the province of Kerman, richly ornate vases cut from green stone (chlorite). At the end of the third millennium this civilization, known as the trans-Elamite, spread in a grand sweep to the boundaries of Central Asia, Bactria and as far as the gates of India.

In the second millennium a dual Elamite kingdom was once more established during the age of the "kings of Anshan and Susa", while the trans-Elamite buildings and the necropoli of Luristan were abandoned. Elamite power then reached its apogee. In the 13th century BC, king Untash-Napirisha founded a new capital at Tchoga-Zanbil, not far from Susa. Dominating the site, was a tower with several stories which is remarkably preserved. Then, during the 12th century BC, kings of a very brilliant dynasty seized Babylonia and carried off to Susa as spoils such masterpieces as the stele of Naram-Sin [10], the Hammurabi Code [18], etc., which were found by the de Morgan expedition alongside Elamite masterpieces. At the same time, new peoples, possibly Iranian immigrants, settled in Northern Iran and left a rich hoard of objects in their tombs, including precious vases. Similarly, the nomad civilization of Luristan, dormant since the 18th century, re-emerged around the 12th century and created extraordinary bronzes in the prehistoric tradition which retain their appeal today.

The Elamites experienced a renaissance in the 8th and 7th centuries, before collapsing under the assaults of the Assyrians in 646. The Persians, established among them, adopted this country as their own. Like the Elamite, the Persian empire had two capitals: Persepolis and Susa. Darius built his Apadana palace in the latter with its rich glazed-brick decor discovered between 1884 and

1886 by Dieulafoy. With the fall of the Persian empire to Alexander the Great, Susa lost its importance as a political and cultural centre. Iran gradually became Hellenized, while retaining its originality which flourished under the Sassanid dynasty from the 3rd to the 7th centuries AD.

28 Goblet from Susa I

Susa: archaic necropolis
Around 4000 BC

Terracotta. H 0.285 m; L 0.160 m

J de Morgan Excavations, 1907-1909. Sb 3174

The painted vases left in the tombs of the first Susians illustrate, on the eve of its extinction, the highest point in the neolithic tradition of the mountain people who came down to the plain. The forms are simple and harmonious and the decoration boldly stylized. At the top is a frieze showing wader birds elongated vertically; below, racing dogs elongated horizontally while below them is a large ibex, geometrical in design, whose vast horns describe an almost perfect oval. This stylization is misleadingly reminiscent of pictographic sign language; it has, in fact, a purely decorative function, as its diversity from one vase to another indicates. Along with these vases, the dead were given access to other objects, such as copper axes, imported from central Iran.

29 Female Votary

Susa, Uruk period
Around 3200 BC

Statuette, alabaster. H 6.3 cm; W 3.8 cm

J de Morgan, R de Mecquenem, 1909

Sb 70

The adoption of the Sumerian-type urban
civilization encouraged the Susians to create work
that would become classic. Breaking with the
purely decorative stylization of prehistoric times,
they adopted realism as their ideal. The statuettes
of the devout were carved in this vein; they are
both delicate and full of humour, kneeling under
their dresses in traditional Iranian manner.

30 Archaic Counting-Pieces

Susa, Uruk Period
Around 3400-3300 BC

Light terracotta. ∅ 6.5 cm

R de Mecquenem Excavations. Sb 1927

Obliged to manage the considerable wealth
produced by urban type development, the Susians
created a system of accountancy. They began by
representing numbers with little clay objects rather
like the *calculi* or pebbles used by other ancient
civilizations which are at the origin of our word
calculation. They kept them in hollow clay balls to
avoid their dispersal. The symbolized number
could be represented by notches on the surface of
the round container; the cylindrical seal of the
scribe could be stamped on it as a guarantee of
authenticity. Strictly speaking, these notches are
the first graphic symbols; they were soon
transferred onto little clay slates or "tablets" before
their meaning was made more precise by

conventional signs. The process that led to the invention of writing was thus triggered off by accountancy.

31 Cultic Stand

Susa, Early Dynastic Period Dynasties
Around 2400 BC

Bitumen Mastic. H 0.183 m; ∅ 0.115 m

J de Morgan Excavations. Sb 2725

In the middle of the 3rd millennium, Susa became a city of the Sumerian type, with an acropolis and a temple which housed statuettes of worshippers and cult objects testifying to the originality of local art. In cheap imitation of exotic stone, artificially hardened bitumen was used - of which there was no shortage in this oil-rich country. It was carved into offering stands with crudely stylised animal motifs. The eagle here protecting its brood is less formidable than in Sumeria where it was given a lion's head.

32 Elamite Goddess

Susa, around 2100 BC

Statue, limestone. H 1.09 m

J de Morgan Excavations, 1907. Sb 54

The Prince of Susa, Puzur-Inshushinak, succeeded in creating a dual empire, containing both the

Susian plain with its Semitic language, and the plateau with its Elamite language. He inscribed his monuments in both languages: Semite Akkadian and Elamite written in a new linear writing that has yet to be deciphered. The statue with its bilingual inscription representing the great goddess portrays her as the Mesopotamian Ishtar, enthroned above lions. Her horned tiara is similar to that of divinities at the time of Gudea, prince of Lagash, contemporary with this.

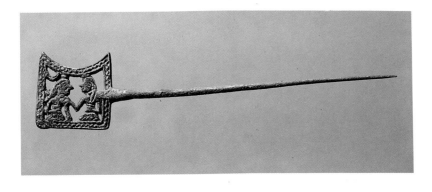

33 Trans-Elamite Pin-head

South-Eastern Iran
Around 2000 BC

Copper. Pin L 24.8 cm

Head H 5.85 cm; W 5.1 cm

Gift of M Foroughi, 1975. AO 26068

Semi-nomadic artisans settled at the Eastern extremities of Iran, beyond Elam, in order to exploit the natural riches of the area. The stonecarvers produced richly decorated chlorite vases and the metalworkers cast real and ceremonial weapons and ornaments like this long pin. The openwork head depicts the intimate conversation of a couple in a dwelling, prefiguring a tradition that was to survive with surprising fidelity in Persian art.

34 Female Statuette

Bactria
Beginning of the 2nd
millennium BC
Chlorite and Limestone. H 0.183 m
Acq. 1969. AO 22918

At the end of the 3rd millennium and the beginning of the 2nd, the trans-Elamite civilization extended beyond Iran to the boundaries of Central Asia, in Bactria (Northern Afghanistan). The items left in tombs dug close to elaborate fortresses included everyday and luxury objects, and reveal a civilization similar to the Elamite. Next to ceremonial axes serving - as in Elam - to denote honours, composite statuettes of women were placed in the tombs. Their "crinoline" dress is similar to that of the queens of Elam. This dress has been given the stylistic treatment of the *kaunakes* from the age of the archaic dynasties.

35 Ibex Cup

Susa, 20th-19th century BC
Bitumen. H 9 cm; L 22 cm
R de Mecquenem Excavations, 1924. Sb 2740

The prosperity that Susa enjoyed at the beginning of the second millennium is evident from the wealth of objects left in tombs. As well as gold and silver jewellery, the dead were supplied with food left in ordinary dishes and in luxury vases carved from bitumen mastic in imitation of exotic stone. This cup is treated as a sculpture; the handle is an ibex head carved in high relief, renewing a tradition founded some thousand years earlier in Mesopotamia. Vases like this, so characteristic of Susian art, were exported to Babylonia in antiquity, where they were highly appreciated.

36 Elamite God

Susa, beginning of the 2nd millennium BC
Copper and Gold. H 17.5 cm; W 5.5 cm
Sb 2823

Susa's cultural dependence on Babylonia remained great at the beginning of the 2nd millennium, even though the town belonged to the Elamite kingdom. Accordingly, the gods were portrayed like those of Mesopotamia, wearing the pleated *kaunakes* dress and the many horned crown which signified divine power. This one differs from Mesopotamian idols because of its smile. One hand retains a layer of the gold plating which originally covered the whole statue.

37 Funerary Head of an Elamite

Susa, 15th-14th centuries BC
Painted unbaked clay. H 0.24 m; W 0.15 m
R de Mecquenem Excavations, 1926. Sb 2836

In the middle of the second millennium, the Susians buried their dead in family vaults under their houses. Next to the head of the deceased, which was probably veiled, they frequently placed a portrait, executed at the moment of death. It is

the only example from the East of a genuinely
funerary art which aims at personal likeness.
This one shows the typical Elamite, with its severe
expression characteristic of a tough population
which had strong links with mountain dwellers.

38 Royal Axe

Tchoga-Zanbil,
formerly Dur-Untash
Around 1250 BC

Silver, Electrum. H 5.9 cm; W 12.5 cm

R Girshman Excavations, 1953. Sb 3973

King Untash-Napirisha of Elam built a religious
capital near Susa, dominated by a storied tower
dedicated to the two patron-gods of the two halves
of the empire, the highlands and the Susian plain.
At its foot, the goddess Kiririsha, wife of the
mountain god, had a richly furnished temple.
Notable among the finds was this axe, bearing the
inscription: "I Untash Napirisha" inscribed on the
blade which issues from a lion's mouth. The
handle is decorated with the figurine of a young
wild boar, harking back to a specifically mountain
tradition, originating in Luristan in the third
millennium.

39 Elamite Worshipper

Susa, 12th century BC

Statuette, gold and bronze. H 7.5 cm; W 2.4 cm

J de Morgan Excavations, 1904. Sb 2758

This statuette, like a similar one in silver, depicts a
devotee in prayer, carrying a kid as an offering to

the divinity. It was designed to perpetuate a ceremonial act in a temple. This one, however, was added to the funerary offerings found in a royal tomb near the temple of Inshushinak, patron god of Susa. It is a fine example of the mastery of Susian metalworkers who were capable of casting a statue of a queen weighing, without the head, 1750 kg.

⁴⁰ Model of an Elamite Cultic Site

Susa, around 1150 BC

Bronze. H 0.60 m; W 0.40 m

J de Morgan Excavations, 1904-1905. Sb 2743

This model carries a dedication from the greatest king of Elam, Shilhak-Inshushinak, who calls it a *Sit Shamshi,* "ceremony of the rising sun". Two naked priests officiate between two temples, next to ritual objects (raised stones, a water basin, a sacred grave) which are similar to those of Canaanite holy places of the same period. The model was not visible: it was enclosed in a block of chalk inserted into the masonry of a tomb.

⁴¹ Vase with Winged Monsters

Marlik Region (Northern Iran)
14th-13th centuries BC

Electrum. H 0.110 m; ⌀ 0.112 m

Acq. 1956. AO 20281

The first Iranian immigrants seem to have settled during the 2nd millennium to the north of the plateau to which they gave their name. Most probably nomads, they buried their dead in cemeteries like the one discovered at Marlik, not far from the village of Amlash. Lacking any artistic tradition, they took inspiration from the art of the old traditions of western Asia in decorating their ornaments. This goblet, made of electrum - a natural alloy of gold and silver - is in a decorative style borrowed from the repertory of the middle empire in northern Mesopotamia: winged monsters with intertwined claws holding animals in their grip.

42 Pin Head from Luristan

Luristan (Western Iran)
8th-7th centuries BC
Bronze. H 0.129 m; L 0.108 m
Gift of P and J David-Weill, 1972. AO 25008

The mountain dwellers of Luristan created from the middle of the 3rd millennium a rich tradition in metalwork which was eclipsed when they became sedentary in the 2nd millennium. The tradition revived with the return to a nomadic way of life from the 12th to the 7th centuries. The mountain bronzeworkers adopted the same shapes as the urbanised peoples of the plains, but stylizing them in a spirit appropriate to nomads who remain on the margins of history. A spirit master-of-animals, descended from prehistoric times, wears the pleated dress - an ancestor of the Persian type - which is here depicted with realism.

43 The Archers of Darius

Susa, around 500 BC
Relief, glazed bricks. H 2 m
M Dieulafoy Excavations, 1884-1886. AOD 488

Darius I (522-486 BC) made Susa his administrative capital, building his palace in the Babylonian

tradition, to which was added a throne room with
columns in the Iranian tradition. The glazed brick
decor of this palace centres on images of the
Persian army. The archers are shown in
ceremonial dress, rather than in fighting gear.
Anxious to depict this pleated dress, in keeping
with the tradition of Luristan, the Susian
enamelers borrowed from the Greek model, but
stylized it in their own inimitable way.

⁴⁴ Persian Vase Handle

5th-6th centuries BC

Silver and Gold. H 0.27 m; L 0.15 m

Former Tyszkiewicz Collection. Acq. 1898.

AO 2748

In all probability, this zoomorphic silver vase handle, partially gold-plated, and its twin in the Berlin Museum belonged to one of those wide-rimmed high-necked amphoras with the fluted ovoid bellies that are shown in the bas-reliefs of Persepolis and of which some examples in bronze or precious metal have come down to us. Like their nomadic ancestors from Northern Iran, the great Persian kings greatly appreciated luxury tableware. Their gold and silversmiths were freely influenced by the art of peoples of the empire. Thus this winged ibex is markedly Iranian, but rests on a mask of Silenus, borrowed from the Ionian Greeks.

⁴⁵ Sassanid Pitcher

Province of Dailaman
(Northern Iran)
6th-7th centuries BC

Silver gilt. H 0.181 m; Ø 0.106 m

Acq. 1966. MAO 426

From the 3rd to the 7th centuries, the Sassanid Empire fostered a brilliant courtly art, reviving a tradition of ornate silverwork which had been important to the early Iranians. Despite a nationalist backlash against the Hellenism of the Parthians, the decoration on these precious vases is often Dionysiac in inspiration, and linked with Indian influences, recognizable in the dancers with their diaphanous veils. The design is in keeping with the atmosphere of drinking parties described by the Persian poets at the dawn of Islam.

Levant

The term "Levant" includes those countries on the Mediterranean side of the Near East, aside from Egypt. Major collections were assembled in the Louvre from the 1850's. They were enriched between the two wars by scientific expeditions, which distributed the antiquities between Paris and the new museums founded at Aleppo, Damascus, Beirut, etc. Since the Second War, archeological finds remain in the country of origin, but the Louvre pursues an active policy of on-site research, sometimes on the very sites which once contributed to the establishment of the museum collections: Mari and Ras Shamra.

Linking the Mediterranean to the Mesopotamian Orient, the Levant connects with Babylonia, beyond the steppe where the nomads dwelt, via the Euphrates valley. The coastal plains, cut off by mountain chains with numerous passes, the course of the Orontes and the Jordan all have very different ecological identities. Doubtless as a result of this geographical fragmentation, the Levant never formed a political entity, and was often a prey to its ambitious neighbours such as the Pharaohs and the 12th dynasty (20th century BC) and the Assyrians (9-7th centuries). From the 7th millennium, small settled communities gradually mastered their environment with livestock breeding and agriculture. These little settlements became cities. During the 4th millennium, agglomerations, or Sumerian-style colonies established themselves along the Euphrates; in the Negev, villages specialized in the extraction of copper invite comparisons with predynastic Egypt (Safadi, near Beersheba).

History begins with the third millennium and the first texts: hieroglyphic names of Pharaohs at Byblos, where the Egyptians came in search of building timber on the mountains of Lebanon, and cuneiform tablets at Ebla or Mari, where the scribes adopted the Mesopotamian system of syllabic writing. The first attempts which led to the invention of the alphabet, perfected by the Phoenicians, were made in the Levant around the middle of the 2nd millennium.

Byblos and Ugarit, city ports and bridgeheads for the commercial routes from the interior towards the Mediterranean prospered; the same is true of Cyprus, Enkomi, Paphos, Kition. Cultural and commercial relations developed with the great neighbouring powers, Egypt, the Hittites and then the Assyrians; these exchanges also extended to the Greek world, from the Mycenaean period (14th century) and throughout the Ist millennium. The Mediterranean of the first millennium was marked by major colonial exploits: white the Greeks settled on the shores of Anatolia, Sicily and Southern Italy, the Phoenicians spread to Cyprus and to the west. The colony of Carthage founded its own satellite towns, in Sardinia, at Ibiza in Spain and all along the Maghrebi coast. There was more contact between Greek settlers and Phoenician and Punic merchants than the Latin historians admit to. The Roman conquest finally united these vast territories into one "mare nostrum".

⁴⁶ Male Statuette

Negev, Chalcolithic Period
3500-3000 BC
Hippopotamus Ivory. H 0.24 m
J Perrot Excavations at Safadi. AO 21406

Carved from a hippopotamus's horn, this schematic image belongs to a set discovered at Safadi, near Beersheba. It is characteristic of the primitive culture of Sinai and the Negev, influenced by pre-Pharaonic Egyptian art. The area around Beersheba developed the exploitation of copper and turquoise mines in the region for trade with Egypt.

Levant   **Oriental Antiquities**

⁴⁷ Seven-Branch chandelier, Palm and Trumpet

Jordan Valley
6th century AD
Synagogue Installation, Basalt. H 0.38 m
Oum Qeis, formerly Gadara.
Gift of F. de Saulcy, 1852. AO 5042

This architectural item, possibly a lintel, is a good illustration of the development and expansion of primitive Judaism in the first centuries of our era.

47 bis Eyed Idol

Northern Syria   Around 3300-3000 BC

Terracotta. H 27 cm

Gift of the *Société des Amis du Louvre* 1991.

AO 3002

These schematic idols are characteristic of the early stages of urban societies which developed in Northern Syria and Anatolia at the dawn of the metal age (Chalcolithic period). Through their extreme schematism, these anthropomorphic figures are comparable with contemporary works from the Cyclades and Troy and illustrate the links that existed between these early metalworking societies, from the Mediterranean to the Persian Gulf: similar idols, though miniature, have been found in regions as distant as Sunna and South-West Iran.

Syria

48 Votive Statuettes

Byblos, 19th-18th centuries BC

Bronze and Gold. H 7 cm

Byblos, Montet excavations.

AO 10945, AO 14678

and seq.

Numerous figurines were given as offerings in the "obelisk temple". This building, notable for the pyramidal steles which were consecrated to it, was dedicated to a storm god, most probably Reshef; it is he who is depicted in these statuettes. They borrow the garment and crown from Egyptian art, while the molten bronze casting covered with gold leaf is a strictly local, Amorite technique.

49 Stele Showing the Storm-God Baal

Ugarit, 14th-13th centuries BC

Sandstone. H 1.42 m

Ras-Shamra, formerly Ugarit.

Schaeffer Excavations. AO 15775

The god is shown brandishing a
mace and a spear, the extremity of
which is tipped with vegetation; this
is an allusion to the beneficial effects
of the rain released by the storm. A
young and popular god, celebrated
in beautiful mythological texts
discovered at Ugarit, Baal is also the
tutelary god the dynasty:
the king of Ugarit is shown in
prayer beneath the arms of Baal. The
style is both attentive to anatomical
detail and nobly hieratic. This stele of Baal is one
of the finest pieces of sculpture that has come
down to us from Oriental antiquity.

50 Gold Plate with Hunting Scene

Ugarit, 14th-12th centuries BC

Gold. ⌀ 0.188 m

Ras-Shamra, formerly Ugarit.

Schaeffer Excavations. AO 17208

Found with another gold-plated dish not far from
Baal's sanctuary at Ugarit, this masterpiece is a
royal offering to the patron-god of the dynasty.
The dish in the Louvre shows the king out
hunting gazelles and wild bulls. The fleeing
animals are shown in the "flying gallop" attitude
which was used by artists from Crete and the
Levant during the Bronze Age. Hunting in
chariots was the royal recreation *par excellence*, as
Egyptian reliefs from the same epoch confirm.

51 Fertility Goddess

Ugarit, 14th-13th centuries BC

Cosmetic Box Cover, elephant ivory.

H 0.137 m

Minet el Beida (port of old Ugarit).

Tomb III. Schaeffer Excavations. AO 11601

This sumptuous cosmetic box, designed for a high-ranking woman, is decorated in a mixed style. The Aegean, or Cretan style of the Ibex woman's dress is combined with an antithetical oriental style of composition and symbolic imagery : a goddess or priestess dominating wild animals. Precious ivory objects like this were common enough property among the rich merchants of Ugarit.

52 Goblet with Human Face

Ugarit, 14th-13th centuries BC

Earthenware. H 0.162 m

Minet el Beida (port of old Ugarit).

Tomb VI. Schaeffer Excavations. AO 15725

Objects like this belonged to women and were connected with fertility rites. The mask of a goddess, in "make-up", is depicted here, similar to the jewel-masks worn round the neck. The style is derived in part from Cretan art, and in part from Oriental and local traditions.

53 Model of a Sanctuary decorated
with Nude Goddesses

Emar, 13th century BC

Terracotta. H 0.44 m

Meskene, formerly Emar on the Euphrates.

Margueron Excavations. AO 27905

Exploration of the city of Emar, capital of a vassal
Hittite kingdom established along the Euphrates,
led to the discovery of a whole urban complex:
palaces, temples and residential quarters yielded a
rich hoard. The existence of household rites is
confirmed by these "models" which were found in
the houses. They possibly served as movable altars,
decorated with symbolic images.

54 Stele of Si Gabbor
Priest of the Moon God

Northern Syria, 7th century BC

Basalt. H 0.95 m

Neirab, Aleppo Region. AO 3027

This monument, which bears an Aramaic epitaph,
is highly representative of the Aramaic culture and
religion at the time when the Aramaeans spread
from the Syrian steppe to Babylonia: the priest's

73

garment is very Babylonian in style. The cult of the moon god, venerated by the Aramaean nomads, took on great importance at that time.

⁵⁵ Lady at the Window

Hadatu, 8th century BC

Ivory, formerly gilded. H 8 cm

Arsian Tash, formerly Hadatu.

Thurau-Dangin Excavations. AO 11459

This decorative motif belongs to an item of furniture, a casket or a seat. Produced in Phoenician or Aramaean workshops, these luxury pieces decorated royal apartments, and most particularly the palace "gynaeceums" built by Syrian kings. They were often taken as spoils of war by the Assyrian kings during their conquest of the Levant.

⁵⁶ Taime and his Mother at a Banquet

Palmyra, 2nd-3rd centuries AD

Relief, limestone. H 0.43 m

AO 2093

The Louvre possesses a fine set of funerary sculptures from Palmyra, a trading city and oasis in the Syrian steppe. The rich merchants of Palmyra erected public monuments and tombs which show the cosmopolitan character of their culture. Eastern elements (language, writing, ornament) combine with western ones such as Roman dress and the naturalist style.

Anatolia

⁵⁷ Double Idol

Cappadocia, Ancient Bronze III
Around 2000 BC
Alabaster. H 0.12 m
AO 8794

These extremely schematized images have some connection with sculptures from the Cyclades.

⁵⁸ Hittite God

Classic Hittite Empire
1600-1400 BC
Gold. H 3.8 cm
Yozgat, Boghas-Köy.
Chantre Collection. AO 9647

This pendent-figurine is characteristic of Hittite art at its height. The dress, turned-up shoes and high conical crown is comparable with the reliefs of divine processions at Yazilikaya.

Cyprus

59 Fertility Idol

*Cyprus, Chalcolithic Period,
end of the 3rd millennium*

Painted and incised terracotta. H 0.129 m

Couchoud Expedition. AM 1176

This is one of the first images related to fertility cults in Cyprus. Goddess or woman, the figurine is remarkable for evoking the stream of milk - the source of life - collected in a basin. The stylization of the features and the angle of the head is comparable with other "primitive" images from Greece, the Cyclades and the Balkans.

60 Vase decorated with Gift-Bearers

Cyprus, around 700-650 BC

Terracotta. H 0.25 m

AM 1142

The richly imaginative style of the Cretan potters is here employed in the service of religious belief. The faithful carry vegetation to the divinity, symbolic of the power of fertility and fecundity.

⁶¹ Redoutable Mask

Carthage,
end of 7th- early 6th centuries BC

Terracotta. H 0.195 m

Dermech Necropolis. Delattre Excavations AO 3242

These objects, which were left in tombs, had a magical function to fend off evil spirits. Oriental in tradition, they are a good illustration of the cultural inter-dependency of the Punic world and Phoenicia.

Levant **Oriental Antiquities**

Islam

After the Crusades, Christian Europe acquired
various art objects from the Muslim world. The
old royal collections housed some major pieces,
such as the rock crystal ewer in the Saint Denis
treasure-house, the great brass bowl inlaid with
silver called the "Saint Louis Baptistery" [68]
and a series of cups in jade which are Turkish or
Indian in origin. But not until the middle of the
19th century, when the Louvre received some
major legacies (1840: Despointes; 1856: Sauvageot)
and at the very end of the century, was any real
interest taken in Islamic art. Bequests and
donations multiplied (1885: Davillier; 1892:
Fouquet; 1893: Arconati Visconti). Thanks to the
interest of certain curators of Decorative Arts, a
"Muslim Art section" was finally put together
which made some significant purchases (1899: the
"Barberini" Vase [67], one of the prize objects in the
collection). A first exhibition, in 1903, showed
more than a thousand pieces from private
collections in the Pavillon de Marsan. A good
many of these pieces were later donated to the
Louvre, the collectors rivalling each other in
generosity: Doistau (who gave a rare, 16th century
"Kilim" carpet of silk and metal thread and a
Syrian bowl inscribed to the Sultan Ayyoubid al-
Malik al-Adil); Dru, Jeuniette and Marteau (who
gave superb metals and miniatures), and Peytel
among others. By its size and the quality of the
pieces on show, this exhibition provided a perfect
illustration of the temporal and spatial scope of the
Islamic world and its works of art. At the time it
included the Maghreb, a region later reserved for
the Musée des Arts Africains et Océaniens.
In 1912, in addition to a number of rare objects
(Iranian and Syro-Egyptian woodwork, ivories and
metals - all of the highest quality, including two
signed and dated ewers), Baroness Delort de Gléon
left the Louvre the sum of a hundred thousand
francs to help pay for a larger room of Muslim
art. A space was allotted to it on the second floor
of the Pavillon de l'Horloge, and after a long
delay due to the war, the room was finally

inaugurated in 1922. Between the wars, Gaston Migeon published two volumes in which the principal pieces in the collection were reproduced alongside his commentary; and Georges Salles published a small visitor's guide.

There were some especially rich legacies, from Baroness Salomon de Rothschild in 1922, from Madame Stern (rare Spanish metals: aquamanila peacock and lion), and from Raymond Koechlin, who left ceramics, including the famous peacock plate $_{70}$, and precious metals.

For their part, the archeologists began to explore the Islamic levels which had been neglected for a long time. Archeological treasures from the digs (the most famous being that of Susa in Iran) gradually entered the collection.

After the war, the section under the directorship of Jean David-Weill came once more under the aegis of Oriental Antiquities.

62 Cup

Mesopotamia, 9th century

Clay ceramic with metal lustre decoration
in brown and yellow on white opaque glaze.

H 6.3 cm; ∅ 22.3 cm

Vignier collection. Acq. 1931. 8179

Metal lustre decoration was one of the greatest
glories of potters working in the Abbassid
caliphate in Irak and Iran during the 9th and 10th
centuries. This expensive and complicated
technique was brilliantly developed in the
medieval Islamic world before spreading to the
West, into Spain and Italy.

63 Panel

Egypt, end of the 9th century
Wood (Aleppo pine). H 0.73 m

Fouquet Donation, 1892-1893. 6023

Egyptian woodcarvings from the Toulounid period
reflect the influence of the developed art of
Baghdad and Samarra. Vigorous bevelled cuts
accentuate the play of light over the supple curves
of a motif that is half-animal and half-vegetal,
depicting a bird in profile.

64 Pyxis of Al-Mughira

Cordoba, 968
Ivory. H 0.15 m

Acq. 1898. 4068

During the period of the Cordoba Caliphat the
workshops of Andalusia turned out a whole series
of masterpieces of sculpture on ivory. Most of
these are rectangular or cylindrical boxes with
curved lids as on this pyxis. Round the bottom of
the lid is an inscription which gives the date, 968,
and the name Al-Mughira, son of the caliph Abd
al-Rahman III. The scenes depicted - fighting
animals, princely recreations (hunting, music,

drinking) - belong to an iconographic repertory common to the whole Muslim world.

detail

⁶⁵ Saint-Josse Shroud

Khurassan (Eastern Iran), middle of the 10th century

Silk samite. H 0.52 m; W 0.94 m

Commune of Saint-Josse. Acq. 1922. 7502

This cloth, which was almost certainly brought home from the First Crusade by Etienne de Blois, brother of Godefroy de Bouillon, was given to the Abbey of Saint-Josse (Pas-de-Calais). The very fine kufic inscription, bearing the name of a Turkish governor of Khurassan, put to death in 961, confirms its provenance from Eastern Iran, which was at that time a province independent from Baghdad. The weaving technique as well as the motifs - elephants meeting head-on, a line of harnessed camels - can be traced directly to pre-Islamic Iran, though they are treated with a new stylization.

⁶⁶ Cup

*Iran, end of 12th - beginning of
13th century*

Silicious Ceramic with over-glaze painted
decoration embellished with gold and metal lustre.

H 6.5 m; ∅ 22 cm

Acq. 1970. MAO 440

For the beauty of its forms and decorations and
the variety of techniques applied, the so-called
Seldjoukid period in Iran was a golden age for
pottery. Long before Europe, the over-glaze
painted decoration was perfected, enabling a wide
chromatic scale to be used. On the most beautiful
pieces, such as this cup showing a falconer on
horseback, finesse of line and delicacy of colour
bring to mind the art of the miniature.

detail

⁶⁷ "Barberini" Vase

Syria, middle of the 13th century

Brass inlaid with silver.

H 0.459 m; ∅ 0.37 m

Barberini Collection. Acq. 1899. 4090

The shape of this large vase which belonged to the
collections of Pope Urban VIII Barberini is more
frequently used for ceramic vessels (spice or
medecine pots). It is decorated with inscriptions
bearing the name of an Ayyoubid Sultan of
Aleppo and medallions showing hunting scenes
of a rare finesse.

68 Bowl known as the Baptistery of Saint Louis

Syria or Egypt,
end of the 13th or beginning
of the 14th century

Brass with gold and silver inlay, signed
Muhammed ibn al-Zayn. H 0.232 m; ∅ 0.505 m
Crown Collection in the Sainte-Chapelle de
Vincennes. Entered the Louvre in 1852. LP 16

This large bowl which was in the French Royal Collections was used for the baptism of certain princes in the 19th century, which explains the arms of France stamped on the interior. A masterpiece of Muslim brassware, it is of the highest standard of metalwork and a proof also of the wealth of the ruling Mameluke class. On the outside surface four circular medallions, each containing a prince on horseback, are set between a line of huntsmen and high officials with emblazoned boots. The decoration here is notable for the unusual size of the people and the absence of inscriptions which are omnipresent on objects of this time.

09 Bottle

Syria, 1342-1345
Gilded and enameled glass. H 0.505 m
Spitzer Collection. Acq. 1893. 3365

Drawing on a long tradition of glass-work in the Near-East, Muslim artisans lent particular brilliance to certain techniques such as gilt and enamel decoration. Used during the Ayyoubid period, this decoration was extremely popular under the Mamelukes, from the middle of the 13th to the end of the 14th century. It appears on numerous mosque lamps commissioned by sovereigns or the principal state official. Rarer in shape, this bottle is decorated with a splendid blue epigraphy, broken by the arms of Tuqutzemur, viceroy of Syria from 1342 to 1345 (a white eagle over a white cup on a red shield).

70 Peacock Plate

Turkey, Iznik, second quarter of the 16th century

Silicious ceramic with under-glaze painted decoration.

H 8 cm; ∅ 37.5 cm

K 3449

A peacock in profile can be seen amidst a floral composition which takes up the whole surface of the plate. The tones used - a very delicate palette based on blue, grey-mauve and lime green - are typical of the Iznik style during the second quarter of the 16th century.

71 Portrait of Shah Abbas I

Ispahan, March 12, 1627

Ink, colour and goldleaf on paper, signed Muhammed Qasim. H 0.275 m; W 0.168 m

Acq. 1975. MAO 494

This drawing is most probably the only portrait in existence executed during the Shah's lifetime. Head shaved, and wearing a broad rimmed conical hat, he tenderly embraces one of his pages who is offering him a drink. The scene is pastoral, at the edge of a stream. Under the foliage is the name of the artist, the date and a short poem: *"May life procure you all you desire from the three lips: those of your lover, the river and the cup".*

72 Horse-Head Dagger

India, 17th century

Grey-green jade, inlaid with gold, rubies
and emeralds; damascened steel blade. L 0.505 m

Salomon de Rothschild Collection.

Acq. 1927. 7891

Numerous objects, in gold, silver, ivory or hard stones, often embellished with enamel and precious stones provide us with a glimpse of the wealth of the court of the Great Moghuls. White or grey-green jade was highly prized and often used for jewels, boxes or the handles of ceremonial arms. The latter were often delicately sculpted animal heads of great expressiveness such as this.

Prehistory
and the first two dynasties

Old Kingdom

Middle Kingdom

The Temple : architecture and
architectural sculpture

New Kingdom

Daily life

Third Intermediate period,
Saite period
and last indigenous kingdoms

Egypt under Greek and Roman
domination

Script

Burial

Coptic Egypt

Egyptian Antiquities

Introduction

The Department of Egyptian antiquities displays the remains of cultures centred around the Nile from prehistorical to early Christian times covering a period of 4500 years. The majority of objects entered the Egyptian Department following its establishment in 1826.

At that time, Champollion's deciphering of Egyptian hieroglyphs was having a wide cultural impact. After fifteen centuries the mystery of the ancient Egyptian script was at last unravelled and the history of Egypt under the pharaohs was rewritten. Meanwhile English and French consuls in Egypt began disposing of collections they had invested in. On Champollion's advice, Charles X of France acquired them, ordering the installation of new rooms for their display on the first floor of the Cour Carrée (now Rooms A to D), the design of which was inspired in part by the ancient Egyptian style. This was the world's first museum of Egyptology.

Around the middle of the nineteenth century, the collection grew with numerous finds by Mariette at the Serapeum, and with the acquisition of the great collection of Doctor Clot. The end of the century saw the emergence of scientific archaeology and a site was seen to be as important as the objects it contained. With excavations conducted by the Institut Français d'Archéologie Orientale at Cairo and by the Musée du Louvre, objects with a precise provenance and context came into the collection from sites such as Assiout, Deir el-Medineh, Medamoud and Tod. Today the collection continues to expand with new acquisitions and gifts from collectors.

Prehistory and the first two dynasties

Thinite period: c. 3100-2700 BC

As elsewhere, Neolithic communities in Egypt are characterized by a settled agricultural existence evolving over thousands of years from a nomadism based on hunting and gathering (the Paleolithic era). Excavations in numerous 4th millenium burial grounds in the Nile valley in Upper Egypt have uncovered objects testifying to a belief in life after death and to a developed craft industry which produced stone vases, ceramics decorated with stylized paintings, small ivory and stone sculptures and plaques. At the end of this period, aound 3200 BC, there are the first signs of Pharaonic civilisation in bas-reliefs on schist plaques and in early picture-writing. According to an historical tradition of the ancient Egyptians the valley peoples were then united under a single authority, the first pharaoh. Excavations of the great burial grounds of these ancient kings and their courts at Abydos and at Sakkara give an indication of the high level of craftsmanship attained in the production of luxury goods such as ivory furniture legs, game pieces, statuettes, jewellery and precious vases. On steles found in the tombs, names of the deceased are written in primitive hieroglyphs.

Prehistory

73 Vase

c. 4000-3500 BC (Nagada I)

Basalt. H. 0.428 m

Gift of L. I. and A. Curtis. E 23175

Even from an early date Egyptian craftsmen worked with the hardest stones such as basalt, and hollowed them out to make containers. In the absence of good metal tools they worked with stones, aided by abrasive agents such as quartz and emery. Both the technical mastery of this vase and the pure beauty of its form deserve our admiration.

74 Vase

c. 3500-3100 BC (Nagada II)

Painted terracotta. H. 0.205 m ; W. 0.155 m

AF 6851

At the end of the prehistoric period Egyptians painted vessels with stylized figurative motifs. On such egg-shaped vases in beige clay they would often depict large rowing boats on which stand cabins bearing various emblems. On this vase a figure appears to be dancing with his arms raised and joined above his head. In the absence of a script, the significance of such a scene remains a mystery.

75 Plaque

c. 3200 BC (late Nagada II period)

Carved schist. H 0.32 m; W 0.177 m

E 11052

From the end of the prehistoric period, plaques or "palettes" carved from schist which were used for the grinding of kohl, were laid beside the deceased. Some of the later versions are larger and decorated with what are among the first examples of Egyptian bas-relief. This one uses relief and silhouette carving for the four molossi around the edges. On one side a creature with an elongated neck recalls similar animals found in Mesopotamian art. On the other, two giraffes serve as reminders that at one time the lower valley of the Nile was savannah grassland.

detail   front view   back view

76 Guebel el-Arak dagger

Probably from Guebel el-Arak,
south of Abydos, c. 3300-3200 BC
(Nagada II)

Silex blade and ivory handle (hippopotamus tooth).

H 25.5 cm; H of handle 4.5 cm

E 11517

Similar daggers to this with finely carved handles
can be found elsewhere, but the scenes depicted
here are unique. On one side there is a battle
scene on land and water; the other side depicts
animals such as lions, ibexes and dogs. At the top,
above the knob, a man in the robes of a Sumerian
priest-king is restraining two rampant lions. The
piece raises questions about artistic contacts with
Mesopotamia. It could depict a battle between
communities whose differences can be seen in the
design of their boats. What is certain is that it is
an early example of Egyptian bas-relief and it is
carved with great mastery. The silex is worked
with a polished blade cut on one side by thin
parallel incisions; this is carving at its most
refined, characteristic of this period of Egyptian
civilisation.

77 Stele of Djet,
the "Serpent King"

*From the tomb of the
Serpent King at Abydos,
c. 3100 BC (1st dynasty)*

Limestone, H 1.43 m; W 0.655 m

Abydos Excavations, E. 11007

Found in the tomb of the third king of the 1st
Dynasty, in the burial ground of the Pharaohs of
the first two Dynasties at Abydos, this large stele
is without doubt the finest example of monumental
sculpture of its period. The slender pillar, arched
at the top and slightly convex, is carved away in the
upper section to leave a crisp hieroglyph of the
king's name above a building (his palace?) and
his incarnation as Horus, the falcon god of
Egyptian royalty. The motif is set deliberately
off-centre to create an harmonious composition.

The Old Kingdom *(c. 2700 to c. 2200 BC)*

The Old Kingdom was the period of the great pyramids at Guiza and Sakkara near Cairo. Although we still have their gigantic monuments, our knowledge of 4th Dynasty sovereigns and even their successors in the 5th and 6th Dynasties, is scant. Nearly all our knowledge of these centuries (from 2700 to 2200 BC) is based on discoveries made in the burial grounds near the capital, Memphis, and in the provinces. In underground chambers, furnishings for the deceased, consisting of domestic and funerary objects, have been found. Tomb chapels provide inscriptions describing the careers of high-ranking officials who are also depicted in steles and statues. People of humbler status can be seen working in the fields or in workshops in scenes decorating chapel walls. Altogether, such documents reflect a rigid hierarchical society dominated by the king or Pharaoh. The pattern appears to disintegrate around the end of the Old Kingdom and, after its demise, Egypt was divided up into several parallel dynasties in a period of relative obscurity, while the foundations of the old society were shaken by social and economic disturbances. This period, known as the First Intermediate Period, has left us with very few works of art (c. 2200-2060 BC).

78 Sepa and Nesa

c. 2700-2620 BC (3rd Dynasty)

Limestone statues, painted.

A 36; H 1.65 m; W 0.40; P P. 55 m

A 36, A 37

These are among the first examples of large statues of private individuals from the Old Kingdom. Their solid forms are indicative of their archaism; it is as if the sculptor did not dare stray too far from the stone. Their rigid postures and smooth, serene faces remind us of their function, for within the tomb they served as durable stone reminders of the earthly form of the deceased. Inscriptions on the pediments identify them as Sepa, an important official and his wife Nesa.

79 The Large Sphinx

Found at Tanis

Pink granite. H 1.83 m; W 4.80 m

Salt Collection. Acq. 1826. A 23

Carved from a single block of pink granite, this large statue depicts a pharaoh with a lion's body. "Sphinx" comes from the Greek word for a type

of monster, and in Egypt sphinxes served to
indicate and protect passages in religious buildings.
This is a particularly fine specimen with a strong
volumetric sense and finely executed detail. Several
kings in turn inscribed their names on it. The
oldest inscription reads Amenemhat II (1929-
1985 BC) and possibly the sphinx was sculpted
during his reign. However certain details (like the
headdress) might suggest an earlier dating, to the
beginning of the Old Kingdom around 2620 BC. If
this were so, this would be a rare example of royal
sculpture from that distant time.

95

⁸⁰ Head of King Didoufri

Abu Roach
c. 2570 BC (4th Dynasty)

Red sandstone. H 0.26 m; W 0.335 m; D 0.288 m

Abu Roach Excavations. E 12626

The head of King Didoufri, successor to Cheops, is very different from the faces of the Great Sphinx and of Sepa and Nesa ₇₈; it quite clearly depicts a particular individual with a slightly receding jaw and high cheek bones. The particular beauty of this fragment lies in its delicate mix of realism and idealism. Cut in red sandstone, it still has traces of red paint on it. The set of the head suggests that it was part of a sphinx. It was found near the remains of the funerary temple beneath the king's pyramid, at Abu Roach, north of Giza.

⁸¹ Stele of Nefertiabet

From Giza
c. 2590 BC (4th Dynasty)

Painted limestone. H 0.375 m; W 0.525 m

Gift of L, I and A Curtis. E 15591

The freshness of the colours and clear composition delight the eye although this stele was intended to be hidden for all time, immured between the funerary chapel and the superstructure or "mastaba" which would have covered the tomb. Its function was magical: to give the deceased power over the offerings essential for her survival. The lady extends her hand out towards a tray full of slices of bread. Hieroglyphs of different dishes surround the table: chops, legs of meat, poultry. Above and to the right are other useful consumer goods such as oil, make-up and cloth. Above her head hieroglyphs designate the dead lady as "daughter of the king, Nefertiabet" ("the beautiful Oriental"), a princess from the time of the great King Cheops.

82 The Seated Scribe

Sakkara, c. 2620-2350 BC
(4th or 5th Dynasty)

Painted limestone statue.

H 0.537 m; W 0.44 m; D 0.35 m

Sakkara Excavations. E 3023

This famous statue was found in the Old Kingdom burial ground at Sakkara, but the identity of the person is lost to us. Doubtless he was someone of importance, judging from the exceptional quality of this statue, remarkable for its treatment of face and body and for the attention given to the eyes inset into copper. We should not be misled by the poised hands. This is not a humble clerk preparing to write. The oldest statues of "scribes" actually depict princes with high political responsibilities. This statue has a particularly striking presence with its original colours, sharp eyes and intelligent expression.

detail

83 Musicians
detail of the
Akhhetep mastaba

From Sakkara
c. 2400 BC (5th Dynasty)
Painted limestone bas-relief.

E 10958 A

This mastaba is one of many funerary chapels of the great burial ground of Sakkara, reconstructed in the Louvre. Inside, family or funerary priests would make offerings of various goods before artificial doors which take up the back wall. Through these magic openings the dead person in his subterranean dwelling was expected to communicate with the living. Bas-reliefs in the chapel show all the activities and produce of a large estate such as the one here owned by the high official, Akhhetep. The main scene shows Akhhetep's funerary meal, with music and dancing accompanying it.

84 Raherka and Merseankh

c. 2500-2350 BC (5th Dynasty)

Limestone painted group. H 0.528 m; D 0.213 m

Gift of L, I and A Curtis. E 15592

Statues of interlocked couples are not uncommon in Egyptian tombs during the Old Kingdom. This is a particularly striking example. The lady, known as Merseankh, seems both to be nudging her husband Raherka forward, and relying on his strength as he advances. It is a refined piece of work and her arm and his leg are clearly and independently articulated. Their round, smiling faces have a calm confidence about them which is typical of the period.

85 Jug and Basin

c. 2350-2000 BC (6th Dynasty)

Copper, Jug: H 0.199 m; W 0.315 m

Basin: H 0.15 m W 0.32 m

E 3912 A and B

While during the 3rd millenium Egyptians were as yet unaware that copper and tin could be combined to make bronze, they were able to work in copper with great success, and even made over-lifesize statues. Copper vessels were common and jugs and basins such as these were set beside the dead in the vaults, indispensable as they were at mealtimes. Hammered and rivetted together, this group is engraved with the name of its owner, a priestess of Hathor known as Pes.

Middle Kingdom *(2060-1786 BC)*

Following the demise of the 1st Intermediate period (c. 2200-2060 BC), Egypt was united again by another pharaoh, Mentuhotep the Great. Originating from Thebes, the kings of the 11th Dynasty and their successors in the 12th Dynasty paid tribute to their god Mentu, adorning shrines at Tod and at Medamoud. French excavations have provided the Louvre with many fragments of the temples there. Royal statues of this period are often impressive. Official sculptors developed an art of portraiture based on the facial features of the great kings Sesostris III and Amenemhat III. Private statues also appropriated royal features and moved towards more geometric volumes, enveloping figures in tent-like robes. Goldwork also flourished during the Middle Kingdom, along with literature and the sciences. Fine examples of painted wooden sarcophagi have been found in tombs along with small wood carvings of groups of people at work. These help to give us a vivid picture of the everyday life of the Egyptians.

86 The Treasure of Tôd

Temple of Tôd, Amenemhat II
1925-1895 BC (12th Dynasty)
Bronze, silver, lapis-lazuli.
Large coffer: H 0.205 m; W 0.45 m; D 0.285 m
Tôd Excavations. E 15128 to E 15328

While excavating the foundations of the Middle Kingdom temple at Tôd, south of Luxor, the archaeologist Fernand Bisson de la Roque discovered four bronze coffers buried in the ground of the temple. They contained a large number of silver bowls, most of which were folded up, gold chains and lingots, and lapis-lazuli in its natural state or worked into cylindrical seals. Both the raw materials and finished products were foreign in origin. The bowls are in the Aegean style. This precious treasure brought into Egypt for political or commercial reasons was dedicated to the god Montu, lord of Tôd, by the pharaoh Amenemhat II.

87 Lintel of Sesostris III

Medamoud temple
1878-1843 BC (12th Dynasty)
Limestone bas-relief. H 1.065 m; W 2.21 m
Medamoud Excavations. E 13983

Architectural elements in Egyptian temples are carved with reliefs relating to the function of the room. This is the lintel to the door of the room storing offerings. King Sesostris III appears in two parallel scenes, making offerings of bread to the god Montu, the lord of Medamoud. On the left the king is shown in his youth, while on the right is the thin face and drawn features of an old man which are familiar from other three-dimensional busts of him. These two stages of the king's life are possibly shown together to express the idea of the cycle of life; unfortunately the text consists of the usual dialogue between king and god when exchanging goods and gives no further clue as to its meaning.

88 King Amenemhat III

1842-1797 BC (12th Dynasty)

Schist statuette. H 0.214 m; W 0.10 m

N 464

Although its inscription is missing, the identity of this statue is not in doubt; the features, the large mouth and aquiline nose of King Amenemhat III are boldly delineated. The exaggerated size of the ears is characteristic of the period. The idealised body coexists with a markedly realistic facial portrait, a feature typical of royal statuary at the end of the 12th Dynasty.

89 Hippopotamus

c. 2000-1900 BC (early Middle Kingdom)

Egyptian faience (glazed silicious pottery).

H 12,7, W 20,5; D 8,1 cm

E 7709

From pictures in Old Kingdom mastabas, it appears that the hunting of hippopotami in the Nile marshes was a sport for noblemen. Hippopotami were placed in tombs at the beginning of the Middle Kingdom so that the sport (which probably had symbolic connotations) could be continued in the afterlife. On the surface of the animal are decorations derived from its natural habitat; blue suggesting river water and aquatic plants such as the waterlily. The chubby outline is rendered with a skill which characterizes Egyptian depictions of animals.

90 Large statue of Nakhti

Assiout
Between 1991 and 1928 BC
(early 12th Dynasty)

Acacia wood. H 1.785 m; W of base 0.495 m; D 1.10

Assiout burial ground excavations. E 11937

The tomb of the chancellor Nakhti was undisturbed for nearly 4000 years. In the entrance chapel two large wooden statues were found; both depict the deceased and are lifesize. Other small representations of Nakhti were laid around the sarcophagus in the tomb. This is the most striking of all the statues; the quality o the woods, its

carving and the facial expression are all
remarkable. The collection of relics from this tomb
are divided between Paris and Cairo; together they
give us a good picture of the funerary possessions
of a member of the privileged class of that time.
Alongside painted wooden sarcophagi, models of
scenes of life along the Nile, gift bearers and
imitation weapons and tools surrounded the dead
man.

91 Model of a boat

*Tomb of the chancellor Nakhti
at Assiout
Between 1991 and 1928
(12th Dynasty)*

Painted wood. L 0.81 m; H of hull 0.385 m

Assiout burial ground excavations. E 12027

Within the tomb, this boat and its crew were to be
of eternal service to the dead man for all river
crossings and would in particular have served in
his pilgrimage to Abydos and to the god of the
dead, Osiris. Eight oarsmen are led by a cox
standing at the prow whose duty was to test the
depth of the water with his pole, given the many
changing sandbanks under the river Nile. The
rudder at the back consists of two oars controlled
by the helmsman by means of wooden interstices
which have disappeared.

⁹² Gift bearer

ι. 2000-1800 BC (*12th Dynasty*)
Painted wood statuette. H 1.085 m; D 0.327 m
E 10781

This attractive Egyptian lady is not the owner of
the tomb where she was found. She is simply an
anonymous servant placed there to bring her dead
master an ox's foot and a jar of water for all of
time. While statues of gift bearers are common at
this period, the beauty of this one is exceptional,
with her slender body, elegant bearing and refined
and attentive face.

The Temple: architecture and architectural sculpture

For anyone fortunate enough to have visited Egypt
and its great temples it is easy to imagine the
many architectural fragments the Louvre contains
(columns and capitals, bas-reliefs, etc.) in their
original setting. The basic layout of the sacred
dwelling, a stone palace designed for daily tending
of the god on the earth, did not change. First
came an open courtyard to which worshippers had
access, then a room with columns, the gentle
shadows from which screened the penumbra of
the private sanctuary beyond. Only officiating
priests were allowed there, for this was the
dwelling of the god incarnate in a statue within
a tabernacle.

93 Naos or small sanctuary

Reign of Amasis, 570-526 BC
(26th Dynasty)

Pink granite. H 2.55 m; W 1.61 m; D 1.50 m

Gift of Drovetti. D 29

Cut from one block of granite this chapel once had a door to hide its precious contents: the statue in which the god was thought to dwell. Placed at the end of the temple, where all the processional axes culminated, the naos was opened every day by priests; the statue or god was offered libations, incense, food and prayers as appeasements. This naos from an unknown temple to Osiris in the region of lake Mariout, near Alexandria, derived its form from archaic sanctuaries of northern Egypt. A multitude of divinities are carved on the outside, a veritable Egyptian pantheon, which protect and accompany the god. The refined style of the bas-relief, showing complete mastery of a hard stone, is proof of the high quality of contemporary craftsmanship.

94 Amun and Tutankhamen

Reign of Tutankhamen
c. 1347-1337 BC (18th Dynasty)

Diorite group. H 2.14 m; W 0.44 m; D 0.785 m

E 11609

Many temple statues are groups consisting of the ruler with one or several gods. In this the god Amun is recognizable from his two high plumes. He was the great god of the temple of Karnak who according to official doctrine gave victory to the great conquering kings of the 18th Dynasty. Suppressed under the religious revolution led by the ruler Amenophis IV - Akhenaton, his cult re-emerged with renewed strength under the young

Tutankhamen. As a testament of his faith, Tutankhamen had many images of Amon made similar to this, with the god protecting him. The almost feminine body and the spiritual cast of features nevertheless derive from the art of Akhenaton's time.

95 Nakhthorheb

Reign of Psammetic II
595-589 BC (26th Dynasty)
Crystallized sandstone statue.
H 1.48 m; W 0.465 m; D 0.70 m
A 94

Nakhthorheb is kneeling in prayer and the text of the statue informs us that he is appealing to the god Thot, "lord of Dendera and Hermopolis". Leader of the officiating priests, he had some important religious duties and his family was recorded in many documents. The statue is in line with the archaising tendency of the time with its simple costume; the smooth loincloth and hairstyle merge into and emphasize the lines of the body. The bare torso provided the sculptor with the chance to display his anatomical skills, though it is idealised like the characterless face.

This is one of many statues which would have filled the courtyards of sanctuaries where worshippers of a god waited to receive some reward for their devotion, in the form of crumbs from the god's table.

96 The Goddess Sekhmet

Reign of Amenhotep III
c. 1403-1365 BC (18th Dynasty)

Diorite statue. H 1.78 m (without restored disc);
W 0.55 m; D 0.95 m

From the Mout temple at Karnak, transported from
its place of origin on the left bank of Thebes.

A 8

The goddess Sekhmet has the head of a lioness
and the body of a young woman; her schematic
headdress cleverly masks the change in form.
Volumes are well-balanced and details are finely
carved. None of the eight statues of Sekhmet in
the Louvre are alike either in size or detail.
Originally there were a considerable number of
them, placed in the temple of the ruler
Amenhotep III in Thebes, a lost temple which is
marked now by the colossus of Memnon. Each
statue represented a daily appeal to Sekhmet,
goddess of great danger, to chase all evil away
from the temple throughout the year.

The New Kingdom *(c. 1555-1080 BC)*

The New Kingdom emerged from a national war of independence against the Hyksos, a people from the Near East who had invaded 150 years earlier under a politically weak late Middle Kingdom. Pharaohs of the 18th Dynasty (c. 1555-1305) the Thutmosis, and Amenhoteps ruled over a huge empire stretching from the Sudan to Syria. The resulting prosperity led to the architectural flowering of great temples at Thebes, Karnak, and Luxor, and palaces, the splendour of which is hinted at in the luxurious furniture of Tutankhamen's tomb. Cultural contacts multiplied, availability of raw materials and wealth increased, and the whole of Egyptian society benefitted, as is apparent from the increasing refinement and enrichment of the arts.

The ruler Amenhotep IV or Akhenaton harnessed the economic strength and great creative energies of his time to his revolutionary ideas, doing away with many artistic conventions and constructing a new capital.

The Ramesside period (19th and 20th Dynasties) saw a return to the old order. The rulers Sethi I and Rameses II made prestigious additions to the large sanctuaries.

By the end of the second millennium Egypt had to defend itself against the first waves of displaced populations which shook the Mediterranean world. The rulers moved their residences to the north, leaving the south in the hands of the powerful priesthood of Thebes. A page of Egyptian history had been turned.

⁹⁷ Patera of the General Djehuty

Reign of Thutmosis III
c. 1490-1439 (18th Dynasty)
Gold. ∅ 17.9 cm; H 2.2 cm

N 713

The patera is made of hammered gold with an embossed and chased pattern. At the centre is a flower, a waterlily, seen from above; around it are stylized fish and papyrus, themes also found on contemporary blue ceramic bowls. An inscription engraved around the edge explains that this magnificent gold piece was offered by the ruler Thutmosis III to general Djehuty for his faithful services abroad.

⁹⁸ Head of a King, Amenhotep II (?)

c. 1439-1413 BC (18th Dynasty)
Red crystallised sandstone. H 0.21 m

E 10896

This fine head belongs to a sphinx because the headdress (the royal "nemes") is raised up at the back. Over the forehead an erect cobra ("ureus") symbolises the pharaoh's powers to destroy the enemies of Egypt. Although the inscription is lost, the style of the face and particularly the eyes link it to artistic developments in royal sculpture around the first half of the 18th Dynasty.

99 A Couple : Senynefer and
Hatchepsut

c. 1410 BC (18th Dynasty)

Painted sandstone group. H 0.62 m; W 0.82 m

E 27161

This lifesize couple, with their fresh colouring, are
strikingly present. They are a good illustration of
the purpose of Egyptian sculpture: to duplicate the
human form, serving as its earthly record. For
once the faces are authentic likenesses; only the
skin colouring is conventional; yellow for the
woman and red ochre for the man. The couple
would have been arm in arm, seated against a
backrest which served as a stele; a prayer is carved
on it, for an offering to ensure their eternal life.

¹⁰⁰ Paser's Stele

c. 1410 BC (18th Dynasty)

Limestone. H 0.985 m; L 0.77 m

C 80

This form of stele served as a funerary monument, designed to be inset into the wall of the tomb to perpetuate the cult of the deceased. Here two offerings are shown; above, the dead man called Paser offers Osiris bouquets and food saying *"I have come to bring you gifts, all sorts of fine products from the land of Egypt for you, oh Osiris, leader of Westerners (the Dead): will you favour me, as the ruler favoured me on earth"*. On the lower scene Paser himself receives an offering made by his wife, daughter and son, who had the stele made for him.

¹⁰¹ King Amenhotep III

c. 1403-1365 BC (18th Dynasty)

Diorite head. H 0.325 m

A 25

This fragment has lost its identifying inscription. However there can be no doubt that it is the ruler Amenhotep III with his recognizable round cheeks, small, flattened chin, thick lips, short nose and almond eyes. His helmet is in a royal style which emerged under the New Kingdom; the body of the "ureus", a royal cobra, uncoils gracefully over it.

c. 1400 BC (18th Dynasty)

Statuette in African red ebony.

H 33.4, W 7 cm; D 17 cm

E 10655

The sculptor of this statuette displays his craft both in the perfection of volumes and treatment of surfaces; the delicate engraving on the braids of the wig screening the face contrasts with the fine polish of the body in its tight-fitting robe. On the base a prayer invokes Osiris, and all the gods of the burial ground so that Touy *"may breathe in the soft Northern wind, so that her soul may enter the burial ground, so that she may be in the company of the blessed next to Osiris, so that she may drink water where she pleases".* The statuette was made for the tomb of this society lady from the flourishing period under the ruler Amenhotep III.

New Kingdom   Egyptian Antiquities

103 Spoon with a Swimmer

c. 1400 BC (18th Dynasty)

Wood and ivory (or bone). H 29 cm; W 5.5 cm

E 218

The 18th Dynasty saw the development of a new genre of decorative spoons with developed forms; handles in the shape of duck's necks or bouquets of flowers etc. They were long thought to be cosmetic spoons. However, the study of certain

inscriptions and pictures of them has left little
doubt that they were actually used to throw myrrh
onto fire as an offering to the gods or to the dead.
Notable for their grace and inventiveness, the
"swimmer" spoons doubtless belong to this group.
Here a young slender girl holds a duck with
outstretched arms, the two wings of which form
the lid of the spoon.

104 Colossus of Amenhotep IV
(Akhenaton)

Amenhotep IV,
c. 1365-1349 BC
(18th Dynasty)

Painted sandstone. H 1.37 m; W 0.88 m;
D 0.60 m. From a temple east of Karnak.
Gift of Egyptian government. E 27112

From the beginning of his reign Amenhotep IV
(who changed his name to Akhenaton) gave a new
direction to art and religion, as is shown in
remnants of a sanctuary he had built at the east of
the Amun temple at Karnak. A large courtyard

was lined with a pillared portico against which stood colossal statues in the ruler's image, his arms crossed over his chest like Osiris. This was a traditional form of architectural sculpture; the novelty resides in the extraordinary and unprecedented style of the statues. The body of the ruler with its strangely feminine hips is crowned by an elongated head, its features heavily stylized like a mask. The colouring which by now has almost entirely faded must have emphasized the extraordinary expression of this disturbing yet entrancing face.

105 Body of Nefertiti (?)

Reign of Amenhotep IV - Akhenaton
c. 1365-1349 BC (18th Dynasty)
Crystallised red sandstone. H 0.29 m
E 25409

Despite being damaged, this fragment is evidence of the mastery of certain artists during the revolutionary period of Amenhotep IV, known as the "Amarnian period". Remaining strictly within the canon imposed by the new official doctrine - slender arms and protuberant belly - the sculptor has created a new style of beauty. The ample but finely chiselled forms give it its originality; the generous proportions of the lower body are emphasised by the radiating folds of the costume, finely carved in red sandstone. Nefertiti, the celebrated queen of Amenhotep-Akhenaton was most likely to be the inspiration behind this fulsome female body and not, as some have suggested, one of her daughters.

106 Head of a Princess

Amenhotep IV - Akhenaton
c. 1365-1349 BC (18th Dynasty)

Painted limestone. H 0.154 m; W 0.10 m

E 14715

Amenhotep IV and Nefertiti had six daughters. Their lives - and the early death of one of them - can be traced in the series of representations of the royal family which were central to the official religious imagery of the period. This adolescent girl with rounded cheeks has her hair styled like other children of the time in a thick mass of long braids which fall over her right shoulder. The satisfiying combination of the "Amarnian" style with a certain realism, most apparent in the treatment of the neck, mouth and chin, is the mark of the finest works of the end of this reign.

107 Piay, the Gatekeeper of the Royal Palace

c. 1330-1300 BC
(end of the 18th, early
19th Dynasty)

Statuette, karite wood (acacia base).

H 0.544 m; W 0.109 m; D 0.31 m

E 124

The statue of Piay is a good example of artistic tendencies at the end of the 18th Dynasty. Artists abandoned Akhenaton's extraordinarily humane canon but his artistic revolution led to a new, milder approach. Piay's gently rounded belly, emphasized by the folded loincloth, derives from work of the preceding period. The finely detailed fuller costume adds elegance to the work and anticipates the voluminous fashions of the next Ramesside period.

108 Wailing Women of Horemheb

Tomb of Horemheb at Sakkara,
Reign of Tutankhamen,
c. 1347-1337 BC (18th Dynasty)
Limestone bas-relief. H 0.75 m; W 0.36 m
B 57

While a general under Tutankhamen, Horemheb had a fine tomb built for himself at Sakkara, the burial ground for the town of Memphis. By that time, the administrative centre of the country had moved there from Thebes. The scene of mourners at a burial, common in 18th Dynasty tombs, takes on a dramatic depth here, thanks to the artistic innovations of the "Armanian" period. Arms and hands turn about, giving an impression of movement and planes are treated freely with incised and raised areas suggesting a crowd.

Horemheb eventually became a pharaoh himself and was buried in another larger tomb in the Valley of Kings.

109 The Goddess Hathor and King Sethi I

Tomb of Sethi I
in the Valley of Kings
c. 1303-1290 BC (19th Dynasty)
Painted limestone bas-relief. H 2.265 m; W 1.05 m.
Brought back from Egypt by Champollion. B 7

This painted bas-relief once faced a parallel scene (now in Florence), half-way down the long corridor cut into the mountain west of Thebes

(present-day Luxor). As always the scene is connected to its location; the goddess Hathor is greeting the king who is leaving the world of the living. She seizes his hand and gives him a necklace, her emblem, placing him under her protection. Particularly venerated in Western Thebes, burial ground of the capital of the New Empire, she took on an important role as receiver of the dead. The bas-reliefs of the largest tomb in the Valley of Kings combine traditional hieraticism with the softened approach of Amarnian art in an elegant classical form.

110 Pendant in the form of
a Predatory Bird with
a Ram's Head

*Serapeum of Sakkara,
c. 1264 BC
(19th Dynasty)*

Gold, turquoise, jasper, lapis-lazuli.

Span 13.7 cm; L 7.4 cm

E 80

At Memphis a sacred bull called Apis was
venerated as the terrestrial incarnation of the god
Ptah. At its death it was buried with the rites of
a person of importance, in a subterranean
necropolis reserved for its kind. In 1851, Auguste
Mariette found a beautiful ornament in cloisonné
gold, inlaid with precious stones in the tomb of an
Apis which died during the reign of Rameses II.
It is thought to represent one aspect of the sun
god Re.

111 King presenting the Goddess
Maât

*c. 1300-1100 BC
(19th and 20th Dynasties)*

Statuette, silver gilt. H 0.195 m

Gift of Ganay. E 27431

The silver statuette, covered with gold leaf in
some areas, was probably part of a larger religious
object, possibly a ceremonial boat borne by priests
when sacred statues were brought out on feast
days. The king is holding up a small seated
woman, Maât, goddess of Order in the world. In
this way he shows his god that he is maintaining
the sacred order on earth.

112 Funerary Servant of King Rameses IV

c. 1162-1155 BC (20th Dynasty)

Painted wood statuette. H 0.325 m

N 438

The successors of Sethi I and of Rameses II (including Rameses III-IX) also had deep tombs cut into the Valley of the Kings. The single unviolated example of Tutankhamen's tomb shows what treasures such underground chambers contained. Unfortunately most were pillaged as early as antiquity. Some objects have nevertheless come down to us, this funerary servant of Rameses IV among them. Placed in the tomb with hundreds of his king, all in the king's image, his function is inscribed on his body; he must replace the king "when his task is to undertake work in the necropolis, looking after the fields, irrigating the banks, transporting sand from East to West..." Clearly the after life, even for royalty, was not without its obligations.

Daily Life

The objects of Egyptian daily life, both humble
and luxurious, are ours to admire only because of
the custom in the 18th Dynasty of placing articles
from everyday life into the crypt near the deceased
to make their new life as comfortable as possible.
Of course an ordinary tomb with its carefully
selected collection of worn and humble articles
such as baskets, headrests, and cosmetics was a far
cry from the tomb of a king like Tutankhamen in
which hundreds of objects of an extraordinary
refinement were found.

Most of the objects on display in the Louvre fall
somewhere between these two extremes. A large
number were found in a burial ground on the
west bank of Thebes (now Luxor). Their middle
class owners had relatively comfortable lives.
Cosmetic articles such as mirrors, ointment jars,
kohl flasks, combs, hairpins, razors and tweezers
are preponderant. Most are decorated with designs
inspired by animals or plants. Jewels, gold rings
with mobile settings of precious stones and
ceramic, and polychrome ceramic bead necklaces,
were appreciated by men and women alike. Tools
and weapons, games and musical instruments have
also been found.

113 Chair

c. 1400–1300 BC (18th Dynasty)

Wood, inlaid with ivory (or bone); the leather strips are modern.

H 0.91 m; W 0.475 m; D 0.59 m

N 2950

The origins of this chair which found its way into the Louvre collection before the mid-19th century are unclear. Undoubtedly it came from a well-furnished tomb, judging from the quality of the woodwork. The curvature of the various sections of the backrest, the carved lions' paws and the use of different woods and inlay are all worthy of note. As always the sections are assembled with mortice and tenon joints, reinforced with dowels. The feline paw motif can be traced back to the time of the Pyramids, but the inclined backrest was fashionable during the New Empire. The original caning was in twine.

114 Flask

c. 1400–1300 BC (18th Dynasty)

Glass. H 10 cm; W 7,2 cm

AF 2032

With increased foreign contacts in the 18th Dynasty and a corresponding development of artistic techniques, Egyptians manufactured glass for the first time, concentrating particularly on small containers like this. Since glass-blowing was unknown, a mould made of compressed sand was dipped into molten glass; coloured glass strands were applied onto the hot surfaces and the garland effect obtained by drawing lines across the unset surface with a pointed instrument. When the glass cooled, the sand core inside the bottle was emptied out. The small size and narrow neck of this jar suggest it was destined for a precious liquid, probably a perfumed oil.

115 Ibex-shaped Flask

c. 1500-1400 BC (18th Dynasty)
Painted pottery. W 0.10 m; H 0.102 m
Dra Aboul Naggah Excavations (western Thebes).
E 12659

During the 18th Dynasty the applied arts, pottery among them, flourished. Decorative containers like these, in the form of women or animals, were produced in abundance. This represents an ibex lying down with its kid; the aperture is in the mother's mouth. The fine red shine was obtained by carefully burnishing the surface before firing. A few black lines indicate details of forms.

116 Kohl Pot

Reign of Amenhotep III
c. 1403-1365 (18th Dynasty)
Egyptian glazed silicious ceramic. H 8.4 cm
E 4877

Egyptians used kohl extensively, both to emphasize and protect their eyes. The wide rim of this small pot meant that small crumbs of this precious

product, from distant Arabian mines by the Red
Sea, were not wasted. It is made of Egyptian
faience, a material made of quartz powder covered
with a fine yellow glaze. The names of
Amenhotep III and queen Tiy are inlaid in blue
faience. During their reign, potteries and
glassworks within the palace grounds developed
their crafts to a high degree of perfection as this
pot illustrates particularly well.

The Third Intermediate Period,
the Saite period and the Last Indigenous Dynasties
(c. 1080-332 BC)

At the beginning of the first millennium BC, the
capital was at Tanis, in the Delta, while the high-
priests of Amun at Thebes enjoyed independence
in the south of the country (21st Dynasty, c. 1080-
946 BC). Political divisions widened; Libyan
families took the throne for a time (22nd and 23rd
Dynasties). Then the kings of Sudan annexed
Egypt into their empire (25th Dynasty), until they
were overcome by the Assyrians (664 BC). Kings
from the town of Saïs, in the Delta, subsequently
reunited the country (26th "Saite" Dynasty, 664-
525 BC). But the Persians then conquered it for the
first time (525-404). The 28th, 29th and 30th
Dynasties saw the last pharaohs of Egyptian
origin, before the Persians returned and made the
country part of their great empire (342-332 BC).

117 Cover of the **Sarcophagus** of Soutymes

c. 1000 BC (21st Dynasty)

Stuccoed and painted **wood**. H. 2.10 m; W 0.79 m

N 2609

Soutymes belonged to the highest class of officials in the powerful temple of Amun, a class gradually closing ranks at that period to form a sort of clergy. His power was principally temporal, in that he was in charge of finances in the temple. The body of this important man was protected by no less than three successive covers, each of which depict him as a mummy, with open eyes. The inside and outside of each case were painted with pictures of the great gods of the dead, Osiris and Re, in all their manifestations, accompanied by winged goddesses.

118 Extract from the "Book of the Secret Dwelling"

Scene of the 12th hour
c. 1000 BC (21st Dynasty)

Papyrus. H 0.435 m; total width 1.60 m

N 3109

A female singer of Amun, Ankheseniset, had an abridged version of what was then a very popular

Egyptian Antiquities

Third Intermediate period

text, the "Book of the Secret Dwelling" copied out for her tomb, a provision for the journey slipped alongside the body of anyone of sufficient wealth. Alongside the text, are pictures showing the journey of the sun during the twelve night hours, triumphing over every obstacle in the underworld to be reborn each morning in the East at the end of the twelfth hour. The god, in the form of a man with a ram's head, has climbed onto a boat hauled along by his companions. At the 12th hour, he crosses over the body of a huge snake to emerge in the form of the rising sun, which the Egyptians represented as a scarab (the hieroglyph for transformation). By means of this book, Ankheseniset participated in the eternal cycle of the sun.

119 Stele of Taperet

c. 900-800 BC

Painted wood. H 0.31 m; W 0.29 m

Gift of Batissier. N 3663

At the beginning of the first millennium BC large funerary steles in stone were partly replaced by small wooden steles, on which the dead were no longer shown seated at their funerary feast, but in adoration before the great gods of the beyond. By the side of Osiris, different manifestations of the sun god are shown. The dead lady Taperet sends a prayer to Re-Horakhty (the sun at its zenith) on one side of the stele and to Atoum (the setting sun) on the other. There are two different symbols for the universe surrounding these scenes; on one side the curving band of sky rests on the strip of black earth via the heraldic plants of northern and southern Egypt. On the other, the sky is the goddess Nout, whose body is traversed by the sun which she swallows every evening and gives birth to each morning. The beneficial effects of sunlight are symbolised by lilies, another novelty in this richly coloured and finely drawn stele.

¹²⁰ The Osorkon Group

*Reign of Osorkon II c. 889-866 BC
(22th Dynasty)*

Gold, lapis-lazuli, glass. H 9 cm; W 6,6 cm

E 6204

Osiris's family are represented here in an original way. Isis, the mother and Horus, the son with the falcon's head, are shown at either side of the god Osiris who is squatting on a pillar, and they raise their hands over him in a protective gesture.

Legend had it that Isis pieced together the severed body of Osiris and breathed life into him again for the time it took to conceive a son by him, the god Horus. The latter avenged his father, challenging his murderer, the god Seth, to a fight.

The name of the king, Osorkon II, is engraved on the lapis pillar, thereby ensuring assimilation with the great king of the dead. The goldwork is of a quality which compares with the best sculpture, despite its small scale.

¹²¹ The "Divine Consort" Karomama

c. 870-825 BC (22nd Dynasty)

**Bronze statuette, inlaid with gold, silver, black and
white paste (eyes).**

H 0.595 m; W 0.125 m; D 0.26 m

Acq. in Egypt by Champollion. N 500

To strengthen links between the powerful clergy of Amun dominating the region of Thebes and the royal family now governing from the north, the pharaohs of the period appointed one of their daughters "divine consort of Amun". As the only wife of the god she was invested with a great temporal power over the area of Thebes. A courtier of one of these Karomama dedicated this statuette in the temple. It is one of the finest Egyptian bronzes known to us. The beauty of it is further enhanced by the inlay of precious metals, over the lavish costume with two large wings, like those of queens or goddesses, folding around her legs and a magnificent necklace, the heavy clasp of which falls at her back and is inscribed with her name "the beloved of Mout, Karomama".

122 The God Horus

c. 800-700 BC

Bronze statue. H 0.95 m

E 7703

Although metal statues were frequent in temples at all periods, bronzes were most common and of highest quality during the Third Intermediate Period. This great statue of Horus was part of a scene in which the two gods of royalty, Horus and Thot, faced each other and purified the king with water before ceremonials. To save metal, large statues were hollow, and made in the "cire perdue" method as follows. A core of clay and sand is formed and covered with a layer of wax of the same thickness as the bronze, which is modelled into the desired shape. It is covered in clay, then heated. The wax melts and runs, leaving a space between the inner core and the clay mould, into which the molten metal is poured. After it is cooled the mould is broken; generally the core is left inside. This statue appears to be unfinished; the face has not been polished, and the tenons linking the arms (cast separately) to the body are still visible. It was probably covered with another layer of plaster or gold which has disappeared.

Saite period

¹²³ Seated Cat

c. 700-600 BC

Bronze statuette; scarab in blue glass.

H 0.33 m; W 0.25 m

N 4538

Bronze ex-voto statuettes offered by devotees in
the temples proliferated during the Late period.
Bronzes of cats, for the most part representing the
goddess Bastet, have been found in large numbers.
They indicate the popularity of this goddess not
only in Bubatis, but in many other large towns
such as Memphis, Thebes and Esna. The
Egyptians also depicted her with her kittens or in
the form of a woman with a cat's head.

¹²⁴ Bust of an Old Man

c. 550 BC (28th Dynasty)

Schist. H 0.252 m; W 0.185 m

N 2454

Unfortunately part of the inscription to this statue
is missing; "under the protection of Ptah-Sokar,
the chancellor of the king of Lower Egypt...".
Two tendencies are linked in this fine piece of
sculpture; a contemporary vogue for archaism
which can be seen in the naked bust and sober
hairstyle, and a concern for realism, confined to
the face. The marks of age are minutely detailed,

perhaps to indicate wisdom. The fine stone, a beautiful green schist, gives the work a perfect finish, with its smooth polished surfaces and precision modelling. It is a remarkable portrait.

Last indigenous dynasties

125 **The Extraction of Lily Juice**

4th century BC

Limestone bas-relief. W 37 cm; H 25.8 cm; D. 4 cm

E 11162

This fragment of a bas-relief comes from a tomb dating from the last indigenous dynasties. There are several contemporary examples of scenes like this. Lily flowers are being collected and their juice extracted. The flowers are placed in a cloth which is twisted with the help of rods, to extract all the juice. The liquid runs into a jar placed on a low table or held upright in a stand. More complete reliefs show the juice being poured into small jars offered to the owner of the tomb. The full figures of the working women and their round faces reveal the influence of Greek art which, combined with the Egyptian clarity of composition, gives this work its peculiar charm.

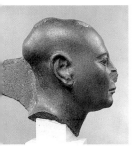

126 **Man with a Shaved Head**

4th century BC

Schist. H 0.129 m

Gift of Lami. E 25577

Under the last Egyptian pharaohs, men of note chose to be depicted without wigs, their heads shaved, as was the practice for temple ceremonies. This work is a fine example of the continuing realistic tendency, showing a middle-aged man, with full features, heavy chin, and lined eyes. The sculptor's skill is clear from the closely observed anatomy of the cranium.

127 **Healing Statue**

4th century BC

Basalt. H 0.077 m

E 10777

This statue is an example of artistic tendencies in the 4th Century BC and reveals the growing interest in witchcraft. The fine, smiling face stems from the idealizing line of Saite sculpture. Smooth, simplified volumes for the costume serve as a base for magic invocations designed to heal snake and scorpion bites. The text is formal; the bitten man must drink water which has run over the text of the statue and has become impregnated with its magical powers. The stele the man is holding shows the young god Horus standing on crocodiles, and is common as an independent sculpture serving the same purpose.

Egypt under Greek Domination *(333-30 BC)* **and under the Romans** *(30 BC to 4th century AD)*

The Greek, Alexander the Great, took Egypt from the Persians. After his death it was governed by one of his generals, Ptolemy. For three centuries Egypt was ruled by Greek "pharaohs" who descended from Ptolemy, with a Greek ruling class which early on, at least, did not mix with natives. In 30 BC the last of these Ptolomaic sovereigns, Cleopatra VII, fell to Octavius. Egypt remained part of the Roman world for several centuries. While the emperors - "promus" pharaohs - continued reconstruction work on the great Egyptian sanctuaries, they diverted the country's economy into the production of cereals for the population of Rome.

Grecian Egypt

128 Compartmented Box

3rd century BC
Egyptian faience (glazed silicious pottery).
H 5 cm. W 12 cm; D 11.6 cm
E 11071

Pottery in Egypt under the Greeks provides a good example of a successful union between traditional Egyptian techniques and the repertoire of Greek forms and decorations. The hollow motifs are a deeper blue than the protruding areas, being more thickly glazed. One of the most important areas of manufacture was Memphis.

129 Body of Isis

3rd-1st century BC
Diorite statuette. H 0.63 m
Gift of Hoffmann. E 11197

Under Ptolemaic rule, the Egyptians experimented
to a limited degree with elements of Greek art.
This body of a goddess in the traditional frontal
position is dressed in a draped garment in the
Greek fashion, though it has the symmetry
beloved of the Egyptians. The knot of material
between the breasts indicates this is a
representation of Isis.

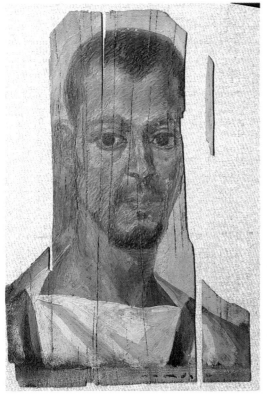

Roman Egypt

130 Funerary Portrait of a Man

2nd century AD (?)
Wax on wood. H 0.38; W 0.24 m
AF 6883

During the Roman period, the skilful wrapping of
bands around a mummy was sometimes used to
attach a board with the portrait of the dead person
to the head. The technique and style of such
portraits is Graeco-Roman; they are painted with a

wax medium in separate brushstrokes. This bust is in a three-quarter view and the face is almost fully frontal. The people painted were members of the dominant class, Greek in origin, though mixed with local blood by this time. Sometimes a portrait was painted directly onto the shroud.

131 **Mortuary Mask of a Woman**

Early 3rd century AD

Painted plaster. H 0.34 m; W 0.62 m; D 0.26 m

Antinoe excavations. E 21360

During both the Ptolemaic dynasty and the Roman Empire, Greek officials governed Egypt. Attracted to the Egyptian religion of the dead which promised eternal life, they adopted various practices such as mummification with the idea that the appearance of the terrestrial body should be preserved. However, their masks are very different from Egyptian "casings", being plaster busts like this one, with realistic features and Roman hairstyles and embellishments.

Script

Alongside painted and sculpted hieroglyphs visible on temple walls, the Egyptians used a cursive script, in which the original hieroglyphs are more or less recognisable depending on the period, rapidity of execution and skill of the scribe. This is known as "hieratic script". From the 7th century BC this evolved into a form where original signs are unrecognizable: the so-called "demotic script" which transcribed the language that was spoken rather than the classical language. In the last centuries of the pharaohs, scribes working on mural inscriptions in the temples played about with signs, inventing hundreds more which could only be interpreted by a few initiates. Invented around 3100 BC, hieroglyphs were still in use during the 4th century AD. As for the old Egyptian language, it survived the Arab invasion thanks to the Christian community. It was preserved in texts of the Coptic religion, written in Greek characters. It was his knowledge of Coptic that enabled Champollion to decipher hieroglyphs between 1824-1826, after fifteen centuries of obscurity.

¹³² Scribe's Palette

c. 1347-1337 BC (18th Dynasty)
Wood and reed. H 37 cm; W 5.5 cm; D 1.3 cm
N 2241

The palette is formed of a strip of wood, hollowed at its centre to hold reed sticks with chewed ends serving as brushes. Two hollows contain little cakes of red and black colour. The red was used for chapter headings in texts such as the "Book of the Dead". The "cartouche" engraved on the object indicates that its owner lived under the reign of Tutankhamen.

133 Burial Scene from the
"Book of the Dead" of Nebqued

c. 1400 BC (18th Dynasty)

Painted papyrus. H about 0.30 m

N 3068

detail

Egyptian books were written on strips of papyrus which could extend to several meters in length, and could be rolled and unrolled as they were read. The writing is divided into columns or pages of lines. Funerary books such as this fine example of the "Book of the Dead" tended to be illustrated. The burial scene is shown at the outset and because of the format of the papyrus it spreads out into the funerary procession and various stages of the ceremony. The Louvre also conserves other religious texts, as well as letters, accountancy books, contracts and even fragments of literary works.

Burial

The Egyptians were not the only peoples to attend to funerary rituals with great care. However, the exceptional condition of preservation of bodies and objects found in tombs and the sheer variety of furnishings and funereal iconography has encouraged the false notion that Egyptians were obsessed above all else with the day of their burial and their afterlife. Still, we do have precise information about the burial ceremony from tombs and illustrated at the beginning of the "Book of the Dead". Aside from the procession of furnishings and the sarcophagus to the burial ground, an important moment was the reanimation ritual performed over the mummy or the sarcophagus before its descent into the tomb.

¹³⁴ Sarcophagus of Madja

c. 1490-1470 BC (18th Dynasty)

Painted wood. H 0.62 m; W 1.84 m

Excavations of Deir el-Medineh. E 14543

detail

The sarcophagus of the lady Madja reflects the sobriety of middle class funerary furnishing. The white background of the bier matches the form of the mummy and accentuates the clear and balanced composition. On one side men are bringing water and meat for the dead; on the other the sarcophagus is being hauled to the tomb where mourners are awaiting it.

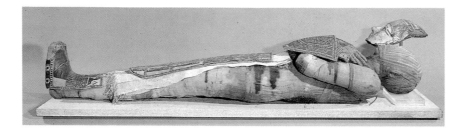

135 Mummy of a Man

3rd or 4th century BC

L 1.67 m;

N 2627

During the Ptolemaic period, mummification became more artistic in nature. Having been disembowelled and dried in natron salt, the body was skilfully swathed in a mesh of linen. Then the mummy was covered with a coating of plastered old papyrus or cloth. A mask was laid on the face, a case on the feet and a large necklace on the chest. The usual winged goddesses and funereal spirits are depicted over the legs along with a picture of the mummy on its embalming bed.

Coptic Egypt

The term "Copt" derives from the Greek word "Aigyptios", meaning Egyptian. By the time the Arabs arrived in Egypt in 641 AD, the whole country was Christian and the term was used to designate not only the native group but their adherence to Christianity as opposed to the Muslim faith of the invaders. Later it came to refer to the Christian practices of Egypt and by extension those of Ethiopia.

The beginnings of Coptic script can be traced to the 2nd century BC and it developed from the 3rd and 4th centuries AD. Made up of Greek letters along with seven signs of Pharaonic origin, it was replaced in official texts by Arabic from the 8th century on, and disappeared during the 11th. It survived only as a liturgical language in the church.

A stylistic change in Egyptian art took place over the 4th century giving rise to an original style which lasted into the 12th century. When, after the 9th century, the Copts were in a minority they gradually turned for inspiration to the art of Byzantium and Islam. But Coptic art at its apogee (from the 5th to the 7th centuries) was strongly marked by Graeco-Roman, Paleochristian and oriental influences.

¹³⁶ Dionysus

Probably Antinoe,
4th century AD
Limestone high relief.
H 0.545 m; W 0.527 m; D 0.175 m
Acq. 1958. E 26106

A Dionysus emerges from a niche covered in vine scrolls. This work is in a new style that appeared during the 4th century, which turned resolutely away from Greek and Roman styles. The disproportionate body of the god is devoid of realistic detail; the round, characterless face, the large lined eyes with holes bored for pupils, the beaded hair are all signs of a new direction in Coptic thought. Of all the pagan divinities, Dionysus was particularly venerated in Egypt. Linked to Osiris, the god of wine, according to the Texts of the Pyramids, he was particularly favoured by the Ptolemaic rulers. The theme of the vine, his main attribute, also appears in the Bible, evoking God the Father and Christ, from whom the faithful spread like vines.

137 **Virgin of the Annunciation**

Late 5th century AD

Fig wood bas-relief carving.

H 28.5 cm; W 14.2 cm; D 2 cm

Acq. 1945. E 17118

Seated on a high stool, Mary is busy weaving the Veil of the Temple as described in the Apocrypha. The Archangel Gabriel, of whom only a foot remains, would have faced her. This carving, which was once painted, probably belonged to a larger panel illustrating scenes from the life of the Virgin, the iconography of which spread throughout the Christian world after the Council of Ephesus in 431 which proclaimed the divine maternity of Christ's mother.

The woodcarving technique was always popular in Egypt despite the fact that wood had to be imported. Coptic craftsmen and carvers were famous for their skill and even in the middle of the Arab period they were brought over to work on the great constructions of the near East.

Monastery of Baouît
7th century AD

Distemper. H 57 cm; W. 57 cm; D 2 cm

IFAO Excavations, 1901-2. E 11565

With a protective gesture Christ is accompanying
the abbot Mena, head of the Baouît monastery.
Both figures are standing in strictly frontal
positions, against a background of hills and red
evening sky. Destined probably to be inset into a
wall, the style of the panel matches the numerous
lines of saints decorating niches and walls of the
monastery chapels. Simplified and boldly painted,
the rounded folds of the garments are typical of
Coptic painting. Byzantine influence shows in the
white highlights of the clothes and the richly
studded and bejewelled binding of the Gospel that
Christ carries, which is offset by the simplicity and
sobriety of the rest of the painting.

139 Sabine's Shawl

Antinoe, 6th century AD

Wool tapestry. H 1.10 m; W 1.40 m

A Gayet Excavations, 1902-3. E 29302

This garment was found in an Antinoe tomb where it covered the shoulders of a lady known as Sabine. It is one of some 35,000 fabrics recovered from Egyptian tombs. Decorated with tapestries on a canvas backing, the shawl is composed of two squares framed by right-angle bands, with a central medallion. The iconography derives from Graeco-Roman mythology: Daphne and Apollo, Diana the huntress, Bellerophon and the chimaera. The Nilotic scenes of the bands can be linked to subjects from ancient Egypt which were adapted to the taste of a wealthy Roman clientele from the 1st century AD. The fashion for lavishly decorated fabrics which started in the Orient, with a few examples dating from the New Empire, developed during the 3rd century AD and spread during the Christian era across the whole Mediterranean.

140 Censer with an Eagle

9th century AD

Perforated bronze. H 0.28 m; ⌀ 0.20 m

Acq. 1925. E 11708

This object, which probably had a liturgical function, consists of an incense burner with three feet decorated with hares, and a dome-shaped cover surmounted by an eagle strangling a serpent. The body of the brazier and lid, which are bolted together, is fretted with elegant foliated scrollwork. It is a showpiece of the skill of Coptic bronze founders which continued to develop into the Arab period. Hares and rabbits are frequently seen on early Christian monuments as well as on lamps, pottery, glassware, seals and fabrics, though their significance (the brevity of human life, a symbol of Christ perhaps?) remains unclear. The eagle strangling the serpent is symbolic of Christ's victory over the devil, depicted elsewhere as pierced by Christ's monogram.

The Prehellenic period
and the Archaic Greek world

The Classical Greek world

The Hellenistic world

The Etruscans

The Roman world

Greek, Etruscan and Roman Antiquities

Introduction

The Department of Greek, Etruscan and Roman antiquities along with the Department of Painting were among the first to be established in the Louvre. Antiquities from all three civilisations come in a wide range of materials including stone, bronze, terracotta, wood, glass, gold and silver, ivory, stucco and amber. They illustrate the artistic activities of a wide area centred principally around the Mediterranean, from the end of the Neolithic age (4000 BC) to the 6th century AD. Starting with the royal collection as a nucleus (begun during the reign of François I), to which was added the collections of Richelieu and Mazarin, the department has grown with new acquisitions over the years, principal among them being the Borghese (1808) and Campana (1863) collections. Because of long-established tradition and the close historical links between certain objects and the palace itself, the Department is located in some of the oldest areas of the building, such as the gallery formerly housing the queens' apartments and the *Salle des Cariatides*, which has witnessed many important events in French history since the 16th century. Owing to their weight and scale the sculpture is displayed on the ground floor. Here, strict chronological order has been observed wherever possible in both the Greek section, which contains original statues along with copies executed in Roman times, and the Roman section. On the same floor, three rooms are devoted to Etruscan art with large and small objects arranged together so as to make the transition from the Archaic style to the Classic and Hellenistic periods as apparent as possible. The first floor, which is being reorganized, is given over to bronzes, principally of Greek and Roman origin, and to the display of a collection of mainly Greek vases and terracotta statuettes, the abundance and diversity of which rank it among the greatest world collections.

The Prehellenic age and the Archaic Greek world

The area of the Mediterranean basin, settled in a series of invasions by what came to be known as the Greeks, was originally occupied by peoples of a non Indo-European origin. The history of their art, from the Neolithic period to the end of the Middle Bronze age, looks first to Thessaly, then to the Cyclades and finally to Crete. Each of these areas benefited from the influence of the most advanced civilizations of the East. The development of Minoan Crete in the first half of the 2nd millennium was to have a profound effect on the early Greeks, the Myceneans, who were notable for their major artistic undertakings. Though centred principally in Argolis, the Mycenean civilisation had a powerful influence over the Aegean world. The Myceneans were the heirs to the art of Crete and they gave it a strength which quite possibly the early Iron age Greeks did not forget.

After the collapse of the Myceneans, Greek art re-emerged in the Geometric style. Becoming more

and more sophisticated, every form of decoration
and sculpture was governed by the Geometric
aesthetic. Within this common language each
region had its own distinctive accent, and Attica
led the way.

However, by the end of the 8th century, the
system broke down. Oriental motifs flooded in,
and the Greeks adopted them in their own unique
way. Every city and province "orientalized" their
art in a different manner during the 7th century,
in a period which also saw the emergence of
monumental sculpture. After exercises in the
"Daedalic" style, the kouroi at the end of the
century marked an advance in the use of marble
and massive scale. Kouroi and korai were
reproduced on a humbler scale, within a
conventional framework, right up to the Graeco-
Persian wars, and bear witness to an increasingly
detailed observation of anatomy. The approach to
relief sculpture became freer as did subjects which
were less constrained by religious tradition.

The independent nature of the ancient cities
favoured the development of artistic centres, from
which painted vases, bronze and terracotta
statuettes emerged in profusion. Athens rivalled
Corinth with regard to pottery. Corinth cornered
the market especially with its small perfumed oil
jars; but having adopted the black figure
technique from Corinth, Attic vases finally
predominated. Remaining the centre of trade,
Athens was by the middle of the 4th century the
home of flourishing workshops which exported
many objects to Etruria. Innovative artists
revolutionized the technique of vase painting.
Reversing relationships, they painted around the
outside of the figures, thus bringing about the "red
figure" style, in which the greatest masterpieces of
the genre were created at the turn of the 6th and
5th centuries BC. A similar creative impetus can be
seen in bronze figurines, and excavations in the
great panhellenic sanctuaries have uncovered an
astonishing variety of objects. Despite such
diversity, however, the combination of religious
function, use of myths and the increasing

importance given to the human form, provide a strong sense of overall unity.

The Prehellenic period

141 **Female Head**

Amorgos (?)
c. 2700-2400 BC
Marble. H 0.27 m, W 0.145 m, D 0.096 m
Gift of J Delamarre, 1896. MNC 2108 (Ma 3095)

This imposing, long head comes from a large family of figures and figurines which artists of the Cyclades produced during the Early Bronze age (3200-2000 BC). In general they represent female nudes, though their size and shape may vary considerably. The Louvre marble is a fragment of a full-size statue, and the complete work must have been around 1,50 m in height.
Although the only detailed carving on this head is around the nose and ears, the sculptor's sensitivity to volumes is clear from the convex plane of the head and the depth of the profile. Similar heads can be seen on full-length figures represented standing, with tapering feet and forearms crossed

at right-angles over their bodies. Belonging to what is known as the "cross-armed" type, these are the most classical versions of the genre; the geometric treatment of form, evident in the construction of this head, is carried through to the body, in planes and volumes respecting carefully calculated laws of proportion.

The precise importance and function of such figures which are generally found in excavations of necropoli, and also occasionally in ordinary dwellings, is not yet clear, although there seems little reason to doubt their religious nature.

142 "Sauce Bowl"

Heraia of Arcadia (Peloponnese?)
Around mid-3rd century BC
Gold. H 0.17 m, W 0.10 m, L 0.144 m
Acq. 1887; MNC 906 (Bj 1885)

The high upright spout of this receptacle has earned it the name of "sauce bowl". With the exception of the solid handle decorated with a herring-bone motif, it is made from a single sheet of gold. Thus its annular base was made by beating out the wall of the bowl. Only one other example is known to us and the presumed origin of this precious object, a site in the Peloponnese called Heraia of Arcadia, is an intriguing one. The shape, however, was common to Early Bronze age potters in the Cyclades as well as in areas around Greece and to the northeast of Anatolia. Its origin is now thought to lie in the Cycladean archipelago where the earliest examples are to be found. A similar origin for this Louvre bowl is possible, although a Peloponnese connection cannot be excluded.

143 Geometric Krater (fragment)

Attic style, c. 750 BC

Terracotta. H 58 cm, W 14 cm, Th 1.3 cm

A 517, S 568

After the destruction of Mycenaean civilisation, Greece seems to have entered a "dark age". However, an artistic revival took place in the 10th century characterized by decorative effects derived from geometry. From an early experimental phase (Proto-Geometric style), it became more assured, as can be seen from the large funerary vases of the middle of the 8th century BC found at the Dipylon necropolis at Athens. This bowl is an example, and boasts a large number of decorative figures. In the midst of ornamentation dominated by zigzags, we see a "prothesis" (a dead man displayed on his bier) with the family gathered around the corpse and his possessions. All are shown in lamentation with arms raised in a distinctive Geometrical manner. A procession of chariots and war boats point to the heroic and noble lineage of the dead man whose tomb was marked by this great vase. The extreme care given to the execution is typical of painters in Athens. The vase is no doubt the work of one of the most proficient, known as the "Painter of the Dipylon".

144 Amphora

Attributed to the "painter of Analatos"
Attica, c. 680 BC

Terracotta. H 0.81 m

Acq. 1935. CA 2985

This vase, with its slender form recalling the amphora of the late Geometric style, must have served as a "loutrophoros", that is, a ritual vase used in marriage ceremonies or at funerals of unmarried people. But while the relief decoration applied around the mouth and handles, and the layout of motifs, conform to earlier designs, the motifs themselves generally break away from the geometric register. The rosettes and braids around the neck, along with animated figures such as the sphinxes, the two couples dancing to the sound of pan-pipes and the coachmen driving their chariots, herald the arrival of the Orientalizing style in Athens.

By the early 7th century BC, interest in the Geometric code was waning and motifs from the East appeared increasingly in Greek decoration; with them, the outlines of human and animal figures became more fluid and proportions more realistic. Many cities produced painted vases in the new style. Despite few exports, the painters of Athens at this period gave evidence of an inquiring spirit and an interest in the human figure, which is amply demonstrated in this vase.

145 **Oenochoe**
jug for pouring wine

Rhodes (?) c. 650 BC

Terracotta. H 0.395 m

Acq. 1891. CA 350 (E 658)

This terracotta jug, which was inspired by a metal receptacle as is indicated most obviously by the form of the handle, has an aperture formed of three lobes to facilitate pouring. Bought by the painter E Levy in Rome in 1855, its origin is unknown, but the shape, technique and style of decoration, ranks it with vases which the cities of Eastern Greece (both on islands such as Rhodes and on the mainland) produced during the orientalizing period of the 7th century BC and after. Applied with a brush on top of a pale-toned slip, the decoration is arranged in superimposed bands. This layout along with the abundance of motifs recalls contemporary texts describing embroidered fabrics which have been preserved. This highly orientalizing style is known as the "wild goat style" after the animal motif which recurs most frequently. The care taken in the detail of each outline around the deer and imaginary animals make this a masterpiece of the genre. There is none of the monotony here, which can be seen on similar but looser compositions of a later date.

146 Aryballos
perfumed oil flask

Corinth, c. 640 BC
Terracotta. H 0.063 m
Acq. 1898. CA 931

Because of its geographical location, Corinth was one of the first Greek cities to be affected by influences from the East from the end of the 8th century BC onwards. Corinthian pottery, an indication of the prosperity of this city on the Isthmus, dominated the market and was known throughout the Mediterranean. The small Louvre aryballos is a good example of craftsmanship during the first phase of activity of the Corinthian artists known as the "Protocorinthian" style. Using the new black figure technique, the artist has managed to give life to two parallel friezes, a battle and a hare-hunt, albeit within a confined area. The quality of this object is further enhanced by the modelling of the neck into the form of a female head. The relationship between the face and hair and the composition, of the latter link it with a work such as the *Dame d'Auxerre* 147. Corinth produced a considerable number of vases between the end of the 7th and the first half of the 6th century BC, but rarely does their quality exceed this.

147 Female Statue known as the "Dame d'Auxerre"

Crete (?) c. 630 BC

Limestone. H 0.75 m incl. base.

Exch. 1909 with Musée d'Auxerre.

MND 847 (Ma 3098)

This small statue was discovered by the archeologist Maxime Collignon in the reserves of the Musée d'Auxerre. Its origin is not certain, although the soft limestone of its composition and the style it emerges from, link it to Cretan sculpture of the 7th century BC which has been called "Daedalic" after the legendary sculptor and inventor of the maze who worked for King Minos in Crete. In contrast to the imaginative contours of the Geometric style, the "Dame d'Auxerre" is very solidly constructed, her body sheathed in a close-fitting costume, her left hand flat against her thigh. There is evidence that the costume was probably painted as traces of pigment remain in the incised designs which would have served as guidelines. Another sylistic feature is the U-shaped face set within a symmetrical Egyptian hairstyle. Whether she does in fact represent a goddess, or is simply a priestess or worshipful follower, is open to speculation. With a greater respect for proportions and a sense of volume, the "Dame d'Auxerre" is a precursor of monumental Greek statuary.

148 Pendant

Rhodes (Camiros)
c. 630 BC
Electrum. H 8.5 cm
Salzmann coll. Depot of the Dept. of
Oriental Antiquities, 1949. S 1209 (Bj 2169)

This pendant is a fine example of the virtuosity of goldmiths working in Rhodes during the Orientalizing period. Its function is not certain, although it is now believed to have been worn at the neck or chest rather than on a belt or over the forehead. The techniques it uses such as granulation and filigree, passed down from Oriental jewellers, clearly demonstrate the skills of their Greek imitators. Motifs such as the rosettes, griffon's protomes and janiform heads (the Daedalic style of which recall the "Dame d'Auxerre"**147**), are also Eastern in origin. On the plate bordered with filigree, a lion and eagle are depicted according to an Egyptian tradition which is here softened by Aegean fantasy. The sheer luxury of this ornament is a mark of the high level of refinement attained by certain Greeks in the 7th century BC.

149 Female Statue

Samos, c. 570 BC
Marble. H 1.92 m with plinth.
Acq. 1881. MNB 3226 (Ma 686)

Found in 1875 in the sanctuary of Hera at Samos, this imposing female figure is one of the first "kore", that is, one of the first Greek representations of a graceful woman shown at the peak of her beauty and offered as a gift to a god or goddess. She is the female counterpart of the male "kouros", a young male nude shown at his athletic peak. Korai and kouroi mark the progress of the Archaic period from the origins of monumental sculpture to the Persian wars. A recent discovery in Samos has brought to light an identical statue with the same costume and a dedicatory inscription: "I have been dedicated by Cheramyes to Hera as an offering". It is thus very likely that it was one of a group of at least two female figures, which is not unusual in Samos; a family group of six figures also exists. The statue is dressed in a ceremonial garment combining a tunic, mantle and veil. It was probably sculpted around 570 BC. The legs are still joined and the right hand, seen under the veil, does not as yet alter the direction of folds in the tunic. It is possible the damaged left hand held some attribute. The quantity and similarity of sculptures discovered at Samos points to the existence of a local tradition which no doubt contributed greatly to the development of sculpture in Greece.

150 Kouros

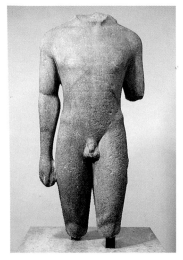

Found in Actium
Naxien style, c. 560 BC

Marble. H 1 m

Acq. 1874. MNB 766 (Ma 687)

The kouros was the principle form of Greek Archaic sculpture from the end of the 7th century up to the Persian wars. Many workshops, scattered all over the Greek world, produced these statues in varying sizes and with diverse functions. The fact that this one was discovered in the sanctuary of Apollo in Actium (Aktion) lends weight to the idea that it represents Apollo. The Louvre kouros should be distinguished from earlier examples because of the satisfying solutions it finds to certain anatomical problems. The effort of Greek sculptors, whatever their origins, was centred on how to render the athletic body of the kouros more realistically. But certain inaccuracies, such as the clumsy junction between arm and

forearm, date the work to 560 BC at the latest.
Aside from growing anatomical accuracy, stylistic
differences can be detected among kouroi. The
decorative harmony governing the treatment of
this particular statue confirms it as being from the
Naxos workshops.

151 Head of a Horseman (the Rampin Rider)

Athens, c. 550 BC

H (head) 0.27 m

Georges Rampin bequest, 1896. MNC 2128 (Ma 3104)

When this marble head entered the Louvre
collections it was deemed unclassifiable, since the

head which was evidently Archaic in style, had asymmetric neck muscles. Furthermore, the hair of this piece, which has a few traces of colour, is atypical, a veritable latticework of marble, under a delicately-worked laurel crown. Things seemed clearer when it became apparent that the head belonged to the body of a horseman, a fragment of which is conserved in the museum of the Acropolis. The victorious rider was no doubt shown turning and bowing his head in response to applause. Understanding of the monument was thoroughly revised when it was discovered that fragments of a second rider remained, clearly a pendent to the first, and together they form a unified group. But the subject is less apparent. Dioscures has been suggested - Castor and Pollux - or, given the originality of the representation, the two sons of Pisistrate, the tyrant of Athens, called Hippias and Hipparque. The face is, in any case, Attic in the way its features are formed, and a touch of Ionian grace enlivens it with a smile.

detail

¹⁵² **Black Figure Amphora**
complete with lid

Signed by Exekias, potter
Attica, c. 540 BC

Terracotta. H 0.50 m with lid.

Acq. 1883. MNC 495 (F 53)

"Exekias, potter" is the signature found on a dozen vases including the Louvre amphora. On two vases, however, he also claims authorship of the painting. The quality of the two scenes depicted here has prompted more than one suggestion that he painted this vase too. On one side Heracles is seen fighting Geryon, a monster with three Hoplite bodies who is struggling to resist the hero's assault. The shepherd Eurytion has already succumbed. Shields are the central compositional pivot of the combat, and the artist gives proof of great narrative powers and an ability to balance elements to create a harmonious whole. The decoration on the lid, an animal procession with deer and sirens alternating, recalls in its miniaturist detail the tall stemmed goblets contemporary with this vase. This was the period when the black figure technique reached its peak, just before red figure painting emerged and revolutionized the art of vase painting.

153 Red Figure Amphora

Signed by Andokides potter
Attica, c. 530 BC
Terracotta. H 0.58 m
Acq. 1843. N 3391 (G1)

Turned by the Athenian potter Andokides who signed the base, this amphora has a continuous design containing two pictures of an exceptional interest and quality. On one side, there is a fight attended by Athena and Hermes, and on the other a female zither player performs before an audience and judge; both are highlighted against the black background. The painter has reversed the usual relationship of black figures on light background, and is thus able to indicate details within each figure with much greater subtelty. This new technique signalled a revolution in the art of the painted vase. The subtler paintbrush replaced the stylet providing a wider range of possibilities. The painter who worked regularly with the potter Andokides seems to have invented this new style which first appeared around 530 BC. The red figure style established the superiority of Athenian workshops which henceforth dominated the painted vase industry.

154 Head of a Sphinx

Thebes, Corinthian style, c. 530 BC

Terracotta.

Acq. 1895. Ca 637

Sphinxes were often part of funerary or votive monuments. In particular, as acroterion, they decorated buildings ranging from edicules (private shrines) to full-scale temples. This head belonged to a small sphinx decorating a corner of a modest sized edifice. Shown seated, in profile with erect forequarters, the sphinx's head would have been turned to the side. The feminine features which are enlivened by a subtle smile are framed by waves of hair spreading from a central parting across the temples down over her shoulders in larger rolls. A diadem painted with lotus flowers and buds crowns the composition. It is a terracotta version of a Greek sculpture of the period dominated by korai. Similar works are known which link it to the production of coroplaths at Corinth. Athenian influence can, however, be seen in the careful modelling and attentive gaze.

155 Red Figure Footed Krater

Signed by Euphronios the painter
Attica, c. 510 BC

Terracotta (the base and some recently recognized

fragments have been reassembled) H 0.46 m

Campana coll., 1863. Cp 748 (G 103)

This red figure vase, the form of which seems to have been developed around 530 BC by the painter-potter Exekias, belongs to the greatest period of Greek pottery. It is signed by Euphronios whose career as a painter in Athens is placed around the end of the 6th century BC, the golden age for such pottery. The decoration around the bowl testifies to an unswerving sense of proportion and balance. The principle scene here describes the battle between Heracles and the giant Antaeus before terrified female spectators. With his armour and the Nemean lionskin laid aside, the naked hero, who is certain of his strength, has a mortal grip on his enemy whose defeat is clear from the expression of anguish on his face. The elaborate detail on the two bodies testify to the artist's virtuosity in capturing anatomical essentials. A scene from daily life on the other side counterbalances the myth. A musical contest is being held. The presence of engraved elements and the quantity of reddish-purple retouches indicate how close it is to the black figure technique which was still actively employed at that time.

¹⁵⁶ Red Figure Cup

Signed by Euphronios the potter, decoration attributed to Onesimos
Attica, c. 500-490 BC
Terracotta, H 0.165 m; Ø 0.40 m
Acq. 1871. MNB 166 (G 104)

Made by Euphronios at the beginning of the 5th century BC, this cup is distinctive not only for its unusual vigour but also for its lavish ornamentation. The subject is Theseus, a hero much loved by the people of Athens where this was made.
The inside of the cup shows an episode from

Theseus' life during his journey to Crete with Minos. Minos threw a ring into the sea, defying Theseus to recover it and prove that he was the son of Poseidon. Theseus dived in, escorted by a Triton shown here holding his feet. In the sea kingdom he is received by Amphitrite. Between them rises the great figure of Athena, protector of heroes. The fluid composition and the complex interweaving of lines is a subtle evocation of the aquatic world. The outside of the cup celebrates Theseus' victories over the bandits plaguing Attica called Skiron, Procrustes and Kerkyon; the capture of the Marathon bull was his last exploit. In this masterpiece of the late Archaic style, there is a deliberate contrast between the divine serenity of the scene within, and the violent images along the outside.

157 **Statuette of a Butcher**

Thebes (Boeotia)
c. 500-475 BC
Terracotta. H 0.12 m
Acq. 1902. CA 1455 (B 122)

The people of Boeotia who are, to this day, unfairly considered by Athenians to be clumsy, have often given proof of their artistic skill, particularly in the making of clay figurines. This one belongs to a group which illustrates various aspects of daily life; figures of cooks, bakers and hairdressers are also known. Here a butcher is knocking out a small pig on a tripod block. Capturing the immediacy of the action very effectively, this small object was modelled by hand except for the face which was cast from a mould. The most probable function of such figurines was as childrens' toys, which were buried in tombs along with other belongings of the deceased.

158 Mirror Stand

First quarter of the 5th century BC

Bronze. H 0.18 m

Acq. 1888. MNC 992 (Br 1688)

Mirrors were among the more elaborate of the various bronze utensils that formed a part of everyday Greek life. Adapting a successful formula from Egyptian art, Greek bronze founders often turned the handle of the mirror into a female figure. Here we have a cariatid bearing a metal disk on her head, and she would probably have held a flower in her right hand. She is standing on a stool with equine feet. This particular artistic genre, of which there are many examples during the transition from Archaism to Classicism, had a part to play in the stylistic developments of this crucial period. But it also has a distinctive regional flavour; it is attributed to the style of Aegina in the early 5th century. The rigid pose and the fine folds down the tunic refer back to earlier influences while the gravity of the face and the suggestion of free movement in the arms look forward to the "Severe style".

159 Cup

Signed by the potter Brygos,
decoration attributed
to the "Painter of Brygos"
Athens, c. 490 BC

Terracotta. H 0.134 m; ⌀ 0.325 m

Acq. 1881. MNB 3047 (G 152)

The influence of Homeric legend on Greek civilisation is proverbial. It comes as no surprise therefore that so many vases should be illustrated with scenes of the heroes of the Iliad and the Odyssey. But this cup has a unique quality. Made by the potter Brygos - who signed one of the handles - it was painted by an artist who knew how to adapt to the constraints of the decoration. Within the circular field of the inner medallion, Briseis, Achilles' captive, is pouring a libation for Achilles' old tutor, Phenix; the relationship between the figures reveals a great skill in balancing the composition. But over the outer bowl the "Painter of Brygos" excels himself; he brings to life the story of the sack of Troy illustrating two episodes marked by violence and passion. On one side Andromache, armed with a pestle, tries to protect Astyanax, her son, from attack by the Achaeans; on the other, Neoptolemus, son of Achilles, brandishes the child's body in an effort to subdue King Priam who has taken refuge at the altar of Zeus.

detail

The Classical Greek World

The tribulations of the Persian wars, when the fate of Hellenism hung in the balance, brought about a decisive change in Greek art. Athens, whose "hoplites" and "trieres" blocked the advances of the Persian armies, emerged stronger from the conflict. Back in their devastated city, the Athenians piously buried the statues which the invaders had dethroned, in order to make way for new works of art.

Here, and in the rest of Greece, forms broke loose from conventions and became more realistic. The real weight of gravity shifted the movement across the hips, costumes fell more plausibly in simpler folds. The mobile athlete took over from the rigid kouros and the increasingly widespread use of bronze facilitated the change. But while bodies moved, gestures no longer sufficed; figures were given a sense of purpose, a feeling of imminent change.

Greek art became committed to realism. But progress finally led to a standstill. The rhythm of athletic composition reached a caesura in the wisdom and equilibrium of the statues of Polyclitus, a symbol of Classical perfection. The Ergastines of the Parthenon move at a unified ideal pace, remote from our world. Everything became subjected to reason, harmony and transparency.

The period which in Athens coincided with Pericles' government and the career of Phidias was, however, short-lived. The atrocities of Peloponnesean war upset the balance; new values, a new belief in the individual emerged and art reflected the change. The female body, images of which multiplied, is seen under a web of drapery; faces are tinged with melancholy and time and space are again linked in the image of the athlete. These tendencies increased during the 4th century BC. In a world where Classicism was under varying degrees of threat, foreign elements played an important role. The fluid grace of the figures of Praxiteles, the passion burning in the faces of Scopas defy their origins. At Xanthus and

Halicarnassus, Greek genius encountered the ideology of the barbarians; new disciplines like portraiture were mastered and three-dimensional work became more common. In this troubled world the exploits of Alexander the Great brought such changes in artistic conditions to an end.

160 **Apollo and the Nymphs**

Thasos, Passageway of the Theoroi
c. 480 BC

Marble relief. H 0.92 m; W 2.09 m

Acq. 1864. Ma 696

During the first third of the 5th century, forms underwent rapid change, becoming both more fluid and more realistic. The Passageway of the Theoroi, a group of reliefs placed at eye-level on the walls of a passage in Thasos, an island city in the North-east Aegean, offers us a rare opportunity to compare figures sculpted in the Archaic tradition with others whose modelling breaks away from the code of the time. While the three Nymphs resemble a group of korai in their conventional presentational poses, Apollo with his lyre has a freedom of gesture and a suggestion of depth, which are signs of the arrival in Thasos of early experiments in the "Severe style". The influence of Athens around 480 BC possibly prompted these; but there can be no doubt the relief was executed in Thasos, with an eclecticism which is characteristic of this island.

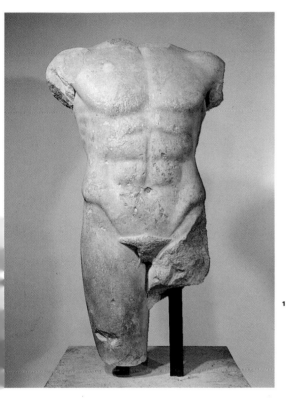

161 Male Torso

Found at Miletos
c. 480 BC
Marble. H 1.32 m
Gift of Rothschild, 1873.
MNB 691 (MA 2792)

The imposing size of the Miletos torso distinguishes it from other athletic sculpture of the transitional period between the Archaic and Classic styles. It is dated to this period because of its somewhat rigid bearing despite the mobility of certain elements such as the back muscles. The position of the shoulder muscles indicates that the right arm must have been drawn back while the left arm moved in front of the body. The anatomical mastery of the body itself combines all the lessons of the Archaic style with a hint of the *contrapposto* developed by sculptors after the Graeco Persian wars. The origins of the sculpture are unclear. Although it was found in Ionia, its forcefulness makes it closer to Peloponnesean styles. However, athletic sculpture was not unknown in Eastern Greece. Pythagoras of Rhegion, a forerunner and rival of Myron, came from Samos. The Miletos torso could well be attributed to his influence.

¹⁶² Statuette of a Young Man

Sicyonian style
c. 480 BC

Bronze. H 0.264 m
Gift of David-Weill, 1937. MND 1891 (Br 4236)

The standing male nude is one of the most eloquent of all statues illustrating the transition from the Archaic to the Classic styles. For almost a century and a half, its original rigid schema, with left leg forward, remained unchanged. At the dawn of the "Severe style", this statuette which was found in Phocis shows how the stiff pose is moderated and the arms stretch out in a more fluid and comprehensive gesture. His position is still that of a Kouros, as is his figure, particularly the pronounced curve of the lower back. But an unprecedented vitality runs through the musculature. The Kouros has become an athlete, and his body has begun to shift in search of the most natural position. The successful combination of strength with suppleness may well be the mark of the school of Sicyon, a Peloponnesian city known for its bronze founders.

163 Funerary Stele

Pharsalos, c. 460 BC

Marble. H 0.60 m

Acq. 1862. Ma 701

The funerary stele, a stone erected over a tomb and sculpted with relief decoration, was a much exploited genre in Greek art. Athens shone most brilliantly at such work from the Archaic period onwards. But the history of the stele in Attica was interrupted for half a century, between 500 and 450 BC. Elsewhere in Greece, such as in Thessaly where this stele originated, production continued. Two women, who would probably have been standing, are shown facing each other in a solemn, serene mood. At the centre of the composition their hands are gathered in an apparent exchange of flowers and bags of grain(?). Perhaps they are mother and daughter, as is suggested by the more solemn majesty of the right-hand figure. Alongside the continuing Archaic style of the left-hand arm, the locks of hair and line of drapery, we find new features such as more developed eyes, heavier jaw-lines and more pronounced expressions.

164 Female Helmeted Head

Aeginetan style, c. 460 BC

Marble. H 0.28 m

Gift of Vogüé, 1917. MND 1053

The island of Aegina, near the Attican coast, was the home during the late Archaic period of thriving workshops of sculptors working in marble as well as bronze. The style of this original head which was part of an idol of the goddess Athena, is the same as that of the pediment of the temple of Athena at Aphaia. The resemblance is striking, particularly with the central scene of the west pediment which shows the same goddess. The holes visible on the temples and ears were points where additional elements were fixed, most probably locks of hair and ornaments attached to the ear lobes. The firm, solemn expression, the round chin and thick eyelids (once lined with metal eyelashes) are signs of the beginnings of the Classic style, the so-called "Severe style".

165 Red Figure Footed Krater

Attributed to the "Painter of the Niobides"
Attic style c. 460 BC
Terracotta. H 0.54 m
Acq. 1883. MNC 511 (G 341)

The decoration of this bowl is unusual and significant in that it distributes the protagonists of the two scenes illustrated across different levels. The black interstices between the clearly drawn figures occasionally partially conceal their form, suggesting a derivation from some well - known painting. The subject of one of the two scenes is easy to recognize, the punishment of Niobe and her children for their offence to Apollo and Artemis, but the second scene remains obscure. It is customary to see the influence here of one of the most famous painters of the 5th century BC, Polygnotus of Thasos, who painted great frescoes as well as easel paintings in Athens and in Delphi during the early Classic period.

166 The Piombino Apollo

*Greater Greece, second half
of the 5th century BC (?)
1st century BC (?)*
Bronze statue. H 1.15 m
Acq. 1901. LP 2801 (Br 2)

Found in the sea near Piombino, this bronze
statue, which was an early-comer to the Louvre
collections, continues to raise questions. Despite
the dedication to Athena in silver letters on the
left foot, the only thing of which we are sure is
the identity of the god; the position of this young
figure ranks it with other idols of Apollo in which
the god holds a bow in his right hand. But the
style leaves one with the impression of a composite
creation. The position is Archaic, as is the fringe
and the browline. However, the naturalism of the
back, arms and legs has nothing Archaic about
them. It is doubtless a later work, combining
stylisation with features closer to observed reality.
However, it is not easy to situate this "archaising"
work more precisely in time and space. Southern
Italy is probably the best guess as to its origins,
while the date could be ascribed either to around
the end of the 5th century when religious fervour
would have favoured preservation of traditional
aspects of a sacred image and the 1st century BC
which saw the creation of many works which
looked back to the Archaic and Classic styles of
the past.

Greek, Etruscan and Roman Antiquities

The Classical Greek world

167 Metope from the Parthenon

*Athens (Acropolis)
447-440 BC*
Marble high-relief. H 1.35 m; W 1.41 m
Acq. 1818. MA 736

This sculpted relief was part of the
Doric frieze of the Parthenon, the
temple on the Acropolis at Athens
dedicated to the city's goddess

Athena. In it stood the statue of Athena by Phidias, who was the artist who evolved the whole decorative conception. The temple and its decoration was finished within the fifteen years which corresponded to Pericles' governorship of Athens. This is the tenth metope of the southern facade, in which the theme of the centauromachy is treated. The man-horse or centaur assails the woman in a wild fury; the scene is cleverly balanced across the confined space. The artist has linked the fluid lines of the horse's body to the firm lines of drapery. Despite the idealized atmosphere in which the forms evolve, an attention to reality has brought out the muscles and veins under the animal's skin. The two figures seem to be moving in front of a screen, in an interplay of lines and volumes which are perfectly ordered thanks to a pronounced sense of harmony.

168 Plaque from the Parthenon Frieze

Athens (Acropolis)
c. 440 BC
Marble bas-relief. H 0.96 m; W 2.07 m
Choiseul-Gouffier coll. Revolutionary seizure.
MR 825 (MA 738)

The sculpted band which ran around the whole length of the Parthenon high up under the peristyle gallery is one of the most accomplished monuments of Greek sculpture. Along over 160 meters of frieze, around 360 figures join in the Panathenaic procession, a great feast when the entire civic body of Athens assembled and walked up to the Acropolis to offer Athena a tunic embroidered by girls from the most prominent families. Here they are proceeding along with two leaders of the ceremony. Their restrained gait expresses the solemnity of the occasion which is orderly without being monotonous. A slow rhythm runs through the figures in which gravity and grace are naturally allied. The figures, it should be remembered, were close to the central scene which showed the gods gathering to attend the homage paid to Athena. Doubtless inspired by Phidias, the Parthenon frieze marks the high point of Classic sculpture.

169 Aphrodite

Roman copy of an original
attributed to Praxiteles,
c. 360 BC

Marble statue (arms restored by Girardon who reworked the area around the breasts and the folds of drapery). H 1.94 m
Found in Arles in 1651. Given by the town of Arles to Louis XIV, 1683. MR 366 (MA 439)

While its identity cannot be confirmed, Louis XIV was no doubt justified in seeing this statue from Arles as a Roman copy of a classical 4th century BC Greek statue of Aphrodite, the goddess of love. Sadly this provided grounds for the sculptor Girardon to restore her arms and add an apple to her right hand and a mirror to her left. These two emblems were most certainly not part of the original intention. This can be inferred from other versions of statues traditionally attributed to the hand of the great Athenian sculptor Praxiteles. It is quite likely that the Arles Aphrodite is a reproduction of the famous Aphrodite of Thespies which Praxiteles sculpted

around 360 BC, using his mistress, the courtesan
Phryne, renowned for her figure, as his model.
The artist's bold representation of nudity was
unprecedented, and he took these revelations to an
extreme in the Aphrodite of Cnidos. The
expression of gentle melancholy and sensual forms
fit in with the ancients' image of Praxiteles as a
sculptor of feminine grace.

¹⁷⁰ Footed Krater

Southern Italy
c. 330 BC
H 0.57 m; ∅ 0.81 m
Acq. 1825. N 3157

A large-scale scene on this high-stemmed krater
depicts several figures using polychrome effects
and an arrangement on different levels so that
some figures seem to be half-hidden by folds of
the land. It was produced in a workshop in
southern Italy during the 4th century BC, when
Greek artists who had settled in the Western
Mediterranean were producing great quantities of
vases which are outside the Athenian tradition and
follow various regional variations. This is in the
style of a workshop that has been located to
Paestum, south of Naples, and to one painter in
particular who signed just one work with his
name, Python. The picture shows the battle
between Cadmus and the dragon. Cadmus, son of
king Agenor of Tyre, went in search of his sister
Europa who had been carried off by Zeus, and
was told by the Delphic oracle to found a city.
Here he is fighting a dragon by a spring where
the city of Thebes was later to arise. This scene
which must have been painted around 330 BC,
probably takes its theme from contemporary
theatre, which often inspired the painters of
Paestum.

171 Bell Krater

Attributed to the painter of Ixion
Campanian style, c. 320 BC

Terracotta. H 0.40 m

Acq. 1985. CA 1724

The well-known scene from the Odyssey in which
Ulysses takes his revenge on rival suitors when he
returns to Ithaca, massacring them in the midst of
their banquet, is very rarely illustrated. However,
this was the subject chosen by an Italiot painter
practising in the second half of the 4th century in
a workshop in Campania. The "painter of Ixion"
(thus named after another vase featuring this
character) succeeded in adapting a composition
from a great painting to the curve of a bowl. The
dramatic aspects of the scene, which confronts
the small group formed by Ulysses, his son
Telemachus and a faithful servant (doubtless the
swineherd Eumaeus), with young suitors who are
either in the grip of death or are trying to escape
their fate, bring to mind descriptions in antique
sources of paintings of great artists such as Zeuxis,
who came from southern Italy. Ignoring the
reverse side of the vase, the artist has concentrated
his energies most profitably into recreating
something of the heroic spirit which must have
pervaded the large picture. The liveliness and the
effects of foreshortening, the psychological detail
on the faces and the polychrome touches (mostly
rubbed off) indicate a 4th century BC origin.

The Classical Greek world

The Hellenistic Period

The conquest of Alexandria (334-323 BC) which
spread Hellenism over a huge area shook the
foundations of artistic activity. From now on in
Greek art, beauty began to be sought for its own
sake, and it was produced in Macedonia, Egypt
and east as far as the Indus. Inevitably the many
workshops over this wide expanse combined local
influences with Hellenistic tendencies to varying
degrees. While Athens still set the example for
others to follow and was a paragon of
splendour - laden with the gifts of princes - other
cities such as Alexandria, Pergamum and Antioch
occupied important positions. Rhodes was the
home of an influential school of sculpture. The
wealth of some of the courts led to increasing
numbers of commissions and more ambitious
undertakings. Amid the multiplicity, in three
centuries of Hellenism during which kingdoms
and empires rose and fell at an unceasing rate, it
would be hard to discern one single line of
evolution in artistic forms which are often as
unexpected as the events of the time. Aside from
this, it should be remembered that there are great
gaps in what work we still have, particularly in
painting; our only records of which are Roman
copies in Campanian villas.

Lysippus, who lived at the turning point between
the Classic and Hellenistic period, introduced
another dimension, the sense of space, into
sculpture and gave his stamp of approval to
portraiture. His followers assimilated his lessons,
carrying the evolution of forms in space and the
study of human physiognomy still further.
Realism, which at times bordered on the scathing,
progressed within certain specific areas. New
subjects enriched the repertoire; artists were at last
drawn to represent children and the elderly,
ugliness and suffering. The sense of movement
increased to the point of violence. Such exuberance
and tragic expression, found particularly in
Pergamum, has often been described, with good
reason, as "baroque" in style. But even at its peak,
at the opening of the second century BC, this was

not the only form of expression. Alongside it we find the most sober realism, the most refined idealized forms in places like Alexandria. Moreover within this plethora of images one can see time and again that the Classic style had not been forgotten. And the gradual, inexorable advance of the Romans onto Greek soil, uncouth soldiers fascinated by Hellenistic culture, only turned artists' attention further back into the past. The last years of the second and first century BC saw the appearance of retrospective styles, in which neo-Classical forms and archaic motifs run alongside and merge in with each other.

172 Statuette of Victory

Myrina
Beginning of 2nd century BC
Terracotta. H 0.278 m
Loan from the Musée de l'Université de Lyon, 1963
LY 1651

Intended to be hung on the wall of a sepulchre, this figurine is one of a great number of statuettes made during the Hellenistic period by workshops which were probably located in Myrina, a Greek city in Asia Minor, close to Pergamum. From what has been found, these workshops started production from the 6th century BC and continued all through the following centuries with little sign of originality. But from the end of the 3rd century new subjects appeared, the Victory among them. Many models can be attributed to several hands, as is indicated by signatures which are more like trade marks. However the recurrence of certain features might indicate a particular hand. The Louvre Victory with its graceful outline and close-fitting garment is one of a similar group produced at the outset of the 2nd century BC and attributed to a single author known as "Coroplathus of the Victories".

¹⁷³ Winged Victory of Samothrace

Samothrace, c. 190 BC

Marble (statue) and limestone (the right wing is a plaster reconstruction). H 3.28 m

Missions Champoiseau 1863, 1879, 1891

MA 2369

This is one of the most famous statues we have preserved from Greek antiquity, and it is also one of the few sculptures the original setting of which we know. It was found in a large number of fragments on a terrace overlooking the sanctuary of the Cabires on the island of Samothrace, in the north east Aegean. Symbolising a sea victory, this awe-inspiring winged woman standing on a ship's prow would have been seen to full effect on top of the hill, thrusting out her wings and surging upward. Her right hand, which was found in 1950 and given to the Louvre, is open. With her face turned to onlookers and her right hand raised, the Winged Victory would thus have been announcing an event. But what event? The vigour and style of the statue are reminiscent of the Pergamum altar which was decorated between 180 and 160 BC. If the limestone prow does indeed come from Rhodes, the Victory of Samothrace might have commemorated a naval victory by the men of Rhodes, which occurred sometime in the early part of the second century BC.

174 Aphrodite known as the "Kauffmann Head"

2nd century BC

Marble. H 0.35 m

Acq. 1951. MND 2037 (Ma 3518)

This delicately modelled female head is a fragment of a statue reproducing the nude Aphrodite which Praxiteles sculpted in the middle of the 4th century BC, and which was placed by the Greeks of Knidos at the heart of the goddess's sanctuary. The Athenian artist had a great impact as much because of the quality of his execution as for being the first to portray a female nude. The marble body of the goddess was coloured by Nicias, the only painter with whom the sculptor would consent to collaborate. Aphrodite is shown having her ritual bath; it is a religious rather than a voyeuristic scene. Her face is appropriately regal, with a certain grace softening her majestic aura. Her hair is pulled back in a chignon to expose the triangle of her forehead and locks of hair are kept in place with bands.

Most copies show these hairbands diverging. On the Kauffmann head they are parallel; a liberty which suggests that the Louvre head is a free Hellenistic recreation and not simply a Roman copy. The remarkable quality of the modelling which is fluid and sensual would lend weight to such a theory.

175 Bearded Fighter

Asia Minor
Second half of 2nd century BC
Bronze statuette (silver inlay for eyes, copper
for nipples). H 0.25 m
Jameson coll. Acq. 1950. MND 2014 (Br 4307)

The growing number of artistic centres across the immense territory conquered by Alexander ensured a high turnover of works of art. Sometimes there is evidence of an alliance between the Greek and local styles; sometimes as here, the work is in the mainstream of the great aesthetic tradition. In the baroque expressiveness of the fierce face and tangled hair, with its exaggerated musculature, this statuette of a naked man in combat can be placed within the 2nd century BC Pergamum tradition of large ex-voto objects. References to classic depictions of Zeus with his thunderbolt or Poseidon with his trident support this attribution. In any case the technique is extremely refined; the reworkings, inlay and correction of faults in the casting are evidence of a consummate skill.

176 Standing Woman known as the
"Venus de Milo"

Melos, c. 100 BC
Marble statue. H 2.02 m
Acq. 1821. LL 299 (Ma 399)

The *Venus de Milo* was uncovered by pure chance
on the Cycladean island of Melos in 1820. The
Marquis de Rivière, French ambassador at
Constantinople, subsequently acquired it and
offered it to Louis XVIII who donated it to the
Louvre in 1821. The statue was made in two
sections which meet in the thick folds of drapery
below the hips. The left arm was detachable and
the right possibly restored in Antiquity. At the

base, the left foot was worked on separately and the plinth would no doubt have been inserted into the top of a pedestal. Her position has been the object of much speculation. The most likely possibility seems that her right arm crossed her body, the hand lightly touching her hip, while her left arm was, unquestionably, raised. The statue is Classical in theme but its lively treatment, the mobility of the silhouette, and realism of certain details make it a Hellenistic work, belonging to the period when the return to the Classic style was taking hold, in other words between the 2nd and 1st centuries BC. Although there is no actual proof, the most plausible subject of this work would be Aphrodite or Venus. This would explain the beauty of the nude body emerging from the folds of drapery.

¹⁷⁷ Battling Warrior known as the **"Borghese Gladiator"**

Antium
Beginning of the 1st century BC
Marble statue. H 1.99 m
Borghese coll. in Rome. Acq. 1808. MR 224 (Ma 527)

This figure has been famous since the early 17th century. Often misinterpreted, the position of the warrior becomes clear if a shield is replaced on his left arm where the buckle can be seen. The warrior is shielding himself - possibly from a horseman if we are to judge from the direction of his gaze - and preparing to deal a blow. The restoration of the right arm, which is not antique, does not seem awkward. The work is signed on the tree trunk at the back of the composition: "Agasias, son of Dositheos, citizen of Ephesos, made (the statue)". Whether this is the signature of the artist who created the subject or that of the copyist who might have copied it from a bronze, as the tree-trunk prop would suggest, is open to question. The elongated figure follows the canon of proportions laid down by Lysippus in the 4th century, while the display of anatomical detail reminds us of the zeal of certain artists of the early Classic period. This combination of tendencies raises the possibility of it being an original work combining the style of Lysippus with certain aspects of Classicism. Its dating (from the style of the inscription) to the early 1st century BC would thus be explained.

The Etruscans

Many different but generally isolated peoples inhabited Italy before Roman times. Of all of them, the Etruscans developed the most coherent and outstanding culture, alongside the Greek colonies of southern Italy, or "Greater Greece" (to which a special room is devoted).

From the middle of the 8th century BC, the cities of Etruria, which never unified, experienced rapid political, economic and cultural growth. The Villanovian culture dominating Italy found its greatest expression in the applied arts - laminated bronze above all - marked by geometric influences then prevailing around the Mediterranean. A highly elaborate art developed, characterized by great technical skill (filigree, granulation) and contacts with the East, and found its greatest expression in the art of the goldsmith.

Etruscan civilization reached its apogee between 675 and 475 BC. Artistic exchanges with Greece were plentiful. Greek artists moved to Etruria and produced works of high quality, notably in the field of funerary paintings. There were massive imports of Greek vases (many Greek vases in the Louvre come from Etrurian necropoli), despite the development during the Archaic period of a truly Etruscan *bucchero* pottery. Etruscan art, however, remained profoundly and radically different from Greek art; less interested in the exploration of forms for their own sake, the Etruscans were more drawn to the expression of movement and immediacy. They were particularly fond of techniques requiring rapidity of execution, such as modelling in terracotta and bronze, at both of which they excelled.

The Hellenistic period was marked by the rise of Roman power over Italy. But the influence of Greek culture remained considerable. Art became more Hellenized, while the peoples of Italy as a whole became more uniform in outlook. Losing its political independence, Etruria gradually became assimilated into the Roman world.

¹⁷⁸ Terracotta Plaque

Caire
Last quarter of the 6th century BC
Painted terracotta. H 1.23 m; W 0.58 m
Campana coll. Acq. 1863. Cp 6627

Terracotta was particularly important in the decoration of Etruscan buildings, on acroteria, antefixes and larger elements, as well as in reliefs and statues. This plaque was discovered in a tomb at Cerveteri. Its funerary significance may be related to the illustration of spirits carrying away the soul of a dead woman or alternatively to the sacrifice of Iphigenia. The series of panels it belongs to appear to have been altered and might initially have been part of a public building. The style of painting is clearly marked by the influence of the Greek art of Ionia.

179 Sarcophagus of a Married Couple

Caire
Late 6th century BC
Terracotta. H 1.14 m; W 1.90 m
Campana coll. Acq. 1863. Cp 5194

This unusual sarcophagus is a proud display of a couple from a great Etruscan family reclining together as was customary at a banquet. Influenced by Ionian art, the artist has expressed the couple's unity with particular sensitivity, relating their upper bodies and hands to each other in a lively harmony. The relationship between upper and lower halves of the body did not however concern him; this lack of interest in physical coherence is typical of Etruscan art. Technical features of this highly-finished work, and the quality of modelling link it to the great statues made in Veii at that time.

180 Achelous

Early 5th century BC

Gold. H 4 cm

Campana coll. Acq. 1863. Bj 498

The river-god Achelous was able to change his form at will in order to confound his enemies. He has often been depicted as a bull-man. On this *repoussé* pendant, some of the locks of hair are in filigree. The rest of the hair along with the beard is granulated in the form of tiny balls of gold applied onto specific areas of the decoration. The Etruscans perfected both these techniques and from the Orientalizing period onward the quality of their work, intended for the ruling aristocracy of Etrurian cities, was superlative.

181 Cinerary Urn: Chariot Journey

Volterra, late 2nd or early 1st century BC

Alabaster. H 0.84 m; W 0.60 m

Ma 2357

On the cover, the bejewelled deceased lady holds a fan in one hand and a pomegranate, a symbol of immortality, in the other. On the side of the urn, two mules are pulling the same woman along in a covered chariot; a horseman and several servants accompany her. During the Hellenistic period workshops in the Etruscan city of Volterra specialized in elaborately carved alabaster urns to hold the ashes of the dead. On some, the influence of contemporary Greek art is very apparent, particularly of styles from Pergamum and Rhodes. This is not the case here. The subject, the journey to the land of the dead, is treated as if it were an everyday occurrence and given a clumsy piquancy which anticipates the vernacular art of the Romans.

182 Portrait of a Man

Environs of Fiesole (Italy)
2nd century BC

Bronze head. H 0.21 m

Acq. 1864. Br 19

The head of this somewhat soft full-featured
Etruscan is crowned by a thick cap of clearly
drawn locks of hair. It is a very attentive portrait
of a man and the artist has done his best to render
his physical appearance, in an analysis of surfaces
which avoids psychological penetration. In this, it
belongs to a group of Italian portraits which are,
nevertheless, a long way behind the almost
excessive observation of detail seen in certain
Roman portraits at the end of the Republic.

The Roman World

For a long time artistic activities were relegated by the Romans to the secondary position. However, wars in southern Italy and in the East during the 3rd and 2nd century BC confronted the Romans with Greece and the Hellenistic world on a massive scale. Attitudes changed profoundly. Art was no longer an indulgence for the privileged few. It became an indispensable tool of political power, of which the Greeks were past masters. Art from earlier periods was brought to Rome; and contemporary artists and works came too. Art nevertheless remained subordinated to the gods, the state and aspiring leaders. Public projects were, therefore, important and an official art developed. This found its supreme expression in architecture and sculpture (the "historical" reliefs). Subjects, forms, and images copied from, or executed in imitation of the Greeks, were adapted sometimes with great subtlety to the new ends that the Romans found for them. But art was also a social tool, enabling an individual to assert himself, and display his real or assumed position in society. Hence the importance of portraits, which also drew a lot on Hellenistic work in that field. The deepening crises at the end of the 2nd century which became more pronounced during the 3rd, marked a decisive artistic turning point. Increasingly clearly, works of art expressed the spiritual preoccupations of the individual. It can be seen most tellingly in funerary sculpture and is also noticeable in the development of portraiture. But art also existed to please the eye, as the development of mosaic floor decoration in Rome illustrates. Different "schools" emerged, each region gave its distinctive flavour to an art which stretched far beyond the Mediterranean basin. While sharing a similar overall direction, it was in no way uniform from one province to another. The production of smaller works in silver, gold and bronze also linked a common language to regional sources of inspiration which, as in the East, often stemmed from long-established local traditions.

183 Portrait of a Man

Rome, c. 100 BC

Head, marble. H 0.375 m

Acq. 1998. Ma 919

Executed in several sections (the top and back of
the head are missing), this portrait of an old man
is unflinchingly realistic (the marks of age, the
toothless mouth and folds in the neck are pitilessly
reproduced) and there is nothing schematic about
it. An intense life animates the mobile features;
the tilt of the head towards the right gives it a
certain pathos which is in keeping with the
tradition of Hellenistic portraiture. From the
resemblance with certain medallion heads, the
sitter has sometimes been identified as Aulus
Postumius Albinus, a consul in 99 BC. It is,
however, a portrait of one of the very first citizens
of Rome towards the end of the 2nd century BC.

184 Scenes from a Census

Rome, c. 100 BC

Marble relief. W 2.05 m.

Acq. 1824. Ma 975

In the Rome of the Republic, the census, which had long been the basis for army recruitment, was taken every four years. Citizens were listed in official registers according to their wealth. The scene here shows this, alongside a sacrifice to the god Mars of a bull, a ram and a pig, which was held at the close of procedures. Part of a larger ensemble divided between the Louvre and the Munich Glyptothek, this bas-relief is one of the oldest historical reliefs beloved of the Romans. As yet unused to rendering contemporary scenes faithfully, the sculptors borrowed certain forms from Greek art, adapting them sometimes awkwardly to their new function.

185 Portrait of Livia

c. 30 BC

Basalt head. H 0.34 m

Acq. 1860. Ma 1233

Livia, wife of Emperor Augustus, is portrayed at around thirty years of age, with one of the most fashionable hairstyles of the early Roman empire: a knot of hair above her forehead, a small bun at nape of her neck and a short plait over the back of her head, hidden here by a close-fitting veil. The hard shine of the basalt gives the head a metallic look, accentuated by the hieratic effect of the strictly frontal pose and fixed features. It recalls contemporary cameo work cut in hard stone, which, under the influence of some exceptional craftsmen, flourished during the Augustan period.

186 Marcellus

Rome, 23 BC
Marble statue. H 1.80 m
Louis XIV coll. Ma 1207

This is a portrait of Marcellus, nephew of Augustus who died prematurely in 23 BC, by the Athenian sculptor Cleomenes. The sculptor's signature can be seen on the tortoise's shell.

Cleomenes chose to depict Marcellus as a funereal Hermes, standing at the tomb of the dead Greeks at the battle of Chaeronea in 447 BC. This revival of Classical art perpetrated by families of Greek sculptors in Rome, complied with the express wishes of Emperor Augustus. Along with the posthumous nature of the commission, it also explains its somewhat cold perfection and idealized features. The young man is transformed into a hero.

187 Juba I

Cherchel
Late 1st century BC
Marble head. H 0.45 m
Acq. 1895. Ma 1885

A king of Numidia, Juba joined Pompey's supporters against Julius Caesar, and killed himself on the latter's victory in 46 BC. The sculptor has emphasized his characteristic head of hair; long corkscrew curls pulled back by a royal band. But the idealized features, framed by the hair and beard, are treated in a deliberately impersonal, Classicizing style; he is more of a god than a real man. The portrait was probably executed during the reign of his son Juba II, restored by Augustus to the throne of a small kingdom, and the capital (which is now Cherchel in Algeria) became an active centre of Greek culture.

188 Imperial Procession

Rome, 13-9 BC
Marble relief. H 1.20 m; W 1.47 m
Campana coll. Acq. 1863. MA 1088

To commemorate the Emperor Augustus's victorious return from Spain, the Roman Senate erected a monument in his honour between 13 and

9 BC, known as the Altar of Peace (Ara Pacis) of Augustus. The carving is unusually elaborate. Assembled behind the Emperor, we see a procession of members of his family, priests, magistrates and senators; it is a conscious transposition of the *Panathenaic procession* 168 of the Parthenon. Athens and the Classic style were chosen by Augustus as the models for official art, as signs of measure, balance and refinement.

189 Sarcophagus: Legend of Acteon

Near Rome
Rome, c. 125-130 AD
Marble. H 0.99 m; W 2.35 m; D 0.75 m
Borghese coll. Acq. 1808. Ma 459

Three young women, the Hours or Graces, are carrying heavy fruit garlands above which are scenes from the tragic story of Acteon; he inadvertently came upon Artemis bathing naked, was turned into a deer and torn to pieces by his own hounds. On the lid is a marine procession. The elaborate borders are influenced by the art of Asia Minor, but the inclusion of small scenes within the garlands was a practice developed by Roman workshops, popular in Hadrian's time. Of great quality and refinement, the execution is notable for its Classicism, which occasionally spills over into a rococo extravagance in the tortuous convolutions of rocks and trees.

190 Hadrian

Second quarter of 2nd century

Bronze head. H 0.43 m

Acq. 1984. Br 4547

The rigidly frontal head with its direct gaze and slight frown gives Hadrian a severity and majesty bordering on the hieratic, which is further emphasized by the nature of the material with its unusual red patina. However, the swirling irregular locks of hair and short beard soften this impression. Looking more closely at the hairstyle (the uniformity of which often characterizes a group of imperial portraits) there is an attention to detail which distinguishes it from most other heads of this Emperor. It is a powerful and original work.

¹⁹¹ Sarcophagus: Marine Procession

Rome, c. 140-150 AD

Marble. H 0.95 m; W 2.37 m; D 0.60 m

Church of San Francisco a Ripa, Rome.

Entered Louvre in 1798. Ma 342

detail

Marine processions were one of the most popular themes on sarcophagi from Roman workshops. They may have served to evoke the deceased's journey to a place of happiness in the afterlife. The models are borrowed from Greek art but are reinterpreted by Roman sculptors more or less freely according to their talent. Here subtle variations enliven the symmetrical arrangement. The harmonious Classically-inspired composition is also given a restrained movement. There is a strong sense of volume with carving deep into the marble. The unfinished left side of the basin shows how sculptors worked in the details progressively on their reliefs.

¹⁹² Portrait of a Young Prince

Annaba (Algeria?) c. 170 AD

Marble head. H 0.21 m

Acq. 1955. Ma 3539

Some of the greatest achievements in Roman sculpture are in children's portraits. This sensitive portrait by a sculptor of Greek origin is probably of one of nine children born to the Emperor Marcus Aurelius, most of whom died young. The delicacy of the modelling and the fine treatment of the marble surface, over which the light plays softly, lend a particular charm to the depiction of this child, whose slightly melancholic expression is a childlike imitation of the gravity that can be seen on the faces of adults in portraits of that time.

detail

193 Sarcophagus:
Bacchus Discovering Ariadne

Rome, c. 235 AD

Marble. Found at St.-Médard-d'Eyrans (Gironde).

H 0.98 m; W 2.08 m; D 0.62

Acq. 1845. Ma 1346

Abandoned on the island of Naxos by Theseus, Ariadne fell into a slumber. Carried along in a tumultuous procession of satyrs and menads, Bacchus came upon her, fell in love and swept her along in his life of joy. For the Romans who, at that period, were in the midst of a spiritual crisis, this image suggested the joys awaiting in the afterlife for those who were faithful to their god. The head of Ariadne, which is unfinished, was intended to portray the deceased woman.

This carefully-polished Greek marble sarcophagus was sculpted in Rome by artists at the peak of their skill. Mastered to the point of giving the marble a translucent quality, their craft centres on the creation of a play of light and shadow which suggests the Bacchic frenzy. The effect is almost Baroque in feel; religious ecstasy is given perfect form.

194 Sarcophagus: Lion Hunt

Rome, c. 235-240 AD

Marble. H 0.88 m; W 2.20 m

Borghese Coll. Acq. 1808. Ma 346

Two episodes from a lion hunt are shown here. On the left they are setting out; on the right the hunter confronts the leaping animal. The hunter is a likeness of the deceased for whom the sarcophagus was made, with the short hair and beard that were fashionable in the 3rd century. He may never have hunted lions, but this combat symbolises the victory that his moral attributes will give him over the grip of death. The clarity of the composition and the direct treatment indicate a concern to give the work movement without violence.

195 The Emperor Julian

c. 360 AD

Marble statue. H 1.75 m

Ma 1121

The sculptor represents Julian (331-363) as a pagan priest (wearing the appropriate crown), and the Emperor who was a talented writer became the ardent defender of the ancient culture and paganism in the face of increasingly dominant Christianity. Here he is dressed not in a toga but in a *pallium*, a Greek costume worn by philosophers, which is draped tightly around the right arm.

The treatment of the costume and above all the face is a conscious evocation of sculpture during the second half of the 2nd century; but the somewhat mechanical treatment of the fringe with a trepanning tool, indicate the later origin of this work.

196 Venus

4th century

Marble group. H 0.76 m

Found at Saint-Georges-de-Montagne (Gironde).

Acq. 1953. Ma 3537

A nude Venus is arranging her long hair. A small Cupid helps her carry the heavy mirror into which she gazes. A Triton to the right and a Cupid on a dolphin to the left remind us that Venus was born from the sea.

Somewhat heavy and awkward in execution, this small free-standing group was found with other statues of divinities in a large villa near Libourne. There was a ready market in the 4th century for such groups which are often devoid of religious significance and have only a decorative value.

197 Wrestler

1st century (?)

Bronze statuette. H 0.27 m

Autun. Acq. 1870. Br 1067

A popular spectacle during Roman times was the "pancratium", a fight between two bare fisted wrestlers. With unusual verve the artist has seized the instant when a wrestler has kicked out and is thrown off balance. It is rare that a bronze statuette fills the space so satisfyingly; it is hard to choose the best angle to view it from. The deliberately exaggerated modelling helps to give this work its particular charm, although it remains firmly within the tradition of Hellenistic period bronze wrestling groups.

198 Old Woman Crouching

2nd century

Bronze statuette. H 9.2 cm
Vichy (Allier). Acq. 1895. Br 2936

The craftsman in bronze has successfully captured the figure of an old woman. She is wearing a long robe, one foot is bare and she is crouching, with the skin of her cheeks and neck falling in folds, her eyes half-closed, looking bewildered as she tilts a cup over in her hand. The artisan has skilfully assimilated her headdress, a veil tied with a ribbon, into the upper half of the vessel which this statuette forms.

In keeping with the artistic tradition of Alexandria, bronze craftsmen were fond of depicting sick and grotesque people. However, it would be hard to find a more powerful evocation of the exhaustion and misery of a human being. The pitiless observation is enlivened with a glimmer of humour.

199 Bacchus and Pan

Second half of the 2nd century

Bronze group inlaid with silver. H 0.187 m
Augst (Switzerland). Acq. 1865. Br 1061

From the end of the Classical Greek period, antique artists often depicted Bacchus leaning on one of his companions, a satyr or Pan himself. But in this small group the two figures are less closely linked. Despite the gesture of his left hand, the god gazes ahead in apparent indifference to Pan who is offering him a bunch of grapes.

The somewhat heavy quality of the modelling and the emphasis given to the eyes (which are inlaid with silver) date the work to the second half of the 2nd century.

200 Aphrodite

Roman period

Bronze statuette. H 0.20 m

From Amrith (Syria). Acq. 1868. Br 4425

Aphrodite was one of the most frequently reproduced figures in bronze workshops of the Near East during the Hellenistic and Roman periods. She is often shown as a fulsome fertility goddess. But she also has the character of a universal divinity with some of the powers and accessories of other gods. Here a nude Aphrodite is laden with attributes; winged like a Victory, she is wearing a towered crown, and carries a horn of plenty and the helm of Fortune. Also on her head she bears the emblem of Isis; at her back is a quiver, and a serpent twists around her arm. These small statuettes produced in great quantities and widely distributed, testify to the religious fervour of the eastern Roman Empire.

201 Calliope

Pompeii, villa of Julia Felix
Between 62 and 79 AD

Fresco wall painting. H 0.46 m; W 0.36 m

Gift of Ferdinand IV, King of Naples, 1802, P 4

The muse of epic poetry, Calliope, stands on a console bearing her name, with a roll of script in her hand. Along with her eight sisters and Apollo, she once occupied the centre of a large yellow panel, in a configuration typical of the last phase of wall painting in Pompeii, before the eruption (the "fourth style"). Her reserved attitude and the attention paid to her costume distinguishes her from her companions, however.

This is the first time the Nine Muses can be referred to with any certainty, thanks to inscriptions bearing their names and functions.

202 **Funereal Procession**

Rome, tomb of Patron
Late 1st century BC
Fresco wall painting. H 1.68 m, W 0.39 m
Acq. 1863. P 37

This enigmatic scene once decorated the wall of the tomb of a Greek-born doctor, Patron. Thanks to the inscriptions we know who the main figures are; the wife of the deceased and her two daughters in the centre, accompanied possibly by her grandchildren. Doubtless this slow and solemn procession had a religious meaning, perhaps a visit to the tomb. Aligning the figures at regular intervals across a simplified landscape, and using a sober and muted palette, the painter has created an exceptional atmosphere of sadness and quietude.

203 The Judgement of Paris

Antioch (Turkey),
"House of the Atrium"
Not long after 115 AD
Mosaic in marble, limestone and glass paste.

1,86 m × 1,86 m

Acq. 1932. Ma 3443

The mosaic once decorated the dining room floor of a wealthy home. It features Paris, the Trojan shepherd-prince to whom the messenger, Hermes, appears, asking him to choose the most beautiful of the three goddesses, Athene, Hera and Aphrodite. Certain of her success, the latter is leaning on a rock on the right. Using very small cubes with a wealth of colour, the artist has sought to rival the delicacy of a brush: his model was without doubt a painting and it came as no surprise to find a fresco very similar to this in Pompeii. For many years the mosaics of the Roman Orient, steeped in the tradition of Greek art, retained this concern to imitate painting in stone.

The border of elegant twists of vines and ivy, trailing from two human heads, and inhabited by insects, lizards and birds, was inspired by a 2nd century BC mosaic from Pergamum.

detail

204 Preparations for a Banquet

Carthage (Tunisia), c. 180 AD

Mosaic in marble and glass paste

2.25 m × 2.40 m

Acq. 1891. Ma 1796

In what is left of this large mosaic, five servants are proceeding with the food, plates and implements required in preparation for a large banquet. The figures stand out against a uniformly white background, and instead of subtle tonal gradations the artist makes use of highly contrasted juxtapositions of light and dark colours to suggest modelling. Stark effects like these were sought after in the expressionistic art of the late 2nd century.

detail

205 Hunting Scenes

Daphne (Turkey),
"Constantinian villa" c. 325

Mosaic in marble, limestone and glass paste.

8.07 m × 8.04 m

Acq. 1939. Ma 3444

This mosaic, at the centre of which was a fountain, once lay in the reception room of a large house in Daphne. From its composition it appears to be an adaptation of a ceiling decoration, including the gold mouldings (imitating stucco) around each section. The outside border is composed of genre scenes taken from Hellenistic art; at each corner is a personification of an abstract idea. Luscious plants surround the flooring; at the corners four young women, the Seasons, stand on acanthus leaves. In the central field are four hunting scenes; one is mythological, illustrating the exploits of Meleager and Atlanta. The sheer variety of images makes it a highly elaborate work but the realistic, and occasionally clumsy treatment of the hunting scenes, contrasts with the highly classical allure of the large acanthus leaves and Seasons. Traditions inherited from the Greeks here confront the new tendencies of late Antiquity.

206 Phoenix on a Bed of Roses

Daphne (Turkey), late 5th century

Mosaic in marble and limestone.

6 m × 4.25 m

Acq. 1984. Ma 3442

The mosaics discovered at Antioch (now Antakaya in Turkey), the capital of Roman Syria, and in the residential environs of Daphne, are a superb illustration of the high quality craftsmanship of one of the biggest cities of the Roman empire. In late antiquity these floorings came to look like real carpets. On this mosaic, a rose pattern is reproduced into infinity. At the centre stands a phoenix, a bird continually reborn from its ashes and a symbol of immortality. It was consciously used by artists to stress the eternal nature of the Roman empire. Around the border, one area of which was clumsily restored during Roman times, ibexes stand on pairs of wings, with ribbons around their necks. The image comes from the art of the Sassanides, whose eastern empire (now Iran)

rivalled Rome's; Antioch was at the crossroads of these two inimical civilisations.

207 Cup Decorated by Skeletons

From the hoard of Boscoreale (Italy)
1st century AD
Silver gilt. H 0.104 m
Gift of Rothschild, 1895. Bj **1923**

This is not the only depiction of skeletons in Roman art. Shown at banquets, they commonly served to remind guests to enjoy the fleeting moment. But never has the subject been treated so elaborately as on the two cups from the silver hoard of Boscoreale, near Pompeii. Rather like in a cartoon, the skeletons are labelled and the scenes explained with inscriptions; they are celebrated Greek poets and philosophers, among them, Sophocles, Euripides and Epicurus and their words and gestures illustrate the vanity of the human condition with a corrosive humour deriding the life of man.

208 Silver Plate with Marine Decoration

2nd and 3rd centuries

Silver dish. ∅ 0.345 m

Found at Graincourt-les-Havrincourt

(Pas-de-Calais) Acq. 1959. Bj 2214

Testifying to the popularity of silverware in Gaul, this dish is decorated with fishing motifs. Fish, shellfish, anchors, oars, lobster pots, fishing nets and seabirds decorate the centre and sides of the dish. The design, however, is not new: many other contemporary objects have identical motifs which originated in the work of goldsmiths most probably from Alexandria during the Hellenistic period. They appeared first in fishing scenes, but Roman goldsmiths tended to use them purely for decorative purposes.

209 Gold Medallion

321 AD
Gold. ⌀ 9.2 cm
Acq. 1973. Bj 2280

A gold coin of Constantine, commemorating the second consulate of his two sons in 321, is inserted in a large mount of perforated gold leaf. This technique *(opus interrasile)* was very popular in goldsmithery from the 3rd century, alongside a fashion for coin jewellery. This particulary elaborate example was one of three that formed a large necklace; most probably it was commissioned by the emperor as a gift. The busts around the edges (originally there were six) have not been identified.

210 Reliquary

Late 4th century
Silver gilt. H 5.7 cm; W 12 cm
From Castello di Brivio (Italy).
Acq. 1912. Bj 1951

With the spread of Christianity, artists had to invent images to illustrate the new faith and biblical texts. This small box in precious metal, designed to conserve relics, is richly decorated with reliefs in the repoussé technique, and the subjects

are drawn from the Old and New Testaments.
Three young Hebrews are thrown into the furnace
on the orders of King Nebuchodonosor and are
saved by an angel. We also see the adoration of
the Magi and the raising of Lazarus.

211 Diptych

5th century AD

Ivory. H 0.29 m

Acq. 1836. SMD 46

Over two ivory plates, six Muses bring inspiration
to six poets and philosophers; pagan in origin, they
were given a wide significance. The refined
execution is steeped in Classicism as is most of
the output of later Antiquity.
The elegant design in strong relief once formed
the cover of a diptych or two-fold panel. It would
have been possible to write on the back of the
panels which shut like a book. This was a much
prized gift offered by men of note to their
associates to commemorate special occasions such
as their entrance into the magistrature.

212 Goblet

Banyas (Syria), 4th century

Glass. H 13.6 cm; ⌀ 7 cm

Acq. 1901. MND 486

The work of Syrian glassblowers was highly
prized throughout the Mediterranean. Here the
craftsman has transformed a relatively simple
object into something quite original by multiplying

the handles around the neck in a sort of cage. Late Antique glassware, consciously used to display skills, exploited effects of transparency achieved by the superimposition of elements.

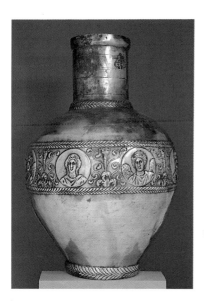

²¹³ Vase

Homs (Syria), 6th-7th centuries AD
Silver. H 0.44 m
Gift of Duighello 1982. Bj 1895

Metalwork made a great advance during the early Byzantine period, particularly in the field of liturgical objects. This large amphora-shaped vase, found on the site of ancient Emesa, was doubtless designed to contain the communion wine of a church. Alternating with foliated scrolls and horns of plenty, the eight medallions on the band where the decoration is concentrated depict busts of Christ, the Virgin Mary, angels and apostles. Although it bears no stamp, the high quality of the reliefs suggests it originated from the capital of the Byzantine empire, Constantinople.

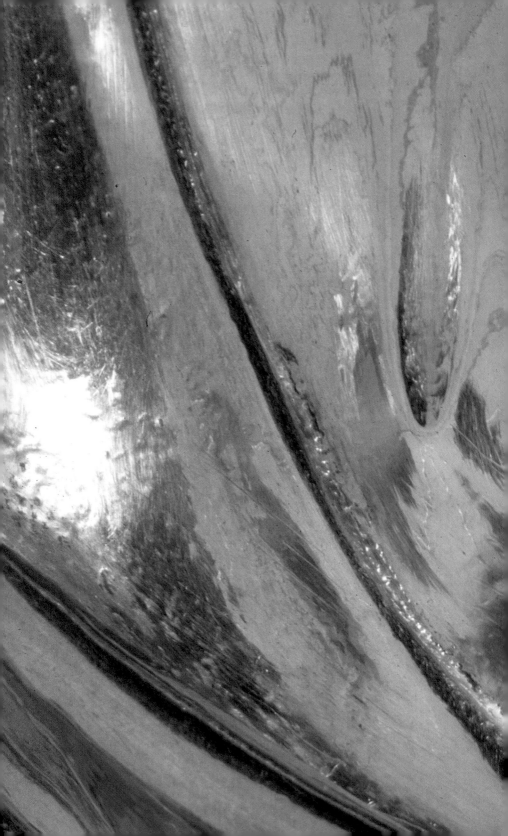

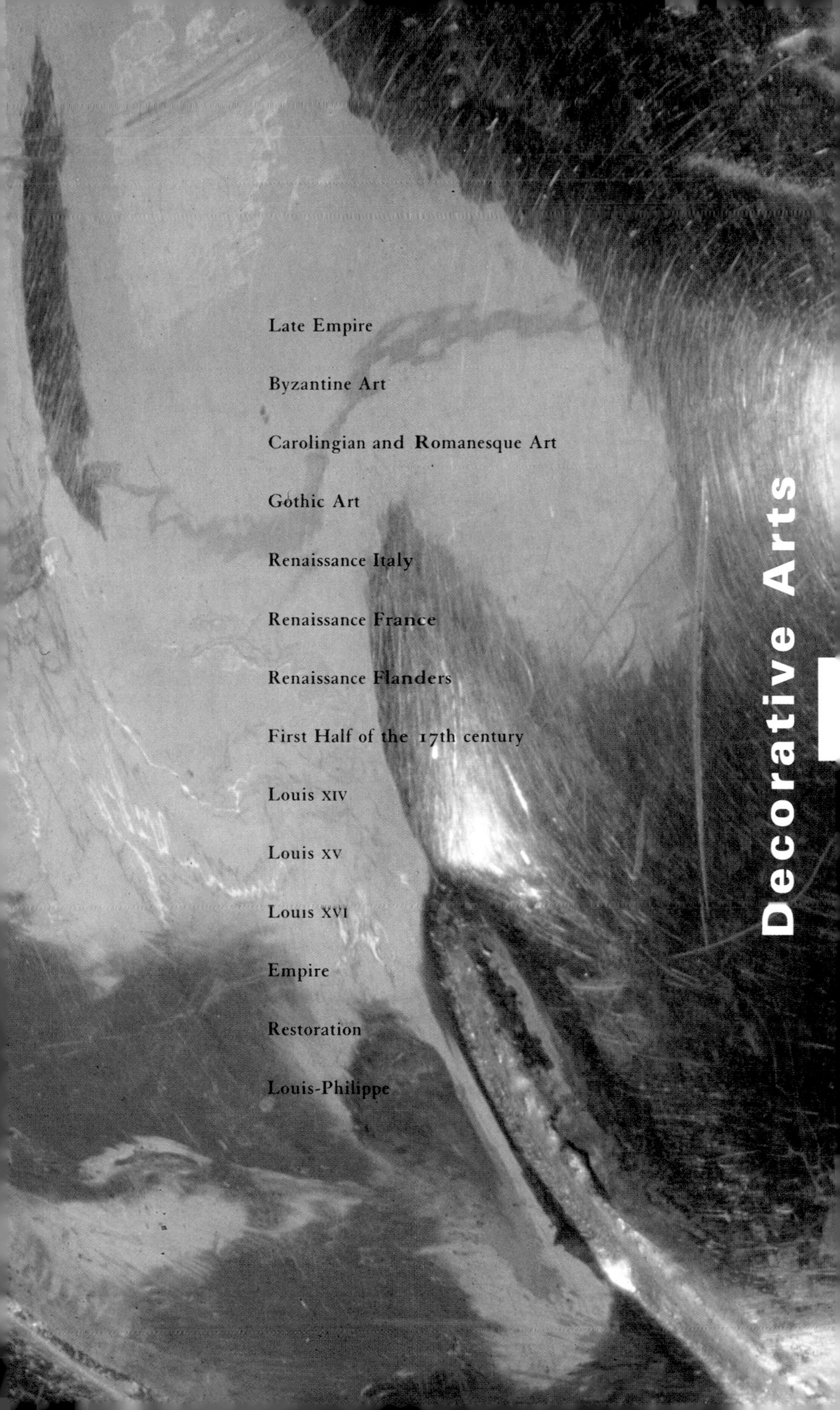

Late Empire

Byzantine Art

Carolingian and Romanesque Art

Gothic Art

Renaissance Italy

Renaissance France

Renaissance Flanders

First Half of the 17th century

Louis XIV

Louis XV

Louis XVI

Empire

Restoration

Louis-Philippe

Decorative Arts

Introduction

A department of decorative arts was envisaged from the beginning, in the decree issued by the convention on 27 July 1793, which founded the Louvre. It was subsequently assembled somewhat haphazardly, mainly thanks to two major sources. At the end of 1793 a small part of the treasure of the Abbaye de Saint-Denis entered the Louvre, including the coronation *regalia* of the kings of France and the precious vases assembled and mounted by Abbot Suger in the 12th century. In 1796, this was joined by the greater part of the royal collections of Renaissance bronzes and stone vases.

This original collection, made up of objects as important historically as they were artistically, gave the future department of Decorative Arts a certain distinction and set a standard that would have to be maintained.

Under the Restoration, two collections of *objets d'art* were purchased; that of Edme-Antoine Durand, wealthy art lover and traveller, in 1825, and that of Pierre Revoil, painter of historical scenes, in 1828. Under the Second Empire, Charles Sauvageot donated his collection in 1856, and in 1863 Napoleon III purchased the Marquis de Campana's collection, which included a remarkable set of Italian maiolica. Thanks to such treasures, the Department of Decorative Arts, created under the Second Empire, gradually assembled a coherent and homogeneous collection covering the Middle Ages and the Renaissance with examples of ivory and metalwork, furniture, ceramics, glass and bronze. The collection continues to increase thanks to gifts (Baron Adolphe de Rothschild, 1901; Baroness Salomon de Rothschild, 1922), and purchases.

In the last years of the 19th century the chronological scope of the department was extended into modern times. The transfer from the *Mobilier National,* in 1870 and again in 1901, of furniture, tapestries and decorative bronzes from former royal residences, formed a prestigious core which was to grow with gifts of furniture

(Count Isaac de Camondo 1911; Baron Basile de Schlichting, 1914; M. and Mme Grog-Carven, 1973), of silver and gold plate (M. and Mme David-Weill, 1946; M. Stavros S. Niarchos, 1955), of porcelain (Mme Adolphe Thiers, 1880) and with dations and numerous acquisitions.

Late Empire

During the 3rd century AD the Roman empire experienced a series of political, social and cultural crises from which it emerged profoundly transformed; this was the beginning of the Late Empire (3rd-4th centuries). The separation of the Western empire, with its Latin civilisation, from the Greek Eastern empire, became definitive at the death of Theodosius (395); Christianity, which had gradually established itself throughout the whole Roman Empire and was recognized by Constantine in 314, became the official religion under Theodosius in 385. In the end, relentless pressure from the barbarians led to the Great Invasions of the 5th century and the downfall of the Western Empire in 476 AD.

The art of the Late Empire complies largely with the traditional forms and techniques of Graeco-Roman art. This revival which took place in Rome around 400, and is especially evident in ivory carving, was nevertheless permeated by original anticlassical currents. While Christian iconography gradually took shape, the continual attraction exerted by the arts of the Orient became increasingly palpable. The resulting primacy of ideas over form represented an infringement of classical illusionism, especially where perspective was concerned. These tendencies became increasingly marked in the Eastern Empire during the 6th century.

²¹⁴ Miracles of Christ

Rome, early 5th century

Ivory plaque. H 0.197 m; W 0.78 m

Acq. 1926. OA 7876-7878

This rectangular plaque formed the lateral side of a large ivory diptych in the Christian tradition, which was divided into five sections. The three scenes depict the miracles of Christ. Another side panel in the same series, but almost certainly from the second leaf, is in the Berlin-Dahlem Museum (Staatliche Museen in Preussichen Kulturbesitz). A third fragment showing the Adoration of the Magi was formerly kept at Nevers cathedral (Nevers Museum). These ivory reliefs are illustrative of the style used by Roman ivory carvers in the first years of the 5th century; the allusions to the classical art of antiquity are still very marked, despite the gradual disappearance of spatial perspective.

²¹⁵ The Emperor Triumphant known as the "Barberini Ivory"

Constantinople
First half of the 6th century
Ivory. H 0.342 m; L 0.268 m
Acq. 1891. OA 9063

A gift to Cardinal Barberini from Claude Fabri de Peiresc, a scholar from Aix, in the early 17th century, the ivory must have been in Provence in the 7th century because on the back is a list of Barbarian kings and officials from the region. The "Barberini Ivory" is the only almost complete surviving leaf of an imperial diptych, each leaf of which was made up of five attached ivory units. The centrepiece shows the triumph of an emperor, Anastasius (491-518) or, more probably, Justinian (527-565) who is associated, in the upper section, with the glorification of Christ. The density of the composition and the very high relief - almost in the round - of the centrepiece, in addition to the fullness of the idealised faces of Christ and the emperor, are characteristic of a group of ivories worked in Constantinople in the first half of the 6th century.

Byzantine Art

Spared the great invasions of the 5th century, the Eastern Empire, now known as the Byzantine Empire, survived until 1453 when its capital, Constantinople, fell to the Turks. After a first flowering under the reigns of Justinian (527-567) and Heraclius (610-641), the existence of Byzantium was soon under threat from the rise of Islam which conquered the Southern Mediterranean coastline over the 7th century. Iconoclasm (726-843), the doctrine which forbad figurative religious art, ended this period of bloodshed. After the return to religious orthodoxy (843), the accession of the dynasty of Macedonian emperors (867-1056) opens the most brilliant period of Byzantine history, prolonged under the Comnenian dynasty (1081-1183). But the Crusades, coming in successive waves from the west, aggravated East-West clashes and the fourth Crusade turned against Constantinople itself. It was sacked in 1204, and the crusaders shared out the spoils of the empire between them. Little by little, however, the Greeks managed to regain their empire, which was restored in 1261. Then the Paleologue dynasty began (1261-1453), the third and final period of Byzantine history, and the last gasp of an empire besieged by the Turks. Byzantine art is a conscious successor to the art of the Christian Late Empire. Each great period of renewal in Byzantine history is matched by a series of deliberate backward turns, known as "renaissances" (the "Heraclian", "Macedonian", "Comnenian" and "Paleologue" renaissances), which derive their central inspiration from the classical mainspring. It is this classicism that gives Byzantine art as a whole its profound unity and which finds expression, in every period, in its finest productions. It was not, for all that, impervious to other artistic currents, as can be seen in the Oriental luxury of Islamic art under the Macedonians, the research into decorative effects proper to the Comnenian period, or the note of pathos in the last period of Byzantine art under the Paleologues.

216 Harbaville Triptych:
Deisis and Saints

Constantinople
Mid 10th century
Ivory with traces of goldleaf. H 0.242 m; W 0.285 m
Acq. 1891. UA 324*l*

The triptych is organized around the depiction of
the *deisis;* the Virgin and St. John the Baptist
intercede with Christ Enthroned, on behalf of
humanity. On the section beneath, and on the two
side panels, apostles, martyrs, bishop and soldier-
saints join in this prayer. This masterpiece of
Byzantine classicism is the most elegant of the
ivories from the imperial workshop known as
"Romanos" (based on the plaque in the *Cabinet des
Médailles* at the Bibliothèque Nationale in Paris in
which Christ is crowning Emperor Romanos II
(945-949) and his wife Eudoxia). It is an important
example of the rebirth of the ornamental arts in
Byzantium under the Macedonian Emperors.

217 St. Demetrios

Constantinople
Beginning of the 12th century
Medallion, gold and enamel. ⌀ 8.4 cm
Gift of Pierpont Morgan, 1911. OA 6457

This medallion and nine others in the same series (New York, Metropolitan Museum) were mounted round the frame of a large icon of the archangel Gabriel, formerly housed in the Djoumati monastery (Soviet Georgia). Three of the medallions depicted the *deisis* with which the saints' heads were associated. This enamel is among the finest things created in Constantinople under the Comnenian dynasty. The striving for decorative effect and the perfect mastery of technique place it chronologically between the Crown Enamels of St. Stephen of Hungary (1071-1078) and the oldest enamels of the Venetian *pala d'Oro* around 1100.

Carolingian and Romanesque Art

As with Byzantine art, Medieval art is descended from the Late Empire. The connection is especially evident in the domain of Carolingian *objets d'art* because a fixed ambition of Charlemagne and his successors - who were fascinated by imperialism - encouraged artists to draw inspiration, in the widest sense of the term, from ancient models and thereby bring about the so-called "Carolingian renaissance". While the art of metalwork was perfected - and this had been the major art form of the preceding period - the end of the 8th and 9th century saw the revival of techniques that had been abandoned; glyptics, bronze casting (an example being the *Equestrian Statuette of Charlemagne* **219**), and above all ivory carving, prime examples of which are displayed in the Louvre.

In the 11th and 12th centuries, workshops multiplied and diversified. Now a cardinal role was played by different enameling techniques. While the *cloisonné* enamels of the *Maastricht*

Binding **222** are direct descendants of Carolingian and Ottonian *cloisonné* enamels, there is a marked development of *champlevé* enamels on copper, in the north and east as well as in the southern regions. The *Resurrection Armilla* **226** and the *Reliquary of St. Henry* **225** are evidence of the achievement of Saxon, Rhineland and Mosan workshops, on a par with the enamelers of Conques (*Griffon Medallion* **227**), and of Limoges (*Alpais Ciborium* **228**).

218 Leaves from the Binding of the Daglulf Psaltery

Workshop of the Palace of Charlemagne
End of the 8th century
Ivory. H 16.8 cm; W. of leaf 8,1 cm

From Bremen Cathedral.

MR 370-371

Charlemagne instructed Dagulf, the scribe, to illuminate a lavish psaltery for Pope Hadrian I. Probably unfinished at the death of the Pope in 795, the psaltery remained in the royal treasury. These two ivory leaves of the binding illustrate the content of the manuscript, showing David overseeing the writing of the Psalms, and singing them, and St. Jerome receiving the order to correct the text of the Psalms and then working on them. These two ivories, which are the only ones that were a direct commission from Charlemagne, signal the start of the Carolingian Renaissance. Their style refers directly to Late Empire models.

219 Equestrian Statuette of Charlemagne

9th century

Bronze with traces of gilding. H 0.235 m

From the treasury of Metz Cathedral.

OA 8260

Inspired by classical equestrian statues, this statuette is made up of several bronze units that were cast separately and then assembled. The horse, which is not in proportion to its rider, may be a Late Empire work. The head and body of the rider are Carolingian bronzes. The sovereign, who is crowned, holds the orb of the world. His plump face with its thick drooping moustache, and his simple attire, correspond to Eginhard's description of Charlemagne. The statuette may have been cast in Aix-la-Chapelle in the early 9th century. It is also possible, however, that the statue is a portrait of Charles the Bald, whose painted portrait in manuscripts shows a resemblance to his grandfather, Charlemagne.

220 Plaque known as the "Earthly Paradise"

France, around 860-870 (?)

Ivory. H 0.358 m; W 0.114 m

Acq. 1863. OA 9064

The plaque is divided into several sections showing, in descending order, Adam and Eve, then fabulous animals, wild animals and domestic ones. It is not, in fact, a depiction of the Earthly Paradise, but an illustration to a text by Isidore de Séville, outlining the different orders of creation, the *Etymologies*. The realism with which the animals are treated and the soft delicacy of the modelling reveal a deep knowledge and a rare understanding of models from antiquity or the Late Empire. This ivory came from the same workshop as the *flabellum* (liturgical fan) from Tournus, in the Bargello Museum, Florence.

221 Serpentine Paten

(stone) 1st century BC or AD
(surround) second half of 9th century

Gold, pearls, precious stones, coloured glass.

∅ 0.17 m

From the treasury of the *Abbaye de Saint-Denis*.

Entered the Louvre in 1793. MR 415

The paten is made up of two parts. The
serpentine saucer, inlaid with golden fish, can be
considered as antique, dating from the 1st century.
The gold surround is decorated with stones,
between which isolated motifs in *cloisonné*
goldwork evolve, a combination found up to the
early 11th century. At Saint-Denis, the Paten
accompanied an ancient agate *cantharus,* the
"Ptolemies Cup", to which a goldwork decoration
was applied which matches that on the Paten
(Paris, Bibliothèque Nationale). An inscription at
the base of the chalice states that it was given to
the abbey by Charles the Bald.

²²² Maastricht Binding-Case

Second quarter of the 11th century

Gold, *cloisonné* enamel, precious stones,
filigree and niello on wood base.

H 0.392 m; W 0.32 m

Acq. 1795. MR 349

This binding-case comes from the treasury of St. Servais at Maastricht (Netherlands); it contained a manuscript of the Gospels on which the Dukes of Brabant took solemn oath. An inscription inlaid with niello, names the donor, Beatrix, who was the wife either of Duke Adalberon of Carinthia, or of Boniface of Tuscany (1036), then of Godefroy le Barbu, Duke of Basse-Lorraine and Brabant. The *cloisonné* enamels are in the style of pieces from the workshops of Trier and Essen, and the style of the gold embossed reliefs is close to that of Ottonian works at the beginning of the 11th century.

²²³ Coronation Sword of the Kings of France

10th-11th centuries (pommel),
12th century (cross-guards), 13th century (spindle)

Gold, steel, glass or lapis pearls.

H 1.005 m; W 0.226 m

From the treasury of the *Abbaye de Saint-Denis*.

Entered the Louvre in 1793. MS 84

The coronation accessories of the kings of France were kept in the treasury at Saint-Denis. The coronation sword dates from the 13th century, and was believed to be the "Joyeuse" that belonged to Charlemagne. The pommel and the small metal plate in the centre of the hilt, with a foliate motif, date from the early Middle Ages; the handle proper, decorated, until 1804, with fleurs-de-lys inside the diamond patterning, has a Gothic appearance; the cross-guards, in the form of two little winged dragons whose eyes are inlaid with pearls, date from the second half of the 12th century. This swords and the spurs (also in the Louvre) are part of the oldest French *regalia* in existence today.

224 Eagle-Shaped **Vase** known as the
"Suger's Eagle"

France, before 1147

Ancient Porphyry Vase, **gilded** silver and niello inlay.

H 0.431 m; W 0.27 m

From the treasury of the *Abbaye de Saint-Denis.*

Entered the Louvre in **1793**. MR 422

Suger, advisor to Louis VI and Louis VII, and abbot
of Saint-Denis, took a particular interest in adding
to the treasures of his abbey and his writings

contain descriptions of the precious vases he commissioned. He writes that he found an antique porphyry vase in a coffer, which he had transformed into a liturgical vase mounted in the form of an eagle. This ewer joins other vases in hard stone which Suger had mounted and decorated: his chalice (Washington, National Gallery), the "Aliénor" vase, and the sardonyx ewer which are both in the Louvre. These were made by one of the groups of goldsmiths who worked for Saint-Denis; in this case, most probably the goldsmiths of the Ile-de-France.

²²⁵ Reliquary of St. Henry

Hildesheim, Lower-Saxony, around 1175

Gilt brass, engraved, *champlevé* enamel and rock-crystal, silver on wood core.

H 0.236 m; W 0.161 m

Acq. 1851. OA 49

This quadriform reliquary, enameled on both sides, rests on a hemispherical base, also enameled. On one side, Christ in Majesty is surrounded by three kings; the other side portrays St. Henry, last Ottonian Emperor of the Germanic Holy Roman Empire, canonised in 1152, with the Empress Cunégonde and a clerk by name of Welandus, probably the donor of the reliquary, on either side. The blue enamel ground flecked with gold, and the subdued colouring are characteristic of a group of works executed at Hildesheim at the time of the Duke of Saxony, Henri le Lion (1142-1181).

226 "Armilla": the Resurrection

Meuse, around 1170

Gilt brass, *champlevé* enamel.

H 0.113 m; W 0.147 m

Gift of the *Société des Amis du Louvre*, 1934.

OA 3261

The *armilla* (a ceremonial bracelet) and its pendant depicting the Crucifixion (Nuremberg, Germanisches Nationalmuseum) might have been found in Russia in the tomb of Prince André Bogoloubski (d. 1174); the latter received them from Emperor Frederick Barbarossa, as a diplomatic gift. The style displays the persistent classical traditions of Mosan art around 1150-1160. But the pure Byzantine grace of the angels, their faces and that of Christ, look forward to the classicizing art of Nicolas de Verdun after 1180.

227 Medallion Decorated with a Fabulous Animal

Conques (?), 1107-1119

Gilt brass, *champlevé* enamel. Ø 8 cm

Gift of the *Société des Amis du Louvre*, 1909.OA 6280

A perfect expression of the Romanesque *"loi du cadre"* (in which the design fits the space perfectly), this medallion is also a very early example of the technique of *champlevé* enamel on brass, proper to the Romanesque period. With nine other similar medallions (New York, Metropolitan Museum, and Florence, Bargello), it was part of the decoration on a casket. A second casket still housed in Conques is decorated with practically identical medallions, two of which bear an inscription which date the construction of the two caskets to the time of Abbot Boniface (1107-1119).

Carolingian and Romanesque Art   **Decorative Arts**

228 Alpais Ciborium

Limoges, shortly before 1200

Gilt brass, chiseled and engraved, precious stones.

H 0.30 m; Ø 0.168 m

Acq. 1828. MRR 98

The ciborium was found in the tomb of Bertrand de Malsang (d. 1316), abbot of Montmajour near Arles, where it might have been used as a funerary chalice. On the inside of the lid, around the form of an engraved angel, runs the inscription MAGISTER G. ALPAIS ME FECIT LEMOVICARUM. It proves that the ciborium was made in Limoges itself, and is an essential document in the history of Limousin enamels of the Middle-Ages. The ciborium is the masterpiece among a group of Limousin enamels executed before 1200.

Gothic Art

Throughout the first half of the 13th century,
Limoges enamellers continued to produce
remarkable works such as the *St. Mathieu* tablet
from the Abbaye de Grandmont [229]. But by the
end of the century, Italian enamellers had
perfected a new procedure which spread rapidly
to the great centres of Western Europe: the
production of translucent *basse-taille* enamels,
executed on silver (*Virgin of Jeanne d'Évreux* [233])
or on gold (*Mirror Case* [231]). The second half of
the 14th century saw the triumph of enamels on
ronde-bosse gold of which the fleur de lys on the
Sceptre of Charles V [235] was originally an example.
These pieces herald the technique of painted
enamel which gradually supplanted other forms of
enamelwork; the *Self-Portrait* by Fouquet [238] is
one of the first examples of the technique.
The growing wealth of the princely courts,
especially of the French court which was
dominated by enthusiastic collectors of precious
objets d'art, greatly fostered the craft of metalwork.
There is, perhaps, no better expression of the
perfection it attained than the two outstanding
masterpieces of Medieval art, the *Virgin of Jeanne
d'Evreux* and the *Sceptre of Charles V*. But the
French Gothic style was even more influential in
ivory carving. The Louvre possesses one of the
largest collections. Statuettes, diptychs, triptychs,
tabernacles and secular objects spread the style of
Parisian workshops throughout Europe.

229 Arched Plaque Decorated with a Figure of St. Matthew

Limoges, around 1220-1230

Gilt brass, *champlevé* enamel.

H 0.29 mm; W 0.14 m

Acq. 1825. MR 2650

The figure of St. Matthew, identified by an inscription, is fixed on a base enameled with vigorous florid scrollwork. There are five other similar plaques with the apostles James (New York, Metropolitan Museum), Philip (Leningrad, Hermitage), Paul and Thomas (Paris, Petit Palais) and St. Martial (Florence, Bargello), the "apostle" of the Limousin whom local worshippers associated with the apostolic college. These plaques come from the high altar of the former abbey of Grandmont near Limoges. Remarkable for their modelling, these apostles are the Limousin version of the classicizing style which appeared around 1200 in the Meuse and the north of France.

230 Virgin and Child from the Sainte-Chapelle

Paris, around 1250-1260

Ivory, traces of polychrome. H 0.41 m

From the treasury of the *Sainte-Chapelle* in Paris.

Acq. 1861. OA 57

In the 13th and 14th centuries, the growth of the cult of Mary led to the production of numerous figurines of the Virgin and Child, especially in ivory. This statuette, described in an inventory of the treasury of the Sainte-Chapelle before 1279, is considered to be the finest achievement of Parisian ivory workers, especially since it seems to have inspired a whole series of ivory statuettes in the second half of the 13th century. The drapery and her triangular face with its narrowed eyes and slightly mocking smile place this statuette in the full flowering of Parisian monumental Gothic, in the middle of third quarter of the 13th century.

231 Mirror Case: the Game of Chess

Paris, around 1300
Ivory. ∅ 0,12 m
Gift of C Sauvageot, 1856. OA 717

Gothic ivory workers produced not only religious pieces but secular articles as well, such as this mirror case. The two sides, held together by a lace or a staple, protecting a small metal mirror, were sculpted with courtly subjects or scenes illustrating episodes from fashionable romances. The game of chess shown here is possibly based on a passage in the story of Tristan and Isolde. The delicate rounded modelling of this relief and the smiling elegance of the figures, clad in long floating robes, are characteristic of art at the court of Philippe le Bel.

232 Arm-Reliquary of St. Louis of Toulouse

Naples, before 1338
Rock crystal, silver gilt, translucent enamels.
H 0.63 m; W 0.20 m
Gift of Mme F Spitzer, 1891. OA 3254

Brother of Robert d'Anjou, king of Naples, St. Louis of Toulouse was canonized in 1317. This reliquary-arm, designed to contain a relic, was made for Sancia of Majorca, the wife of Robert d'Anjou. The translucent enamels that cover part of the structure may have been executed by a Sienese metalworker (Lando di Pietro?). With its pair (the reliquary-arm of St. Luke, also made for Sancia of Majorca), this is one of the rare surviving works from the Angevin court of Naples collaborated on by French and Italian metalworkers.

233 Virgin and Child of Jeanne d'Evreux

Paris, between 1324 and 1339

Silver gilt, *basse-taille* translucent enamels, gold, rock crystal, precious stones and pearls. H 0.69 m

Given to the *Abbaye de Saint-Denis* in 1339 by Queen Jeanne d'Evreux; entered the museum in 1793.

MR 342 and 419

In the 13th and 14th centuries a new type of statuette came into vogue, in which the central figure holds the reliquary itself out towards the spectator. The Virgin in silver gilt holds a lily in gold plate and rock crystal which enclosed relics of the clothes, hair and milk of the Virgin. The rounded face of the Virgin, the layered hems and the folds of her robe that fall in long cones extending her form are characteristic of Parisian art in the first half of the 14th century. The enamels on the base (scenes from the Childhood and the Passion of Christ) are an early dated example of translucent *basse-taille* enameling, perfected by Tuscan goldsmiths at the end of the 13th century.

234 Tabernacle

Paris, second quarter of the 14th century
Ivory
H 0.29 m; W 0.235 m
Acq. 1882. OA 2587

Amidst the multifarious productions of Gothic ivory workers, the "tabernacles" stand out because of their elaborate design. These little polyptychs are made up of folding shutters that close around a central section, shaped like a tiny chapel, which houses one or several statuettes. The centre of the Louvre tabernacle presents a Virgin and Child in high relief. Her tall and sinuous silhouette, the delicate cascading drapery and the full face recall works of monumental sculpture. The scenes on the shutters, however, are closer to contemporary diptychs and triptychs.

235 Charles V Sceptre

Paris, before 1380
Gold, pearls, precious stones, glass. H 0.60 m
From the treasury of the *Abbaye de Saint-Denis*.
Entered the Louvre in 1793. MS 83

Charles V set aside a quantity of vestments and royal insignia - this sceptre among them - for the coronation of his son, the future Charles VI. The detailed description of the sceptre in the inventory of the Royal Treasury, dated 1379-1380, shows that it has not undergone much modification. The major difference is that the fleur-de-lys was originally covered with opaque white enamel. The statuette of Charlemagne on the top of the sceptre, and scenes from his legend on the knob are doubtless allusions to the first name of the king and his son (Charles), but also express the desire of the first Valois monarchs to link their power with that of the legendary Carolingian emperor.

236 Mirror Cases

Paris, before 1379

Gold, translucent *basse-taille* enamels. ∅ 6.8 cm

Acq. 1825. MR 2608-2609

Jean Le Bon and his sons, Charles V, Louis d'Anjou, Philippe de Bourgogne and Jean de Berry were all avid collectors. There is almost nothing left of the vast treasure amassed by Louis d'Anjou and described in an inventory dated 1379 but these two mirror cases. The first depicts a Virgin and Child between St. Catherine and St. John the Baptist, while the second shows God the Father between St. John the Baptist and St. Charlemagne. The bold style of these figures is influenced by the art of the Low Countries and the Rhineland. It is also typical of the milieu of the court of Jean le Bon, and especially of Charles V, at which many artists from these regions worked.

237 Support Figure: Kneeling Prophet

Paris, 1409

Gilt bronze. H 0.14 m

Gift of J Maciet, 1388. OA 5917

The kneeling prophet in the Louvre, and its pendant in the Cleveland Museum, were two of the bronze figures that supported the gold reliquary of St. Germain in the church of Saint-Germain-des-Prés. The reliquary, which was destroyed in the Revolution, is known to us from a 17th century etching and from a contract drawn up in 1409 between the Abbot and the three Parisian goldworkers who were to make it: Guillaume Boey, Gautier Dufour and Jean de Clichy. The fullness of the drapery and the vigour with which the heads are chiselled has been compared to the art of the best sculptors of the 1400's. It is a tangible expression of the "international" stylistic current in Gothic art around 1400.

Jean FOUQUET
c. 1420 - c. 1477-1481

238 Signed Self-Portrait

c. 1450

Painted enamel on copper. Ø 6.8 cm

Gift of H de Janzé, 1861. OA 56

This medallion, showing Fouquet's signature, was set into the frame, now lost, of his diptych in Notre-Dame de Melun. Shortly after his journey to Italy, Fouquet painted this diptych for Etienne Chevalier, secretary and counsellor to Charles VII, and treasurer of France in 1452. The diptych is now divided between the museums of Berlin-Dahlem (Etienne Chevalier presented by St. Stephen) and Antwerp (the Virgin and Child surrounded by angels). On the copper plaque, covered first with black, then grey-brown enamel, Fouquet laid his gold in thin hatched strokes, and then uncovered the black ground shining beneath it with the aid of a needlepoint. These techniques are early examples of the art of painted enamel which became popular at the end of the century and during the Renaissance.

Gothic Art   **Decorative Arts**

Renaissance Italy

Evidence of a new lifestyle and new techniques, Italian Renaissance *objets d'art* are well represented in the Louvre in the main with maiolica and glassware along with bronze statuettes. These give us a good idea of decoration in homes at that time, as well as contemporary interest in the art of antiquity.

Faience (the name derives from the town of Faenza) is Italy's great contribution to ceramics. Faience is earthenware covered with a tin oxide glaze, usually white, onto which the painted decoration is then added. The Louvre conserves major examples from the principal centres of production, Faenza, Urbino, Casteldurante, Gubbio and Deruta.

Glassmaking made such a rapid progress at the end of the 15th century in Venice that the two names are still linked. Thanks in part to the invention of a white glass known as *"cristallo"*, the fame of Venetian glass brought in its wake a flood of imitations throughout Europe in the "Venetian style", encouraged by the emigration of Italian artists. Despite its fragility, Venetian glassware has survived from the Renaissance and the Louvre collection is one of the greatest in the world.

Bronze nevertheless remains the material most typical of Renaissance Italy; after the precious metals, it was the most highly favoured for its diverse qualities and the illusion it gave of working "in the antique manner". Florence, Padua and Venice were the main centres of a flourishing industry in little statuettes and everyday objects, that were highly sought after.

239 Bowl Inscribed with the Arms of Florence

Florence, around 1425-1450

Tin-glazed earthenware.

H 8 cm; ⌀ 64 cm

Acq. 1897. OA 3946

The word *Maiolica,* the name given to Italian tin-glazed earthenware, derives from Majorca; throughout the 14th century the island was a transit point for luxurious glazed artefacts from Spanish workshops in Valencia, destined for Italy. Although they were great admirers of these pieces, a good many of which carry the arms of families from Pisa and Florence, the Italians developed their own original style, which reflected the general artistic climate of the Florentine *quattrocento.*

The iconography on this bowl, a heraldic banner borne by a lion who stands on a field of lily stems (denoting the city of Florence), testifies to the great quality of this city's production in this area in the first quarter of the 15th century.

240 Cup Decorated with an Allegorical Procession

Venice, last quarter of the 15th century

Enameled glass.

H 0.275 m; ⌀ 0.140 m

Gift of Baroness Salomon de Rothschild, 1922

OA 7564

During the 15th century, the glass-making tradition of ancient Rome was revived in Venice thanks to numerous contacts with Byzantium and Mameluke Syria where the tradition had been

Renaissance Italy **Decorative Arts**

maintained. One of the most spectacular aspects of Syrian glassware was its enameling, a technique widely used by the master glass-makers of Venice. Prominent among the latter was Angelo Barovier who died in 1460. Although this cup appears stylistically to date after the death of Angelo Barovier, it gives us a good idea of the splendour of Venetian glassware at the end of the 15th century. The meaning of the allegorical procession around the bowl remains obscure, although it is generally thought to be an allegory of marriage.

Bartolomeo BELLANO
c. 1440-1496/7

241 Saint Jerome and the Lion

Padua, end of the 15th century

Bronze with crackleware black patina.

H 0.25 m; W 0.205 m

Gift of Mme Gustave Dreyfus and her children, 1919

OA 7250

A pupil of Donatello and a native of Padua where the art of bronze flourished, Bellano is renowned for works with a strong narrative bias. This bronze statuette illustrates the famous episode in which the saint extracts a thorn from a lion's paw. As the only one of its kind, the statuette seems to have been cast directly from the wax model. It can be dated to around 1490-1495 because of close similarities to sculptures on the monument to Pietro Roccabonella in San Francesco, Padua. Bellano began work on these in 1491; they exhibit a similar simplified treatment of volumes and an equally sensitive rendering of the human face.

detail

Andrea Briosco known as RICCIO
1470-1532

242 Paradise

Padua 1516-1521

Bas-relief, bronze with brown patina.

H 0.37 m; W 0.49 m

Entered the Louvre in 1798. **MR** 1711. OA 9099

This bas-relief, which is one of a series of eight, comes from a tomb in the church of San Fermo Maggiore in Verona. The tomb was constructed by Riccio, the famous Paduan sculptor, in honour of Girolamo della Torre, a physician and professor of medicine, along with his son Marcantonio, also a professor of medecine and a friend of Leonardo da Vinci. The reliefs derive from Book VI of Virgil's *Aeneid,* and depict - in pagan mode - the journey of the dead soul into the underworld. *Paradise* depicts the soul of the dead (on the left) in the form of a winged cupid carrying a book who is welcomed by dancers on the Elysian Fields of the pagan underworld. Top right, in the same form, the soul is shown drinking the waters of Lethe, the river of oblivion, while at bottom right he is shown sleeping in his earthly form, that of a bearded old man, crowned with Fame, awaiting his return to earth. Known for his many mythical and fabulous creatures, Riccio's achievement here is based on the alliance between a classicism derived from antique models, and a lyrical realism typical of artists in northern Italy.

Nicola da URBINO
known between 1520 and 1538

243 Plate from the Service of Isabella d'Este

Urbino, c. 1525

Tin-glazed earthenware. H.4 cm; ⌀ 27 cm

Gift of Baroness Salomon de Rothschild, 1922

OA 7578

The most original contribution made by the Italians to the history of faience was with the

Istoriato, a decorative genre in which pieces were painted with historical scenes. During the first half of the 16th century, centres like Casteldurante and Urbino brought this art to a unsurpassed degree of perfection. Nicola di Gabriele Sbraga, who signed his works Nicola da Urbino - after the name of his town -, stands out among the most brilliant painters of *Istoriati.*

One of Nicola's most prestigious achievements was the service commissioned around 1525 by Isabella d'Este, the famous patron and connoisseur of the arts. The plate in the Louvre was part of this service. Isabella d'Este's coat-of-arms is in the foreground of the decoration, and her motto is on a scroll on the ground. The scene itself is an imitation of a work by Raphael in the Vatican - an illustration from Genesis, *Abimelech spying on Isaac and Rebecca.*

244 Gnome on a Snail

*Florence, second half of the
16th century*

Bronze with black and brown cracklework patina.

H 0.375 m; W 0.195 m

Acq. 1933. OA 8252

Sitting astride a snail, holding a whip handle in his right hand, the naked gnome seems in a ludicrous way to want to speed the animal along. The bold association of a deformed human figure with a monstrous snail, treated naturalistically, is typically Mannerist in feel. This gnome could be compared with a marble of the same subject, housed in the Villa Careggi near Florence, and attributed to the workshop of Valerio Cioli (1529-1599). Despite its diminutive size it is related to sculptures designed for villa gardens. The gnome's complex position has been worked out so as to stand scrutiny from different angles.

GIAMBOLOGNA (Jean BOULOGNE)
1529-1608

245 Nessus and Deianira

Florence, around 1575-1580

Bronze with red-brown patina.

H 0.421 m; W 0.305 m

Collection of the French Crown. Inv. Cour. 176

A native of Douai, Jean Boulogne made his career in Florence where his name was Italianized into Giambologna. In addition to large marble sculptures, Jean Boulogne made numerous models for small bronzes. These were cast in his workshop and disseminated by his pupils. They were much sought after throughout Europe, and served as diplomatic gifts at the Court of the Medici. The Louvre group is of exceptional quality and one of the very rare examples which has the artist's signature ("IOA BOLONGIE" on the centaur's headband). It was most probably the bronze given to Louis XIV by Le Nôtre in 1693, and shows Jean Boulogne's genius for capturing two figures in action.

Renaissance France

In France, during the Renaissance, *objets d'art* - along with the arts in general - came under Italian influence. The presence of Italian artists in France, especially on royal sites like Fontainebleau, was a stimulus to local artists. And there was another new phenomenon: the circulation of prints which familiarized the French with forms and decorations developed not only in Italy but in Germany and Flanders as well. In return, the brilliance of the "School of Fontainebleau", and the dissemination of models created by a new type of artist, the ornamentalist - Jacques Androuet du Cerceau for example or Etienne Delaune - ensured that France had a place of honour in the domain of *objets d'art*.

Works in precious metal from the period are extremely rare today, but they convey something of the luxury of the Court of France, in particular its taste for polychrome enamel effects, decorations inspired by the Grotesque or the Mauresque, and historical scene-painting.

Enamel painting on copper was a speciality of Limoges during the whole of the 16th century; originally designed for devotional paintings, it was later used on decorative tableware. Like Italian maiolica, its popularity was immense both in France and abroad.

French ceramics belonged to one of two camps; on the one hand Italianism, introduced at Lyon and Nevers, and assimilated by an obscure Rouen artist, Masséot Abaquesne, who produced tin-glazed earthenware using the Italian technique; on the other, the traditional production, which flourished in provincial centres such as the Beauvaisis or the Saintonge, which was dominated by the mythical figure of Bernard Palissy.

Léonard LIMOSIN
c. 1505-c. 1575

246 St. Thomas with the Features of François I

Limoges, around 1550

Enamel on copper, H 0.915 m; W 0.435 m

Entered the Louvre in 1816. **MR 211**

From the 15th to the 17th century Limoges was the centre of production for enameled copper plaques. Léonard Limosin brought the technique to perfection. In 1547 he finished twelve paintings in enamel depicting the apostles which are now in the museum at Chartres. The mounts were painted by Michel Rochetel after drawings by Primaticcio. The series was a gift from Henri II to Diane de Poitiers for her Château Anet; Léonard Limosin may well have reproduced the series as the Louvre possesses two other apostles from the Feuillantines Convent which were shown in Alexandre Lenoir's Museum of French Monuments during the Revolution. This portrait of St. Thomas differs from the one at Chartres in that the head is a portrait of François I, and the surrounding motifs are inverted.

Léonard LIMOSIN
c. 1505-c. 1575

247 Portrait of the Connetable de Montmorency

Limoges, 1556

Enamel on copper, mount in gilt wood.

H 0.72 m; W 0.56 m

Seized during French Revolution. Entered the Louvre in 1794. N 1254

In 1556, Léonard Limosin - who was an enameller at the court of François I and of his successors -

painted this portrait of Anne de Montmorency (1493-1567), High Constable of France in 1538. Most probably painted from a pencil drawing, the portrait a good example of Léonard Limosin's masterly skill. It is still in its original frame which is made up of eight panels of different shapes, depicting the High Constable's motto, heads of children and of the Medusa, and two satyrs, the model for which came from the Galerie François I at Fontainebleau.

Masséot ABAQUESNE
known in 1526-died before 1564

248 Altar Step for La Bastie d'Urfé

Rouen, 1557

Tin-glazed earthenware. H 3.260 m;

W 1.840 m and 0.540 m

Gift of Beurdeley, father and son, 1880. AO 2518

In a contract drawn up at Rouen, on the 22 September 1557, Claude d'Urfé commissioned enameled paving flags from Masséot Abaquesne up to a value of 559 *livres*. These were almost certainly the tiles used to pave the chapel at his home, La Bastie d'Urfé in the Forez. The Louvre possesses the altar step from this chapel, and it is dated the same year as the contract. It is not known whether Masséot Abaquesne was a businessman or artist, or where he trained in the latter case. Both the earthenware technique and the *Raphaelesque* decoration, commonly used in Urbino workshops at the time, indicate an Italian influence.

Bernard PALISSY
c. 1510-1590

249 **Dish Decorated with "Rustic Figulines"**

France, around 1560
Glazed Clay. H 0.074 m; L 0.525 m; W 0.403 m
Acq. 1825. MR 2293

Bernard Palissy is the most famous figure in the history of French ceramics. As a writer, architect, Chemist, and devoted artist he was an archetypal Renaissance Humanist.

One of the most characteristic aspects of his work can been seen in the large dishes decorated with reptiles, shells and plants cast from life. Known as *"rustique figulines"*, they can be linked to the design of two grottoes which have now disappeared, designed for Catherine de Médicis, in the Tuileries, and for the *Connétable de Montmorency* at Ecouen.

Pierre REYMOND
c. 1513-after 1584

250 **Oval Plate**

Limoges, 1578
Enamel on copper. H 0.390 m; W 0.515 m
Acq. 1825. MR 2419

The 16th century saw the emergence of decorative table services in enamel which is often monochrome with highlights - as here - in salmon, pink of gold enamel. These dishes are decorated either with monthly tasks or with illustrations from the Bible. Here, Shaphan reads the Book of Law to king Josias who promptly sets about major religious reforms. The rim is decorated with a frieze of monsters and animals with an escutcheon bearing the date 1578 at the top. The motifs often derive from contemporary etchings: in this case from a vignette by Bernard Salomon published in Lyon after 1554.

251 Charles IX Shield

Paris, around 1572

Embossed metal and gold plating, enamel.

H 0.68 m; W 0.49 m

Acq. 1793. MR 427

This shield is a rare example of the luxury enjoyed by the last Valois kings; it is accompanied by a matching helmet. Charles IX (1550-1574) first received the helmet, and a scimitar, from Pierre Redon, metalworker and page-in-waiting to the King. The shield, which was made later, was paid to Redon's widow, Marie de Fourcroy, in 1572. Round the rim, the King's monogram K alternates with medallions in *cloisonné* enamel. The central bas-relief depicts the victory of Marius over Jugurtha, King of Numidia, in 107 BC. This is surrounded by the favourite motifs of the School of Fontainebleau: cuirasses, masks, trophies, and ornamental fruit.

252 Mace from the Order of the Saint-Esprit

Paris, 1584-1585

Silver gilt and enamel.

H 1.10 m; W 0.32 m; wght 4.24 kg

Formerly in the treasury of the Order of the Saint-Esprit. MR 564

The Order of the Saint-Esprit was founded in 1578 by Henri III (1551-1589) who ordered a set of ten silver gilt objects to be made for the Order in Paris between 1579 and 1585. They were given to the Louvre when the order was disbanded in 1830. The mace was duly delivered in early 1586 by the metalworker François Dujardin. It is surmounted by the royal crown, and the upper part of the mace has four bas-reliefs depicting ceremonies of the Order, after drawings by Toussaint Dubreuil (kept in the *Cabinet des Dessins* in the Louvre). Below, in enamel, are the arms of Henri III, king of France and Poland. The rod is decorated with fleurs-de-lys, flames, Crosses of the Order and the crowned letter H. The mace is evidence of the quality of Parisian metalwork in the 16th century. Such objects were often melted down subsequently, and few examples have survived to this day.

Renaissance Flanders

detail

253 **The Month of September**
7th piece of the set of
Maximilian's Hunt
after Bernard van ORLEY

Brussels, around 1528-1533

Tapestry, silk and wool, gold and silver thread.
7 warps per cm. H 4.48 m; W 5.58 m
Collection of the French Crown. OA 7320

Woven in Brussels, the largest centre of tapestry weaving in the 16th century, this piece belongs to a set of twelve tapestries depicting hunting scenes in the countryside around Brussels. The set is organized around the twelve months of the year; it has been attributed to Bernard van Orley, a Flemish painter who was prominent in tapestry design.

In all probability woven in the workshop of Jan Ghieteels, the set has been dated to sometime between 1528 (from the communal stamp which became obligatory that year) and 1533 (from the building progress on the old ducal palace in Brussels shown in the month of *March*). Called *Maximilian's Hunts* because of the supposed portrait of Maximilian I killing the wild boar in the month of *December,* the set belonged to Mazarin and then to Louis XIV.

First Half of the 17th Century

French *objets d'art* from the first half of the 17th century are still not widely known. The period, however, was a productive one, due in part, no doubt, to Henri IV who encouraged artist-craftsmen by allotting apartments in the Louvre itself to them. Contributions from abroad, (Flemish weavers, and cabinetmakers from Flanders and Germany) favoured the introduction and development of various techniques.

The Louvre collections take account of all this activity. The various tapestry manufacturers which were grouped in Paris, for example, are represented by hangings designed by Simon Vouet **257**, painter to Louis XIII. As for furniture, the traditional solid wood carving by Parisian and provincial furniture makers came up against a new, imported technique which was to revolutionize the history of furniture: that of veneered wood or cabinetmaking. Ceramics are represented by tin-glazed earthenware from Nevers. While much fine French metalwork from the 17th century was melted down, we have an example in the golden coffer said to have belonged to Anne of Austria and in certain mounts in enameled gold, made for hard stone vases. A new technique was introduced in watchmaking, as examples show, from Blois: painting on enamel. Decoration in general, on tapestries, cabinets, tin-glazed earthenware and watches displays a similar contrast of modes; scenes of mythological, religious or literary derivation are framed by naturalistic images such as burgeoning flowers.

Barthélémy PRIEUR
1536-1611

254 Henri IV as Jupiter

Paris, around 1608

Statuette in bronze, black lacquer and light brown patina. H 0.67 m

Acq. 1986. OA 11054

Barthélémy Prieur was one of the greatest French sculptors at the end of the 16th century and beginning of the 17th. There are, sadly, very few works that can be safely attributed to him **312** - hence the importance of his signature on the

base of *Henri IV*.
The portrayal of the King, which is typical of the
classicizing Renaissance, is quite unique. Henri IV
is shown as a nude god. This bronze has a
pendant in the Louvre showing the queen, Marie
de Médicis, as Juno.

Ottavio MISERONI
d. 1624

**255 Cup Belonging to Emperor
Rudolph II**

Prague, 1608

Bloodstone, silver gilt.

H 0.190 m; W 0.575 m; D 0.330 m

Collection of the French Crown. Entered

the Louvre in 1796. MR 143

The Louvre came into the possession of hard stone
vases which Louis XIV had assembled at Versailles.
He began with the acquisition of almost the entire
collection of Mazarin after his death, which
included this cup. It had been made for Emperor
Rudolph II (1552-1612) and his monogram is
inscribed on it. In the 16th century, Milan was
famous for its hard stone vases. In 1558, Rudolph
II invited the engraver Ottavio Miseroni to Prague
to run a workshop specializing in this type of
artefact. This vase is typical of his style, both in
form and in the carved motifs. It is one of the
largest hard stone vases ever produced.

256 Cupboard

France, 1617

Walnut. H 2.54 m; W 1.82 m; ⌀ 0.80 m.

Révoil Collection. Acq. 1828. MRR 61

This cupboard is carved with decorations of an uncommon exuberance and virtuosity. Its form is typical of French cupboards from the Renaissance and the first half of the 17th century, divided into two parts with four doors. As so often, the reliefs on the doors derive from Flemish etchings. Top left we see *Bellonius leading his troops* and right, *The Victory of Wisdom over Ignorance*, after Barthélémy Spranger; below, the reliefs are copies of two prints from the series of *Planets*, after Martin de Vos; to the left is *Mars*, standing above *Virility* accompanied by *Prudence*. To the right is *Jupiter*, placed above *Memory* leaning on his alembic and conversing with a man who symbolizes *Old Age*.

257 Moses in the Bullrushes
3rd piece from a set of
The Old Testament
after Simon VOUET
*Paris, Louvre workshop
Around 1630*

Tapestry, wool and silk,

7 to 8 warps per cm. H 4.95 m; W 5.88 m

Transferred from the *Mobilier national,* 1907.

OA 6086

In 1627 the painter Simon Vouet was called home
from Italy by Louis XIII. The King immediately
commissioned him to design, among other things,
a set of eight tapestries on the *Old Testament.*
Moses in the Bullrushes was one of two pieces
woven in the Louvre workshops, installed by
Henri IV under the *Grande Galerie,* where the
weavers Pierre Dubout and Girard Laurent
worked. These workshops were the beginning of
the Gobelins factory, created after 1662. The
tapestry was intended for the Louvre Palace.

258 Cabinet

Paris, middle of the 17th century

Oak and poplar, ebony veneering, blackened fruit-tree wood.

H 1.85 m; L 1.58 m; D 0.56 m

Transferred from the *Mobilier national*, 1900. OA 6629

The Parisian cabinetmakers (*menuisiers en ébène*) of the first half of the 17th century devoted themselves to one item of furniture, the cabinet, for which they elaborated a formula of their own. The upper part contains a row of drawers under which two large doors open; the interior contains two rows of five drawers which surround two little doors that conceal a niche. The separate base consists of a row of drawers with aprons beneath; these stand, at the front, on columns and caryatids, at the back they rest on columns, pilasters and panelling. The carved and incised decoration of the ebony veneering is often framed by undulant mouldings. The Louvre cabinet, which is further enhanced by statuettes in ebony and, on the inside, by small ivory columns, is one of the most elaborate examples.

Louis XIV

As part of his policy of self-agrandisement, Louis XIV called upon every aspect of the applied arts for support. The Royal Manufactory of the *Meubles de la Couronne* was founded in the Gobelins in 1667. It was here, under the guidance of Charles Le Brun, that the items of decoration required by the royal residences were produced, including tapestries, furniture, metalwork (especially silver) and marble mosaics. The royal carpets were woven at the factory of the Savonnerie. In the Louvre, André-Charles Boulle dominated the cabinet-making of the period. Commissions from the sovereign were so abundant that, as under Napoléon, they determined the general style of the period: a combination of stylized foliate motifs and themes from the Graeco-Roman repertory.

The Louvre houses some particularly spectacular examples of the activity of this period. The Gobelins factory is represented by several tapestries woven after the 16th century and contemporary cartoons as well as two tables in mosaic marbling bearing the royal arms. The Sun King's silverware has disappeared, but a large silver mirror in the French style, made in Augsburg around 1700, gives us some idea of it. Huge carpets designed for the Louvre and the Tuileries display the art of the Savonnerie factory **262**. New types of furniture appeared and Boulle's technique is exhibited in works of marquetry in brass and shell, horn and pewter, showing the importance that bronze ornaments began to have on furniture. Gilding was used to decorate cabinets and other furniture, one of the oldest gilt pieces being the pedestal table in the Louvre which passed from Fouquet to Louis XIV. The Louvre collections testify to the latter's qualities as a great collector; the larger part of his collection of Renaissance bronzes and hard stone vases passed to the museum during the Revolution.

259 Vase

Italy, 16th century (stone)
Paris, middle of the 17th century
(mount)

Lapis, gilt silver, enameled gold.

H 0.415 m; W 0.375 m; D 0.185 m

Collection of the French Crown. Entered
the Louvre in 1796. MR 262

The vase is made up of four sections in lapis: a
particularly voluminous fluted body, a baluster in
two sections and a base. The mounts of hard stone
vases were often modified as fashions changed, as
is true of this vase which was not given its present
mount until the mid-17th century in Paris. It is
done in a style typical of the period, combining
naturalism - in the sprays of flowers in enameled
gold - and mythology, in the silver gilt statuettes
(Neptune and four Egyptian sphinxes), and in
enameled gold figures (head of a satyr and shark,
and two grotesque masks). This vase was part of
Louis XIV's collections before 1673, and later it
decorated Marie-Antoinette's bedroom at
Versailles.

260 Chancellerie Tapestry with Louis Boucherat's Monogramme

Beauvais, 1685

Tapestry, wool and silk.

8 to 9 warps per cm. H 3.61 m; W 4.40 m

Transferred from the *Mobilier National,* 1902.

OA 5703

The *Chancelleries* were tapestries on blue
backrounds printed with fleur-de-lys bearing the

Louis XIV   **Decorative Arts**

arms of the King and the attributes of the Seal, designed as a gift to the Chancellor. The Louvre tapestry, woven in Beauvais, was purchased by the king in 1686 for five thousand *livres,* and given to Louis Boucherat, Chancellor of France from 1685 until his death in 1699. His monogram and the date of his appointment can be seen in the middle of the lower border.

The Beauvais factory was created by Colbert in 1664, but remained a private enterprise under the king's protection. The Louvre *Chancellerie* was woven after a motif by François Bonnemer for the central section, and by Jean Le Moyne for the borders.

261 The Arrival in Africa
First piece from a set depicting
the **History of Scipio**
after Jules ROMAIN

Paris, Gobelins factory,
1688-1689

Tapestry, wool and silk,

8 to 9 warps per cm. H 4.50 m; W 5.48 m

Transferred from the *Mobilier National,* 1901. OA 5393

After 1683, the new Superintendant of Buildings, Louvois, kept the Gobelins tapestry workshops active by having them copy tapestries stored in the royal furniture depot; this also avoided commissioning new cartoons which would have been too costly. He selected masterpieces of 16th century tapestry from Brussels. The *History of Scipio,* after Jules Romain, made for the Maréchal de Saint-André in 1550, was copied in ten pieces. The *Arrival in Africa* shows the moment when Scipio first catches sight of the coast where he will disembark in pursuit of Hannibal, whom he will vanquish at the battle of Zama. The Gobelins copy perfectly reproduces the delicate weaving of the Renaissance original, and shows the standard of excellence achieved by the weavers of the royal factory.

262 Carpet for the Louvre
Grande Galerie,
Bearing the Arms of France

*Paris, Savonnerie factory,
around 1670-1680*

Wool 8.95 m × 5.10 m

Collection of the French Crown.

Transferred from the *Mobilier National,* 1901

OA 5432 bis A

Set up in a former soap factory in Chaillot during the reign of Louis XIII, the Savonnerie carpet factory flourished under Louis XIV. First there was an order for 13 carpets for the *Galerie d'Apollon* in the Louvre, and then one for 93 further carpets to cover the floor of the *Grande Galerie* nearly five hundred metres in length, as part of the King's redecoration scheme. These carpets were woven in the workshops of the Lourdet and Dupont families between 1670 and 1689, following cartoons by François Francart, Baudoin Yvart and Jean Le Moyne, after Le Brun. They celebrate the theme of glory and royal virtues. The carpets were sadly never laid in place. Some went to royal residences and others served as diplomatic gifts.

André-Charles BOULLE
1642-1732

263 Wardrobe

Paris, around 1700
Made of oak and pine, with ebony, tortoiseshell,
brass and tin veneering, gilt bronze.
H 2.65 m; W 1.35 m; D 0.54 m
Collection of the French Crown.
Transferred from the *Mobilier National.* OA 5441

Working in the Louvre from 1672 until his death, Boulle did not invent the marquetry technique to which he gave his name, but he did make the best use of it. The technique comprised cutting a motif out of two superimposed, contrasting materials, one light and the other dark; the motif obtained from one is then inserted into the space left in the other. When the decoration is light on dark, it is called *en partie;* an example is the centre of the wardrobe where brass arabesques are fitted in a tortoiseshell background. *En contrepartie* is the name for dark colours used on a light background, as round the edge of the doors here, where tortoiseshell scrolls wind over a brass background. Boulle applied this technique to luxury furniture in original shapes of his own creation, richly ornamented in gilt bronze. The ebony veneering recalls furniture of the preceding period.

264 Table

Paris, beginning of the 18th century

Gilded walnut, portor marble.

H 0.86 m; W 2.00 m; D 0.87 m

Transferred from the *Mobilier National*, 1901. OA 5049

Gilt wood furniture - tables and chairs - became more widespread during the second half of the 17th century. This table illustrates the ornamental style at the end of Louis XIV's reign. It bears the crest of the Malon de Bercy family (3 gold ducklings arranged 2 and 1 on azure) under the crown of a marquis. The table comes from the château de Bercy, in the east of Paris. In the early 18th century, when the table was made, the owner of the château, Charles-Henri de Malon de Bercy (1678-1742), superintendant of finances, son-in-law of the *Contrôleur Général des Finances*, Desmaretz, and great-nephew of Colbert, had major alterations made to the building under the direction of the architect Jacques de La Guêpière; the interior decoration was renovated in 1713-1714 by the team of wood carvers who worked for the Royal administration.

Upholding the curved line and asymmetry in decoration, and drawing inspiration from the art of gardening (rockeries, trellissing, flowers), the Louis XV style, many elements of which can be found in the last objects created for Louis XIV, enjoyed universal and lasting success.

Ornamentalists (Meissonier, Pineau, the Slodtz), artists (Boucher, Cressent), and *marchands merciers* (dealers in furniture and works of art like Hébert and Duvaux), encouraged by patrons such as Madame de Pompadour, turned out an endless succession of new models in every branch of the decorative arts.

Furniture increased in diversity. After a brief eclipse at the start of Louis XV's reign, marquetry came back into fashion. Cabinetmakers worked not only in wood and bronze but in lacquer and 0porcelain. Gilt bronze was used for a range of purposes and Parisian goldsmiths were employed by every court in Europe. Jewelers covered their snuffboxes and watches with polychrome materials from enamel and tortoiseshell to porcelain and hard stone. Although high-temperature kiln firing *(grand feu)* reached a peak of perfection at Rouen and Moustiers, it declined after the middle of the century when a technique of muffled kiln firing *(petit feu)* was perfected at Strasbourg and Marseille, which enabled a wider range of colours to be used. Meanwhile, the factory at Vincennes produced outstanding examples in the new technique of porcelain before moving to Sèvres in 1756.

However, certain connoisseurs (Caylus, Marigny) and architects (Blondel, Soufflot) grew tired of the Rococo style *(style Rocaille)*. This current of opposition became increasingly active after 1760, and led to the Greek or Transition style, which derived both from classical models and the art of the Louis XIV period. Forms became rectilinear and architectural, while decoration, drawing on archaeological finds, made use of pilasters, Greek borders, vases, marks, scrolls and laurel wreaths. Furniture made by Leleu **278** for the Prince de

Condé is a perfect illustration of this reaction which gave rise to the Louis XVI style.

265 The Regent

Diamond, 140.64 metric carats.
Diamond collection of the French Crown. MV 1017

Although it is now surpassed in weight by other famous diamonds, the exceptional limpidity and perfect cut of the *Regent* give it an uncontestable reputation as the most beautiful diamond in the world. Discovered in India in 1698, it was acquired by Thomas Pitt, Governor of Madras, who sent it to England where it was cut. In 1717 the Regent purchased it from Pitt for the French Crown. It first adorned the band of Louis XV's silver gilt crown (in the Louvre) at his coronation in 1722, going then to Louis XVI's crown in 1775. Later in 1801 it figured on the hilt of the First Consul's sword (Fontainebleau, Musée Napoléon Ist), and then on the Emperor's two-edged sword in 1812. In 1825 it was worn on the crown at the coronation of Charles X, and during the Second Empire it embellished the "Grecian diadem" of the Empress Eugenie.

Daniel GOVAERS or GOUERS
1717 - before 1754

266 Snuffbox

Paris, 1725-1726
Enameled gold, gold-inlaid tortoiseshell,
miniatures, diamonds.
H 3 cm; W 8.5 cm; D 6.5 cm
Anonymous gift, 1978. OA 10670

From the time of Louis XV, French sovereigns would make gifts, particularly to foreign diplomats, in the form of boxes decorated with

Louis XV **Decorative Arts**

their portraits and adorned with precious stones. Govaers was one of Louis XV's suppliers for this purpose. This snuffbox is the oldest in the Louvre's considerable collection. On 3 February 1726 it was given by the King to Baron Cornelis Hop, the Dutch ambassador (1685-1762). The top and bottom are in tortoiseshell inlaid with gold, the sides in enameled gold. Inside the cover are two miniatures attributed to Jean-Baptiste Massé, after Jean-Baptiste Van Loo, portraying the young Louis XV and the Queen Maria Leczinska, married in 1725.

Henri-Nicolas COUSINET
d. around 1768

267 Chocolate-Maker and Small Stove of a Set Made for Queen Maria Leczinska

Paris, 1729-1730

Silver gilt, ebony. Chocolate-maker: H 19.4 cm

Stand of Chocolate-maker: 12 cm

Stove: H 4.5 cm

Gift of the *Société des Amis du Louvre*

with the support of M Stavros, S Niarchos, 1955

AO 9598

The set which originally bore the arms of Queen Maria Leczinska (now effaced) was probably made when the Dauphin was born, after three older sisters, in 1729. Motifs linked to the Dauphin recur on these objects. They also testify to the arrival of the *rococo* style in official art with reeds, waves, shells, asymmetrical cartouches, clasps and flowers. The work on these motifs is eloquent testimony to the quality of Parisian silversmiths, and in particular to the skill of Cousinet, who later earned the title of Sculptor to the Prince de Condé.

268 Winter

Rouen, around 1740

Tin-glazed earthenware with "grand feu" decoration.

H 2.09 m; W 0.60 m

Acq. 1882. OA 2611

This bust is one of a set, illustrating the four seasons. A statue of Apollo, now in the Victoria and Albert Museum in London, originally completed the ensemble.

Although there is no signature, this sculptural bust can be attributed to Nicolas Fouquay's factory at Rouen. The decoration is very similar to examples signed by the painter Pierre Chapelle.

Charles CRESSENT
1685-1768

269 Wall-Clock:
Love Conquering Time

Paris, around 1740

Gilt bronze, brass and tortoiseshell marquetry.

H 1.40 m; W 0.50 m

Collection of the French Crown. Transferred from the *Cour de cassation,* 1953 OA 9586

Cressent, who was a cabinetmaker by trade though he trained as a sculptor, attached great importance to the bronzes on his furniture. He created the models and supervised their execution. Their quality is especially impressive on this wall-clock, where the cabinet work is limited to side panels done in Boulle marquetry. A cupid dominates the composition, the asymmetry of which is typical of the *rococo* style. Cressent was obliged to sell up three times, and included a wall-clock of this type in his 1749 sale. This clock comes from the royal collections. The dial and mechanism is by Nicolas Gourdain, who was received as a master clockmaker in Paris in 1724 and died in 1753.

270 Wall-Clock

Paul Hannong factory
Strasbourg, around 1750
Tin-glazed earthenware with "petit feu" decoration.
H 1.12 m; W 0.45 m
Gift of Count Isaac de Camondo, 1911. OA 6568

Around the middle of the 18th century, growing competition from porcelain manufacturers forced potters to develop new techniques. The use of decoration *au petit feu,* in which successive layers of various metal oxides were fired at a low temperature onto fired enamel greatly extended the range of available colours. This clock comes from Paul Hannong's factory at Strasbourg. It is an example of the *petit feu* process at its best, combined with a form of great complexity, possibly inspired from a model by the Parisian cabinetmaker Charles Cressent **269**.

Jacques DUBOIS
c. 1693-1763

271 Desk from the Château du Raincy

Paris, mid-18th century
Oak, pine and fruit-tree wood, black lacquer,
gilt bronze, leather.
H 0.81 m; W 1.87 m; D 1.02 m
Château du Raincy, seized during French Revolution
Transferred from the Ministry of Justice, 1907
OA 6083

Before the Revolution this desk was housed in the *Château du Raincy* (Seine-Saint-Denis), which belonged to the Duc d'Orléans. It bears the stamp of Jacques Dubois, a cabinet-maker in the faubourg Saint-Antoine. Alongside its standard production, this workshop turned out some of the most luxurious examples of 18th century furniture. This desk reflects the taste for lacquered furniture at its best. The great Parisian *marchands merciers*

(cf. Introduction) were responsible for this, having, during the 1730's, conceived the idea of producing furniture adorned with lacquered panels taken from objects imported from the Far East (chests, cabinets, screens). The skirting around this desk is decorated with lacquer paintings of landscapes; the framing and feet are in black lacquer.

272 Naiad

Vincennes, Royal Porcelain Factory, 1756

Soft-paste porcelain, gilt bronze. H 0.26 m

Gift of Mme Adolphe Thiers, 1880. TH 693

The *Naiad*, more familiarly known by its 19th century name *La Source*, was undoubtedly the most important figure produced at the royal porcelain factory at Vincennes. This model is dated 1756, the same year the factory moved to Sèvres. Its modeller is unknown, but the fine painted decoration is by C-N Dodin, one of the most prolific artists in the factory. The *marchand mercier* Lazare Duvaux purchased it in 1757 and sold it to his colleague Hébert. The latter most probably added the extraordinary bronze mounting.

François-Thomas GERMAIN
1726-1791

273 Fire-dog

Paris, 1757

Gilt bronze. H 0.59 m; W 0.60 m; D 0.45 m

Acq. 1935. OA 8278

This fire-dog is signed in full by the goldsmith
François-Thomas Germain who took over his
father Thomas Germain's title as sculptor-
goldsmith to the King, on his death in 1748, along
with his Louvre lodgings. This freed him from
guild regulations, and allowed him to extend the
scope of his craft. He produced several major gilt
bronze ensembles, including the fireplace in the
Bernstorff Palace in Copenhagen (1756), the wall-
lights in the Getty Museum (1756) and this fire-
dog. The scrollwork is *rococo,* but the pan, tripod
and its hangings are early signs of what came to
be called at that period the «Greek» style, the first
phase of Neoclassicism.

François-Thomas GERMAIN
1726-1791

**274 Centrepiece Belonging to Joseph I
of Portugal**

Paris, 1758

Silver.

H 0.475 m; W 0.573 m; D 0.536 m

Acq. 1983. OA 10923

Germain made silverware for several foreign
monarchs, as well as for Louis XV, including

Joseph I of Portugal (1714-1777) for whom he made several dinner services and this centrepiece, between 1756 and 1765. Centrepieces, which first appeared at the end of Louis XIV's reign, were originally functional objects holding table accessories such as salt cellars, oil cruets, and lights. This centrepiece made for Joseph I is on the contrary purely decorative. A brilliantly executed genre scene rests on a fluted base - a reminder that Germain was a precursor of Neoclassicism. In the 19th century, some of the gold and silverware belonging to the Court of Portugal went to Emperor Pietro I of Brazil, who stamped his monogram on this article.

Edme-Pierre BALZAC
1705 - after 1781

275 Wine Cooler from a Service Belonging to the Duc de Penthièvre

Paris, 1759-1760

Silver. H 0.245 m; ∅ 0.235 m; W 0.285 m

From a pair. Acq. 1987. OA 11117

This wine cooler was part of a famous table service, eight items of which are in the Louvre. In the 18th century it belonged to Louis-Jean-Marie de Bourbon, Duc de Penthièvre (1725-1793), grandson of Louis XIV and Mme de Montespan. In the 19th century it passed to his grandson, the Duc d'Orléans and future king Louis-Philippe (1773-1850), who added his coat-of-arms to each piece. The service consists of two sets made at different times. The earlier set was made by Thomas Germain around 1730. The second set, ordered some thirty years later and made in the *rococo* style to match, is the work of two other great silversmith, Balzac and Antoine-Sébastien Durand.

276 Pot-pourri Vase and Cover Belonging to Mme de Pompadour

Sèvres, Royal Porcelain Factory, 1760

Soft-paste porcelain. H 0.37 m; W 0.35 m.

Acq. 1984. OA 10965

The form of this pot-pourri recalls the gold vases that decorated royal tables. The design is by J-C Duplessis, a goldsmith responsible for models at the Sèvres factory. The delicate pink ground surrounds a palm-fringed escutcheon in which C-N Dodin painted a *chinoiserie* scene. Purchased by Mme de Pompadour in 1760, this pot-pourri was found on her bedroom mantelpiece in her Parisian *hôtel* - the present Elysée Palace - at her death in 1764.

277 Eros and Psyche

after François BOUCHER

Paris, Gobelins Factory c. 1770

Tapestry, wool and silk,

10 to 11 warps per cm. H 4.25 m; W 3.80 m

Palais Bourbon, 4th piece of an alcove set from the

bedroom of the Duchesse de Bourbon. Collection

of the French Crown, 1825

Transferred from the *Mobilier national*, 1901. OA 5118

This tapestry belongs to a set of four, celebrating the *Loves of the Gods*, woven in Jacques Neilson's workshop in the Gobelins. François Boucher was acting artistic director of the Gobelins Factory, supervising work there from 1755 until his death in 1770. It was he who made the sketches for the central scenes which simulate paintings hanging on a wall. The crimson surround follows designs by Maurice Jacques. These two artists collaborated on numerous tapestries on the theme of the *Loves of the Gods* - considered the most successful and spectacular of the Factory productions.

Jean-François LELEU
1729-1807

278 Commode Belonging to the
Prince de Condé

Paris, 1772

Oak, purple-wood panelling, marquetry in different woods, gilt bronze, red-veined marble.
H 0.88 m; W 1.17 m; D 0.56 m.
Acq. 1953. OA 9589

Louis-Joseph de Bourbon, Prince de Condé (1736-1818), purchased the Palais Bourbon in 1764 and subsequently entrusted its decoration to innovative architects. From 1772 to 1776 several items of cabinetwork were ordered from Leleu (now in the Wallace Collection and the Petit Trianon), this commode among them, which was delivered in 1772 and installed in the Prince's bedroom.
With its architectural appearance and Graeco-Roman bronze decoration, it is typical of the "Greek" style which came into vogue in the 1760's. The remarkable marquetry is a reminder that Leleu worked under the great master of marquetry Jean-François Deben who was himself apprenticed to the youngest son of André-Charles Boulle at the Louvre.

Louis XVI

Under Louis XVI, there was an ever-increasing interest in interior decoration, furniture and the decorative arts. The quality of workmanship improved and new ideas were plentiful. Architects and ornamentalists (Gondoin, Belanger, Dugourc) supplied patrons with highly imaginative designs which were realised by *marchands merciers* like Poirier, Daguerre or the Darnault brothers, by cabinetmakers like Riesener and Carlin, and metal-founders like Gouthière and Thomire. Forms were more graceful than during the Greek-style period, and decoration combined classical motifs, scrollwork and « arabesques » with more figurative themes, flowers and trophies. Some objects affecting a Turkish or Chinese style were naively exotic in appearance. Fabrics and trimmings became so important that they provided inspiration for subjects in other forms. Materials increased in variety. While Boulle marquetry came back into fashion, it was not unusual to find furniture veneered in mother of pearl, marble mosaic or made almost entirely out of metal like the Weisweiler table [281]. Mahogany became popular. New techniques took over in ceramics: hard-paste porcelain and Creamware.

The Louvre ensembles, such as the vases belonging to the Duc d'Aumont, Bellevue's lacquered furniture, the furniture by Riesener for Marie-Antoinette in the Tuileries, the Jacob and Sené chairs designed for the Château de Saint-Cloud are typical of developments in progress on the eve of the Revolution.

Robert-Joseph AUGUSTE
1723-1805

279 Service Belonging to George III
of England

Paris, 1776-1785
Silver.
Acq. 1976. OA 10602-10624

R-J Auguste - succeeded by his son Henri who
became a supplier to Napoleon - made numerous
items, which have since been lost, for the French
court under Louis XVI. The Louvre ensemble gives
us some idea of his abilities. This selection from
the service stamped with the monogram of
George III of England (1738-1820) offers a sample
of the different types of table objects to be found
in the 18th century: tureens, cloches, dishes, wine
glass coolers, cruet stands, mustard pots and
candelabra. The grace of the three-dimensional
figures (pairs of children on the tureens, feminine
traits and cupids on the candelabra) soften the
severity of the classical motifs.

Georges JACOB
1739-1814

280 Armchair from the Turkish Room
of the Comte d'Artois at the Temple

Paris, 1777
Gilt walnut. H 0.94 m; W 0.70 m; D 0.76 m
Gift of Baronness Gourgaud, 1965. OA 9987

Under Louis XVI, the fashion for "Turkish Rooms"
which conjured up an imaginary Orient owed
much to the Comte d'Artois, brother of Louis XVI
and future Charles X (1757-1836). In his priory-
house of *Le Temple* in Paris, he had a "Turkish
Room" fitted out for him by the architect Etienne-
Louis Boullée in 1776-1777. The imaginatively
designed chairs, one of the first sets made by Jacob

for the royal family, include two "ottomans", two armchairs - one shown here - and four chairs which were originally painted white and covered with a *lampas* in yellow, white and grey. The daring line of this furniture prefigures that of chairs from the Empire period.

Adam WEISWEILER
1744-1784

281 Writing Table Belonging to Queen Marie-Antoinette

Paris, 1784

Oak, ebony veneering, lacquer, mother of pearl, steel, gilt bronze. H 0.82 m; W 0.47 m; D 0.44 m

Collection of the French Crown. Transferred from the *Mobilier National,* 1901. OA 5509

270

The famous *marchand mercier* on the *rue Saint-Honoré*, Dominique Daguerre, delivered this writing table to the royal stores in 1784. It bears the mark of Weisweiler the cabinetmaker, promoted to master craftsman in 1778. On the outside, cabinetwork plays only a minor part in a table which is very modern for its use of steel for its skirting and bronze feet. The top surface is made up of three lacquered panels ; the central panel can be raised like a sloping desk top. But Weisweiler's artistry is most obvious in the style of the cross-piece and in the refined decoration on the drawers, veneered on the inside with a diamond-shape mosaic. In 1789, the table was in Marie-Antoinette's inner room in the Château de Saint-Cloud.

Charles OUIZILLE
1744-1830

282 **Incense Burner Belonging to Queen Marie-Antoinette**

Paris, 1784-1785

Gold, agate, bloodstone, miniatures

H 0.275 m; W 0.120; D 0.092 m

Acq. 1982. OA 10907

This agate incense-burner stands on a square base made of bloodstone, decorated with four miniatures, like imitation cameos, by the painter Jacques-Joseph De Gault. The gold mount is from Ouizille the jeweller, purveyor to Queen Marie-Antoinette.

This exceptionally refined piece is evidence of the Queen's love of precious stones; it belonged to her personal collection of *objets d'arts* at Versailles. When she left the Château in October 1789, she entrusted them to the *marchand mercier* Dominique Daguerre who kept them until her death.

Georges JACOB
1739-1814

283 **Armchair from the Games Room
in the Château de Saint-Cloud**

Paris, 1787-1788

Gilt walnut. H 0.01 m; W 0.75 m; D 0.64 m

From a pair. Acq. 1948. OA 9449

In 1785 the Duc d'Orléans sold the Château de
Saint-Cloud to Louis XVI; sumptuous furniture
was produced to decorate it during the last years
of the Ancien Régime. Jacob supplied the
furniture for the Games Room, though it is now
dispersed. It comprised two sofas, two *bergères*,
twenty-two armchairs, sixteen of which were
meublants, à la Reine (i. e. with straight backs, like
the one shown) and six *courants, en cabriolet* (with
curved backs). There were in addition twenty-four
chairs, six *voyeuses,* four stools, a fire-screen and a
folding screen. The set was covered with a silk by
Pernon, the Lyon manufacturer. It was decorated
with a rose tree motif, the model for which has
survived; new covers were thus made for the
Louvre ensemble so they retain their original
appearance.

Empire

Under the Empire (1804-1815), the luxury industries benefited from the stability and prosperity of the regime, and in particular from the support which Napoleon lavished on them, with orders, purchases, and the organization of exhibitions displaying their products.
A remarkably coherent style spread throughout the Empire.
The Louvre collections combine furniture from various imperial residences. They are typical of the dominant style which was imposing and rather severe; made in gilt wood or mahogany, with a rigid line, they are embellished with very high quality bronzes. Many were made by Georges Jacob's son, Jacob-Desmalter, an abundant supplier of Imperial furniture. Collaborating with him at times was the bronze-worker Pierre-Philippe Thomire, who was also one of the principal purveyors to Napoleon I.
Reviving the sumptuous tradition and court ceremony of the Ancien Régime, the Emperor commissioned splendid services in porcelain and precious metals. The Louvre exhibits a representative cross-section of pieces by Biennais (1764-1843), private goldsmith to the Emperor. Aiming both for prestige and promotion of the national industry, the Sèvres *Imperial Porcelain Factory* produced items designed for use at Court or as official presents.

François-Honoré-Georges
JACOB-DESMALTER
1770-1841

284 **Jewel Cabinet Belonging to the
Empress Josephine**

Paris, 1809

Oak, yew and purple-wood veneering,
mother-of-pearl, gilt bronze.

H 2.75 m; W 2 m; D 0.60 m.

Deposit from the *Musée National du Château
de Fontainebleau*, 1964. OA 10246.

In 1809, Jacob-Desmalter, principal supplier of
furniture to the Emperor, delivered his most
valuable order, the jewel cabinet designed for the
Empress Joséphine's great bedroom in the
Tuileries (and soon to be used by Marie-Louise).
This impressive piece of furniture which was
designed by the architect Charles Percier is
embellished with several bronze ornaments: the
central panel depicts the "Birth of the Queen of
the Earth to whom Cupids and Goddesses hasten
with their Offerings" by P-P Thomire, after a
sculpture by Chaudet. Jacob-Desmalter completed
the "great jewellery box" in 1812, with two smaller
items of furniture in the same style but using
indigenous woods.

Martin-Guillaume BIENNAIS
1764-1843

285 **Part of a Tea Service
made for Napoleon I**

Paris, 1809-1810

Silver gilt.

Hot water urn: H 0.80 m; W 0.45 m.

Teapot: H 0.18 m; W 0.32 m

Tea-caddy: H 0.145 m; W 0.155 m

Milk jug: H 0.27 m; ⌀ 0.11 m

Gift of the *Société des Amis du Louvre*, 1952.

OA 9537 (2, 4, 5)

Shortly after his marriage to Marie-Louise of Austria in 1810, Napoleon I ordered a 28 piece tea and coffee-set from his goldsmith Biennais. Half the set is now on show in the Louvre. The forms and decoration (the latter supplied by Percier the architect) are classical in inspiration, with an "Etruscan" form for the teapot, palm fringes and water leaves, winged figures and a reproduction of the Augustan frieze, the "Aldobrandine Nuptials", on the tea-caddy. The style is typical of the prolific production of Biennais, which is remarkably consistent with the ovoid form of the milk-jug, and wide rims with motifs engraved on a dulled ground.

286 Fuseau Vase Belonging to Madame Mère

Royal Porcelain Factory
Sèvres, 1811

Hard-paste procelain and gilt bronze.

H 1.07 m; W 0.36 m; ⌀ 0.33 m

Gift of Mme Maria Teresa Castro de Polo, 1986.

OA 11056

The baptism of the King of Rome on 10 June 1811 gave the Emperor the opportunity of offering a large number of gifts in Sèvres porcelain. The spectacular vase in the Louvre was destined for Madame Mère, godmother of the new-born. Standing out from the precious tortoiseshell ground is the portrait of the Emperor crossing Mont-Saint-Bernard painted by J Georget, after the famous painting by David.

Restoration

The accession of Louis XVIII (1815-1824) did not bring about any real change in the development of the decorative arts. The king, who was economically minded, settled into Napoleon's quarters, content merely to do away with the symbols of Empire. The Court was quite austere, and only the Duchesse de Berry provided any real patronage. Charles X (1824-1830) proved more demanding; he commissioned a ceremonial bed in gilt and carved wood from Brion.

The period is represented in the main by porcelain and bronzes in the Louvre collections. Biscuit-ware (unglazed porcelain), in the 18th century tradition, was used for numerous statues and busts of members of the royal family. Painted motifs, in the style of miniatures, had great success on Sèvres and Paris porcelain.

Paul-Nicolas MENIÈRE *1745-1826*
Evrard BAPST *1771-1842*

287 Pair of Bracelets Belonging to the Duchesse d'Angoulême

Paris, 1816

Gold, rubies, diamonds. L 18 cm; 17.6 cm

Gift of Claude Menier, 1974. OA 10576

This pair of bracelets is part of a jewelry set which included a diadem, a necklace, a comb, earrings, a belt and three clasps. The rubies and diamonds came from an adornment made in 1811 by the firm of Nitot for the Empress Marie-Louise. On his accession, Louis XVIII had the imperial jewels dismantled and brought up to date. In 1816, Menière reset Marie-Louis's rubies and diamonds — following designs by his son-in-law Evrard Bapst - for the duchesse d'Angoulême. The Duchesse de Berry and the Empress Eugénie also wore this ensemble.

288 Casket for the King's Snuff-box

Royal Porcelain Factory
Sèvres, 1819
Hard-paste porcelain, silver gilt.
H 0.20 m; W 0.35 m; D 0.25 m
From the *Musée des Souverains*. MS 214

This casket was designed to contain Louis XVIII's snuff-box and a collection of small oval plaques in porcelain that could be fitted onto the snuff-box. The painter Béranger is responsible for the spectacular imitation cameo painting which decorates the top. According to the catalogue entry for the 1820 exhibition of products from the royal factories where this casket was displayed, the painting depicts "Cybele (earth), Vulcan (fire) and Pluto (metals) offering to Painting the means and materials to practise the art of porcelain and to render the results ineradicable". This iconography reflects the theories of A Brongniart, the director of the factory, who saw the transfer of easel paintings onto porcelain as a means of preserving their original colours.

Louis-Philippe

The reign of Louis-Philippe (1830-1848) was a period of diversification and renewal in the decorative arts. Artists returned to previous styles for new sources of inspiration. This led to a wide range of new directions: neo-Gothic, neo-Renaissance, neo-Louis XV. Eclecticism affected techniques in every domain. Ornamentalists such as Chenavard or Liénard, sculptors such as Feuchère, goldsmiths like Froment-Meurice played a leading role here. Sculptors were of particular importance creating the taste for three-dimensional figurines and modelling. The return to the past led to the revival of some neglected techniques such as niello, enamel and chased metal.

289 Lattice-Work Chinese Breakfast Set Belonging to Queen Marie-Amélie

Royal Porcelain Factory,
Sèvres, 1840

Hard-paste porcelain. H 0.295 m; ⌀ 0.50 m

Gift of M. and Mme Jean-Marie Rossi, 1987

OA 11098-11111

The taste for exoticism which was widespread under Louis-Philippe is clear from this breakfast set, which is a free interpretation of Chinese models, adapted for Western purposes. One of the most remarkable aspects of this borrowing from China is the lattice-work in which elements are worked on both sides, with the outer side pierced to let in the light.

The first complete lattice-work Chinese breakfast set incorporating a tray, was shown in the exhibition of products from the royal factories in 1835. Queen Marie-Amélie seems to have been very taken with this type of breakfast set since she ordered several. The set in the Louvre was presented to her on March 1, 1840.

François-Désiré
FROMENT-MEURICE
1802-1855

290 **Feuchères Vase**

Paris, 1843

Silver gilt, malachite. H 0.60 m

Gift of Baronness de Feuchères, 1891. OA 3253

In 1843 the City of Paris commissioned two large vases in silver gilt from its master silversmith Froment-Meurice. The vase shown was presented to general Baron de Feuchères as a token of thanks for his generous gift to the civic hospices of Paris. The vase, an official commission, is Neo-classical in spirit, unlike the *Coupe des Vendanges*, exhibited alongside it at the 1844 exhibition. The contrast reveals the eclecticism of Froment-Meurice. Two figurines in finely engraved cast silver - the spirit of War and Charity - serve as handles. A malachite medallion by the sculptor James Pradier, showing the Baron in profile, decorates the centre of the vase.

Louis-Philippe **Decorative Arts**

Romanesque France

Gothic France

Renaissance France

17th century France

18th century France

France, first half of the 19th century

Italy

Germanic countries

The Netherlands

Sculpture

Introduction

When the *Museum* opened, the sole examples of "modern" sculpture were the *Slaves* ₃₄₇ by Michelangelo in the *Galerie d'Apollon*. Not until 1824 did the *Galerie d'Angoulême*, on the ground floor of the Cour Carrée, exhibit sculptures from the Renaissance to the contemporary period. The collections originated from the royal palaces, the French Academy and the *Musée des Monuments Français* assembled under the Revolution by Alexandre Lenoir. From the palaces, the Louvre received what remained of park statuary, such as those from Marly, and collections of bronzes; from the Academy the wonderful series of admission pieces which give us a complete picture of the evolution of sculpture from Louis XIV to the Revolution. Finally, from the *Monuments Français*, came statues and, in particular, monumental tomb sculpture which had been saved from churches and squares during the revolutionary upheavals. Gradually, the rooms took shape. Commissions from artists in the early 19th century provided the basis for the Neoclassical and Romantic collections. But the first medieval statue was not acquired until 1850 and the first Italian work (door of the Stanga Palace) arrived in 1876. At this period (1871) the Department of Sculpture became entirely independent of the Department of Decorative Arts. While the *Musée du Luxembourg* funnelled off contemporary work, generous donations from Campana, Davillier, Piot, Arconati-Visconti, Schlichting and Zoubaloff enriched the collections of the Department of Sculpture. In addition the Department had an active acquisitions policy, and it also received works on deposit from major institutions such as the *Château de Versailles, Monuments Historiques* and the *École des Beaux-Arts*.

The move to the *Pavillon des États* in 1932 enabled works from the Middle Ages to the 17th century to be exhibited. But not until 1969 and 1971 could the majority of works (over a thousand) be displayed when the *Pavillon de Flore* was opened.

Romanesque France

The presentation of French sculpture begins with various Romanesque art workshops. A major revival in sculpture followed a general cultural rebirth which coincided with the emergence of royal power, feudal reorganisation, and religious fervour following the Gregorian reform, along with the growth of commercial networks and agriculture and the development of a communal village life. The religious revival, stimulated by new forms of monasticism, was under the protection of great powers which can be seen in the reconstruction and embellishment of the great abbeys and centres of pilgrimage; Conques, Autun, Vézelay, Toulouse, Saint-Gilles. The influence of workshops spread from these centres across priories and parishes.

Romanesque sculpture, essentially religious in nature, is on the whole architectural in function. Vast historiated tympanums welcomed the pilgrim; naves and cloisters were decorated with capitals and reliefs. Isolated statues are, in contrast, rare, having been made of precious materials or polychrome woods that have rarely survived the passage of time. Unable to match the great centres of Romanesque art, the Department of Sculptures provides us with a broad overview. There are capitals from the Roussillon and the Ile-de-France (*Daniel among the Lions* 201), from Poitou and Burgundy; a relief from the Rhône area, a tombstone and door to the floral tympanum of the priory at Estagel. Three sculptures in polychrome wood, the *Virgin in Majesty* 293, the *Christ Courajod* 292 and the *Head of Christ* from Lavaudieu are rare examples of religious devotion.

291 Daniel Among the Lions

Paris, 6th and end of the 11th century

Marble capital.

H 0.50 m; W 0.53 m; D 0.48 m

Church St. Geneviève, Paris. Entered the Louvre in 1881. RF 457

This capital testifies to a long period of Parisian history. On the reverse are acanthus leaves from a Corinthian capital, carved for the Basilica des Saints-Apôtres, founded by Clovis and Clotilde after the victory at Vouillé (507). The Normans destroyed this church in 857, and this capital was re-used in the new church dedicated to St. Geneviève at the time of its reconstruction which coincided with the spread of Romanesque art. The architectonic structure of the capital is clearly apparent, emphasized by the volutes at each corner. The composition, showing the prophet Daniel seated meditatively between two lions, fits into this framing with his head beneath the central rosette, and the lions' heads under the volutes. The linearity of the folds and curled manes co-exists with the skilfully rendered volumes of the main figure who stands out boldly from the concave ground.

292 Descent from the Cross

Burgundy, second quarter of the 12th century

Statue in wood with traces of gilt and polychrome.

H 1.55 m; W 1.68 m; D 0.30 m

Gift of Louis Courajod, 1895. RF 1082

Romanesque polychrome woodcarving is rare in France. But by comparing it with examples in Catalonia and Italy, one may assume that this dead Christ, with his right hand unnailed from the cross, figured in a Descent from the Cross surrounded by a sizeable group of figures. The style is typical of Burgundian Romanesque art. While the face recalls the Christ in Judgement on the Vézelay tympanum, the markedly linear folds are close to sculptures in Saint-Lazare d'Autun. The belt is remarkably complex, knotted at the top of the *perizonium* (loin-cloth), as is the fine pleating which falls in a pattern of concentric semi-circles over the legs to increase the sense of volume outlining the knees.

293 Virgin and Child

Auvergne, second half of the 12th century

Reliquary-statue, woodcarving with traces of polychrome. H 0.84 m; W 0.27 m

Acq. 1894. RF 987

As Romanesque art developed, a popular theme proved to be the Virgin in majesty, seated on a throne and holding the Child on her knees. Linked to the throne of the new Solomon, this throne signifies divine wisdom (*Sedes Sapientae*). Some examples were made of precious materials, such as one, since destroyed, from Clermont cathedral. Most of the free-standing Virgins in majesty that have been preserved, are carved and painted in lifelike colours. Similar hieratic images with frontal poses can be seen on the earliest Gothic portals. The graphic linearity of Romanesque art, expressed in the pleating of drapery in concentric waves, is allied to a bold and simplified treatment of volumes.

294 Head of St. Peter

Burgundy, third quarter of the 12th century

Stone. H 0.21 m; W 0.143 m; D 0.185 m

St. Lazare, Autun. Acq. 1923. RF 1783

The pilgrim's sanctuary dedicated to St. Lazarus in Autun contained a highly decorated architectural aedicula, fragments of which survive in the *Musée d'Autun*. Inside it, a series of

under-lifesize stone statues were arranged, as if on stage, to illustrate the raising of Lazarus, surrounded by Sts. Peter, Andrew, Martha and Madeleine. An inscription stated that the stone for the mausoleum had been cut by the monk Martin under the episcopacy of Etienne, probably Etienne II (1170-1189). But several sculptors seemed to have worked on this ambitious mausoleum. The head of St. Peter and the famous free-standing statue of St. Andrew *(Musée d'Autun)* are rare examples of a monumental art which remains linear in spirit, as reflected in the parallel curls of Peter's fringe, with all the locks falling from the same point. This late Romanesque style can be associated with works from Provence and the Rhone area.

295 Altarpiece with Virgin and Child

Ile-de-France, third quarter of the 12th century

High relief, polychrome stone.

H 0.85 m; W 1.24 m; D 0.190 m

From Church of Carrières-Saint-Denis.

Acq. 1910. RF 1612

The theme of the Virgin in majesty reappears at the centre of one of the oldest altarpieces preserved in France. The structure of this highly architectonic work is organized around two scenes from the Gospel, the Annunciation and the Baptism of Christ. The tall, thin silhouettes are separated from the central figure by little columns decorated with chevrons. While the base and sides are covered in a scrollwork pattern peopled with figures, the upper part of the altarpiece is decorated with an architectural system of multiple

arching bays, like those found on Romanesque
capitals and on the royal portal at Chartres. The
vaulted design adapts to the figures it glorifies.
But some of the scenic details such as the waters
of Jordan and the angel Gabriel's wings overlap
the borders. The overall style in this church,
which was a dependent of the *Abbaye de Saint-
Denis,* is typical of the Ile-de-France at that
delicate point, the transition from Romanesque to
Gothic. The altarpiece is still recognizably
Romanesque in its elongated forms and linear
treatment of drapery.

Gothic France

While the South of France remained faithful to
Romanesque art for some time, a new form
appeared in the Ile-de-France to which the
classicizing purists of the 18th century gave the
derisive name of Gothic, stemming from the
"barbarian" Goths. The flowering of the Gothic
style accompanied urban, economic and political
(communal) developments, alongside a growing
role for the Universities. The new master builders
applied the stylistic innovation of intersecting ribs
and pointed arches first to Saint-Denis, and then
to the cathedrals in the Ile-de-France. Where
sculpture is concerned, however, the frontier is less
clear-cut between Romanesque forms and the
more naturalistic freedom of the Gothic style. The
Altarpiece of Carrières-Saint-Denis **295** is visibly
situated at the confluence of the two styles.
The 13th century was the golden age of
equilibrium. It was the highpoint of the building
of Chartres, Reims, Amiens, Bourges - indissoluble
from the art of architecture. The Louvre can only
offer a glimpse of this classic monumental style
removed from its context; *King Childebert* **297** and
St. Geneviève for example, which come from
Parisian churches.
The collections are, however, rich in sculpture
from the 14th century, that age of contrasts, of
plague (in 1348), of war (the Hundred Years), but
also of increasing royal power, princely patronage
and the beginnings of humanism. Two
contradictory styles developed in sculpture: a
naturalist tendency, with portraiture as its
springboard, which led to the demonstrative
strength of Burgundian art revitalized by Claus
Sluter, and on the other hand an art of
sophisticated research into drawing and stylization.
Early in the 15th century, this stylistic evolution
was uninterrupted in centres under the control of
the Dukes of Berry and of Burgundy. There is a
marked change of pace in the middle of the
century when, with peace restored after the long
Hundred Years War, the process of rebuilding the
kingdom began again. This moment of *relaxation*

is reflected in new centres like the Languedoc, Burgundy and above all in the Valley of the Loire. The *Virgin and Child* ₃₀₄, statues by Chantelle, *St. John on Calvary* ₃₀₂ and works by Michel Colombe exemplify this art of the Loire valley, sharp and tender by turns, in which late Gothic becomes infused with a new humanism.

296 The Angel Dictating to St. Matthew the Evangelist

Chartres, second quarter of the 13th century

High relief, stone. H 0.66 m; W 0.50 m

Chartres Cathedral.

Acq. 1905. RF 1388

This fragment was part of the rood-screen (*jubé*) from Chartres cathedral. Comprising several columns of narrative reliefs, some large reliefs remain, illustrating the Childhood of Christ (in the treasury of Chartres cathedral), and small reliefs from the Last Judgement to which the figure of Matthew the Evangelist, as narrator, was attached. The serene figure here reflects something of the monumental scope developing at the transept portals of the cathedral. St. Matthew is enveloped in a cloak with broken folds which give it volume, in contrast to the close-knit pleats which were the norm up until then. With its bold, flattened planes, the style of this piece is linked to the workshop of the Western façade of Notre-Dame in Paris.

297 King Childebert

Ile-de-France, around 1239-1244

Statue, stone with polychrome traces.

H 1.91 m; W 0.53 m; D 0.55 m

Abbey Church of St. Germain-des-Prés, Paris.

Entered the Louvre in 1851. ML 93

This retrospective statue of the Merovingian King Childebert was fixed between 1239 and 1244 to the central pillar of the portal leading to the refectory of the abbey at St. Germain-des-Prés. This was done to honour the founder of the original abbey, at that time dedicated to the Holy Cross and to St. Vincent. With its expressive smile, the statue is characteristic of a monumental classical style, with soft but straightened drapery. Naturalistic detail, such as the metalwork belt encompassing the waist, is of a piece with the animated frontality of the arms and slight turn of the hips that give the torso a gentle motion away from the position of the feet.

298 Virgin and Child

Ile-de-France, second quarter of the 14th century

Statue, marble. H 1.07 m; W 0.28 m; D 0.23 m

Gift of Arconati-Visconti, 1914. RF 1632

In the 14th century the Marian cult prompted wealthy donors and humble labourers to offer images of the Virgin-Mother to the churches. These numerous statues in stone, polychrome wood or in marble (in the case of the wealthy) have many traits in common. Iconographic constraints imposed the floral-patterned crown over a veil framing the Virgin's face and a large draped mantle which sometimes rises apron-like over the dress. The striving for refinement dictated a somewhat unnatural posture, which is often turned at the hips, arched, and undulating. At the same time the interest in line is seen in complex folds falling in cones and arabesque

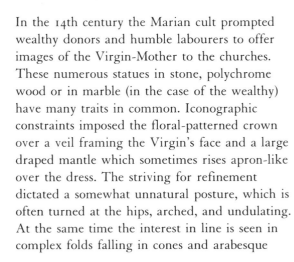

shapes. The statue shown here belongs to a group of Virgins preserved in the Ile-de-France; the sculptor has gone beyond mere viruosity to stress the intimate nature of maternal love. The eyes of Virgin and Child - who holds and apple an a bird - meet in an expression of tender trust.

Attributed to Evrard d'ORLÉANS
known from 1292-1357

[299] Angel with Cruet

Ile -de-France, around 1340

Wall Statuette, marble.

H 0.527 m; W 0.14 m; D 0.083 m

Abbey Church of Maubuisson.

Gift of the *Société des Amis du Louvre*, 1904.

RF 1438

Alongside the development of the single, devotional statue, the sculpted altarpiece proved remarkably popular. It often consisted of narrative reliefs in white marble applied to a black marble ground. The altar-piece in the *Chapelle Saint-Paul et Sainte-Catherine*, founded in 1340 by Queen Jeanne d'Evreux in the Royal Abbey of Maubuisson, was one of the most prestigious ensembles. It featured, among other scenes, a large representation of the Last Supper (now in the Carmelite church), and a narrower one of the Communion of St. Denis, with a row of prophets and the Angel with the cruet holding the wine as a reminder of the overall Eucharistic meaning. This angel, which has been ascribed to an important sculptor from the royal court, is not stylized in any way, and stems rather from a calm and serene aesthetic emphasizing the monumentality of the masses treated.

Sculpture

Gothic France

300 Resurrection of a Girl from
l'Isle-sur-Sorgue
Fragment from the Tomb of
Elzear de Sabran

Comtat Venaissin, around 1370-1373
Bas-relief, alabaster. H 0.34 m; W 0.214 m; D 0.10 m
Franciscan Church, Apt. Gift of Maurice Sulzbach, 1919. RF 1676

Elzear de Sabran, a young Provençal nobleman
who had joined the fortunes of the Angevins as
far as Naples, took vows of chastity and prayer. A
tertiary in the Order of St. Francis, he was buried
in the church of the Cordeliers d'Apt. Miracles
during his lifetime, during his funeral cortège and
on his tomb led to his canonization in 1371. A
sumptuous ciborium, on the model of that for
St. John Lateran, was created to hold his relics.
The decoration, composed of reliefs illustrating the
miracles of the saint, is now dispersed. The
fragment in the Louvre shows a girl who was
drowned, coming back to life in the arms of her
mother in front of the saint's coffin. The sculpture
is typical of art from Avignon, enriched by every
stylistic current due to the presence of the papal
court.

301 Charles V, King of France

Ile-de-France, last third of the
14th century
Statue, stone. H 1.95 m; W 0.71 m; D 0.41 m
Collection of the French Crown.
Entered the Louvre in 1904. RF 1377

detail

This image of King Charles V who reigned from
1364 to 1380, and its pendant, the statue of Queen

Jeanne de Bourbon, were long thought to have come from the portal of the Parisian hospice the *Quinze-Vingt,* or from the Parisian Abbey des Célestins and to have represented St. Louis and his wife with the features of the reigning monarchs. A recent hypothesis suggests they came from the Palais du Louvre which was enlarged and embellished by Charles v.

Although the hands are restored, the king's face is a striking portrait, firm and sardonic; the drapery, which is gathered round and then falls in an ample movement, is also treated with vigour. The king's profoundly human expression coincides with the development of the art of portraiture in the middle of the 14th century.

302 St. John on Calvary

Loire Valley, third quarter of the 15th century

Statue, wood. H 1.40 m; W 0.46 m; D 0.39 m

Church of Loché.

Acq. 1904. RF 1383

With his arms crossed, and bowed in his grief, this sculpture of St. John, and its pendant the *Virgin* (now in the Metropolitan Museum of New York) were part of a Calvary group, at the feet of a crucified Christ. These groups were frequently placed at the entrance to the Choir, high up on a so-called "beam of glory". In the 19th century this work was kept in the little church of Loché in the Touraine; it is typical of the austere grandeur of art from the Loire Valley. The pure volumes of the face, which recall the style of Jean Fouquet, the Master of Tours, and the voluminous drapery with its broken folds contribute to an expression of quiet sadness. Any picturesque detail that might distract from this study of interiority has been banished. Other examples of this can be seen in the art of Touraine wood-carvers.

Gothic France Sculpture

303 Tomb of Philippe Pot
(d. 1494)

*Burgundy, last quarter of the
15th century*

Painted stone. H 1.80 m; W 2.65 m

Abbey Church of Cîteaux.

Acq. 1889. RF 795

This funerary monument which has haunted
many people's imaginations, was commissioned by
the lord of La Roche-Pot, Philippe, seneschal to
the Duc de Bourgogne, then chamberlain to
Louis XI, rallying to his side on the death of
Charles the Fearless. The quality of the sculpture
owes more to its extraordinary, monumental and
expressive composition, than to any stylistic
refinement. The dead knight is borne on a slab by
eight hooded official mourners. This funerary
cortège evokes the grandiose and spectacular
funeral processions of the time, and recalls the
figurines of mourners on the great tombs at the
end of the Middle Ages. It differs from them in its
monumental size, the lack of individualisation, and

the significance of the eight emblazoned shields - which testify to the dead man's noble lineage - carried by the mourners.

304 Virgin and Child

Bourbonnais, end of the 15th century

Group, stone with polychrome traces.

H 0.79 m; W 0.59 m; D 0.45 m

Acq. 1955, RF 2763

The "relaxation" of the Gothic style was most apparent in the Loire Valley. This work which was housed for a long period in the private chapel in the hamlet of Longvé, not far from Moulins, is a good example. The group depicts the Education of the Holy Child, who plays in his mother's lap, distractedly turning the pages of an open book. The composition is concentrated and serenely pyramidal in outline, enlivened by voluminous folds breaking at the base into deep planes. The Virgin has a delicately absent expression, a wide curving brow, looking languidly from under lowered eyelids, with a small, fleshy mouth and full cheeks. This striving for a simplified purity, which is contained and all-encompassing, is in keeping with the refined aesthetic which reigned at the court of the Ducs de Bourbon at Moulins with artists such as the Master of Moulins, Jean de Chartres and Michel Colombe.

Gothic France **Sculpture**

French Renaissance

Gradually Gothic forms were abandoned. New inspiration came from Renaissance Italy which French knights discovered during the wars with Italy. The desire for novelty led first to the adoption of a Lombard style of ornamentation using grotesques, candelabra, scrollwork and volutes. This "Early Renaissance", centred round the royal and aristocratic houses in the Loire Valley and in the Norman Château de Gaillon, was accompanied by the arrival of Italian sculptors, like the Juste family, who were responsible for the tomb of Louis XII at Saint-Denis. The great French sculptors like Michel Colombe and his nephew Guillaume Regnault, introduced into the "relaxed" Gothic style a new feeling of humanity and a concern for clarity of expression and composition.

Under François I, after the troubled years that followed the defeat at Pavia and the captivity of the king at Madrid, the palace of Fontainebleau fairly bristled with Italian artists who came with Rosso and Primaticcio, and the name of the Château is used to designate the Mannerist school. After Italian sculptors like Domenico Fiorentino - who sculpted the tomb of Claude de Lorraine - and Benvenuto Cellini who executed his *Nymphe de Fontainebleau* **348**, the French took up the challenge: François Marchand, created the reliefs on the rood-screen at the church of St. Père at Chartres, Pierre Bontemps and Jean Goujon gave a new fluidity to the bas-relief, in which the conceptual spiralling line is filled out with "wet" drapery emphasizing volumes. Barthélémy Prieur, and Germain Pilon adopted the elongated female figure characteristic of Mannerist art, linking it successfully to the realism of portraiture and the expressive strength of a new religious fervour - that of the Counter-Reformation.

After years of internecine struggle, during which only Pilon sustained his art, the accession of Henri IV heralded a revival of Mannerist art. Known as the "Second School of Fontainebleau", a group of sculptors - Pierre Biard, Pierre

Francqueville and Mathieu Jacquet gave new life
to the turbulent Mannerist style.

Michel COLOMBE
around 1430 - after 1511

305 Saint George Fighting the
Dragon

Tours, 1508-1509

Relief, marble. H 1.75 m; W 2.72 m

Chapel in the *Château de Gaillon*.

Seized during the Revolution. **MR 1645**

The great image-maker of Tours, Michel
Colombe, who designed the tomb for Queen Anne
de Bretagne's parents in Nantes cathedral, was
commissioned in 1508 to carve a marble altarpiece
for the high chapel in the Château de Gaillon,
home of the Archbishop of Rouen, Georges
d'Amboise. This was a centre of the early French
Renaissance, and Louis XII's minister - aided by
French and Italian artisans - introduced Lombard
ornamentation into what was an unchanged
Gothic architectural setting. Michel Colombe gave
depth to a pictorial image of the Cardinal's patron

saint, George, shown as a contemporary knight fighting the dragon which terrorized the town of Trebizond, and freeing the imprisoned princess. This first large Italian-style relief, in which the sculptor has not quite mastered perspective, or the depiction of nature (a few meagre groups of trees) and myth (the dragon is naive in style), nevertheless testifies to a drive for compositional unity and clarity which heralds the Renaissance. Italian ornamentalists, probably under the Florentine, Jérôme Pacherot, were responsible for the surround which is typical of decorations based on pilasters and grotesques imported from Italy.

306 Louise de Savoie

Loire Valley, beginning of the 16th century

Bust, terracotta. H 0.47 m; W 0.54 m; D 0.23 m

Château de la Péraudière.

Gift of the *Société des Amis du Louvre*, 1949. RF 2658

This intriguing bust was found in a niche in a small *château* in the Touraine, La Péraudière. With its cut-off shoulders and fullness of form, it is like the Italian busts which were widely known from Tuscany to Lombardy in the second half of the 15th century but which were unknown in France. Comparison with a medallion has established it as a portrait of Louise de Savoie, mother of King François I. A concern for realism accentuates her features which are firm and powerful, like those found on the bust that is a pendant to this, which probably portrays Duprat, later Chancellor to François I. Special techniques, such as the construction of the headdress, made from superimposed layers of clay held together by brass pins, the iconography and its realism give this bold work its uniqueness. This might, however, be attributable to the variety of influences at work on Court art, fascinated as it was by the Italian model and enlivened by visiting artists.

Workshop of Guillaume
REGNAULT
c. 1460-1532

307 **Virgin and Child**

Loire Valley, first third of the
16th century

Statue, marble. H 1.83 m; W 0.60 m

Château de Couasnon, Olivet near Orléans.

Acq. 1875. RF 202

This statue is a perfect example of the serene grandeur of art in the Loire after the death of Michel Colombe. With her two feet in rounded shoes firmly planted on the ground, and her drapery set within a rectangle, she is finely balanced and monumental. A fashionable detail, a scarf fixed with a monogrammed brooch, enlivens the costume. The celebration of the Virgin-Mother for her serenity and grandeur is accompanied by idealized features: oval face, straight nose, small mouth, and heavy-lidded, almond-shaped eyes. The pride of the mother presenting her fine laughing child is mixed with a tender melancholy which looks forward to the Passion.

Jean GOUJON
c. 1510 - around 1565

308 **Nymph and Putto**

Paris, around 1547-1549

Relief, stone. H 0.73 m; W 1.95 m; D 0.13 m

From the Fountain of the Innocents, Paris.

Entered the Louvre in 1818. MR 1738

The architect and sculptor Jean Goujon introduced a new form of bas-relief; his figures are perfectly contained within the frame and are autonomous. Without seeking to compete with painting they

command their own illusory perspective within the thin slab of stone. Goujon sculpted elegant, slender figures contained within graceful spirals like these on the façade of the Louvre, on the rood-screen in Saint-Germain-l'Auxerrois (fragments of which are in the Louvre), and on the Fountain of the Innocents, a section of which was dismantled and reassembled in the 18th century, the rest going to the Louvre. His sense of the ideal is conveyed by the strong conceptual outline to the figures, which are further emphasized by the fluid draperies surrounding them.

309 Diana the Huntress

France, mid-16th century

Group, marble. H 2.11; W 2.58 m; D 1.345 m

Château d'Anet. Seized during the Revolution.

Entered the Louvre in 1823.

Mr 1581

Diane de Poitiers, mistress and counsellor to Henri II, had a monumental fountain built by Philippe Delorme in a courtyard of her *Château d'Anet.* It was surmounted by a marble sculpture of Diana caressing a large stag, surrounded by her dogs. The sculpture recalls Cellini's *Nymphe de Fontainebleau* [348] which figured in the portal of the *Château d'Anet*. Diana recalls the royal favourite although this is not a portrait.

Ascribed successively to Jean Goujon, Pierre Bontemps, Benvenuto Cellini and Germain Pilon, the work displays the elaborate and high-flow elegance characteristic of the School of Fontainebleau. The chaste goddess, who is distant yet gentle, has a certain cold sensuality about her which recalls the *Girl extracting a Thorn* by Ponce Jacquiot.

Pierre BONTEMPS
c. 1505-1568

310 Charles de Maigny

Paris, around 1557

Funerary statue, stone.

H 1.45 m; W 0.70 m; D 0.42 m

Church of the Celestines, Paris

Seized during the Revolution. Entered the Louvre in 1818.

MR 1729

With the Renaissance, tomb figures which by tradition were recumbent became more varied in posture, leaning forward or kneeling in prayer. In 1557 Pierre Bontemps, responsible for the tomb sculpture for François I, was commissioned to sculpt the figure of Charles de Maigny, captain of the King's Guards. He was to be portrayed sitting, like a guard who has fallen asleep at his post, in front of the king's door. The massive body, slumping against a heraldic stool, is brought into relief by the fine carving of decorative elements.

Germain PILON
c. 1528-1590

311 Monument for the Heart of Henri II:
The Three Graces

Paris, around 1560-1566

Group, marble. H 1.50 m; W 0.755 m; D 0.755 m

Church of the Celestines, Paris.

Seized during the Revolution. Entered the Louvre

in 1818. MR 1591

Working by turns on antinaturalist themes and on
realistic portraits, Germain Pilon managed to
reconcile the contradictions of the Mannerist style.
Commissioned by Catherine de Médicis to execute
the funerary sculpture for Henri II who died
accidentally in 1559, Pilon decorated the tomb for
his body in the abbey-church of Saint-Denis with
shapely figures of Virtues. To carry the casket
containing the King's heart he was commissioned
to sculpt the Three Graces in a circle, standing on
a pedestal decorated by Domenico Fiorentino. He
adapted an etching by Marco Antonio Raimondi
after Raphael, creating a group of graceful
caryatids holding the heart casket on their heads.
While rejecting the exuberance and the serpentine
line of Mannerism, he retained its elongated forms
which he clothed in crumpled drapery which
tumbles down in graceful curves.

Barthélémy PRIEUR
1536-1611

312 Funerary Spirit

Paris, 1583-1585

Statue, bronze. H 0.46 m; W 1.07 m; D 0.35 m

Church of Saint-André-des-Arts, Paris. Seized during

the Revolution. Entered the Louvre

in 1824. MR 1684

Barthélémy Prieur was a Protestant who owed his
fortune to the protection of politicians anxious for

reconciliation to bring an end to the wars of religion. The family of the Connétable de Montmorency, who was a friend of Henri II, commissioned two funerary monuments from Prieur which are now in the Louvre. For his part, the politician de Thou ordered two tombs to be sculpted, one for his father and one for his first wife. Prieur juxtaposed a characterful, realist bust with two thin and tormented spirits, inspired by Michelangelo's statues on the Medici tombs.

Germain PILON
c. 1528-1590

313 Virgin of the Sorrows

Paris, around 1585

Statue, polychrome terracotta.

H 1.68 m; W 1.19 m; D 0.78 m

Sainte-Chapelle, Paris. Seized during

the Revolution.

Entered the Louvre in 1890. RF 3117

The other side to Pilon's art is a refined but pointed and troubled pathos which finds expression in the reliefs depicting the *Descent from the Cross*, on the pulpit in the Grands Augustins and on the altarpiece in Saint-Etienne-du-Mont. The *Virgin of the Sorrows* - unlike a Pietà in which the Virgin holds Christ's body - introduced a new mystical contemplation of despair and solitude which corresponded to a revived Catholic spirituality. Used as a model for a statue in marble, now in the Parisian church of St. Paul and St. Louis, it was designed to fit in with an ensemble, the *Resurrection* (in the Louvre) and *St. Francis* (in the church of St. Jean of the

Armenians), commissioned by Queen Catherine de
Médicis for Henri II's funerary chapel in Abbey of
Saint-Denis, the *"Rotonde des Valois"*.

Pierre BIARD
1559-1609

314 Fame

Paris, 1597

Statue, bronze. H 1.34 m

Chapel in the *Château de Cadillac*.

Seized during the Revolution.

Entered the Louvre in 1834. LP 361

The Duke of Epernon, governor of Gascogne,
embellished his *Château de Cadillac* and built a
tiered funerary mausoleum - modelled on the royal
tombs in Saint-Denis - in his chapel. Surmounting
this was the statue of Fame, holding the trumpet
of ill-repute in one hand and blowing into that of
good repute. The same iconography can be found
later, on certain great aristocratic tombs in
Westminster Abbey. Commissioned in 1597, the
statue is a Mannerist figure balancing precariously
on one leg like the *Mercury* by Giambologna. The
art of the second School of Fontainebleau, less
refined in its attention to grooming and ornament
than the First, concentrated on the thrust of
volumes turning in space.

17th century France

Several major movements affected French sculpture between 1600 and the death of Louis XIV (1715). A latter-day Mannerism persisted under Henri IV and Louis XIII alongside the solid realism of sculptors of tombs. A new style appeared around 1640, dominated by figures like Simon Guillain, Jacques Sarazin and the Anguier brothers. Their training in Italy during the emergence of the Baroque style led to a use of scenic and dynamic forms. Contact with classical art disciplined them, however, and the combination of a classical ideal with a tempered Baroque style gave rise to a classical, balanced and intellectually-based sculpture in France. Art under Louis XIV was at the outset dominated by Colbert's meddlesome administration (1665-1663) which supplied royal artists with the means of production. The establishment of the Royal Academy of Painting and Sculpture devoted both to training and theory, the creation of the French Academy in Rome and the great building projects at the Louvre, Versailles, the Invalides and Marly, all called for a great deal of sculpture in keeping with the canons laid down by the Court painters. Only Puget, in Provence, escaped Court interference and managed to create bold and passionate works.

Under his influence, and under that of colourist painters, official art took a more dynamic turn, By 1700 or so, the "Rocaille" style, or French Rococo, an interpretation of the Baroque, held sway most spectacularly in the Park of Marly.

Pierre FRANCQUEVILLE
1548-1615
Francesco BORDONI
1580-1654

315 Slave

Paris, 1614-1618

Statue, bronze. H 1.55 m; W 0.66 m; D 0.70 m

From the equestrian monument of Henri IV on the Pont Neuf.

Seized during the Revolution.

Entered the Louvre in 1795. MR 1668

The arrival of Pierre Francqueville, who was already famous in Florence under the name Francavilla, with his son-in-law Bordoni, marked the arrival of Tuscan Mannerism to the court of Henri IV. As official sculptor to the king, he was asked to collaborate on the equestrian statue of Henri IV, erected on the tip of the *Ile de la Cité*, by the Pont Neuf. While the statue itself, commissioned by Queen Marie de Médicis in Florence as early as 1604, was by Pietro Tacca, another pupil of Giambologna, the four slaves at each corner of the pedestal were cast by Bordoni in 1618 after models made by Francqueville before his death (1615). Symbolizing enchained passions, subjugated nations and the ages of man, these captives with their unstable postures are very agitated. The fine chiselling accentuates their tortured, suffering bodies.

Jacques SARAZIN
1592-1660

316 Prudence

Paris, around 1645

Relief, marble. Medaillon H 1.02 m; W 0.74 m

Monument for the heart of Louis XIII.

Church of St. Louis of the Jesuits, Paris.

Seized during the Revolution. Entered the Louvre

in 1881. RF 607-610

After a long period in Rome, Jacques Sarazin was responsible for introducing the new concepts of Italian art into France. The Louvre possesses a large selection of his work, which is classical in character though infused with a Baroque warmth. From the joyful, generous group, the *Children with a Goat*, to the statue of Bérulle in Ecstasy, founder of the *Ordre de l'Oratoire*, including statuettes and reliefs for private devotion, *St. Peter* and the marble *Madeleine*, along with the terracotta *Virgin and Child*, the variety of materials and forms allowed for a great liberty of treatment.

The monument for the heart of Louis XIII decorated an arch in the choir of the Jesuits church (now St. Louis). From the keystone hung two angels in vermeil melted down during the Empire to make Chaudet's sculpture *Peace*. On the jambs were epitaphs on a red marble ground held out by crying cherubs, and in the ovals figured the Cardinal Virtues in an Antique style.

François ANGUIER
1604-1669

317 Strength

Paris, around 1660-1663
Statue, marble. H 1.48 m; W 0.63 m; D 0.52 m
Monument for the heart of the Duke of Longueville.
Church of the Celestines, Paris
Seized during the Revolution. Entered the Louvre
in 1824. MR 1749

The Anguier brothers, François and Michel, went to Rome to study from the Antique. While there, they collaborated with Algardi, the leading light of Roman classicism. Back in France they encouraged a taste for quality materials - marble and bronze - and for a harmony derived from an interpretation of the Antique, seeking to achieve a subtle mobility. Among the great funerary monuments by Anguier housed in the Louvre, like those for de Thou and de Souvré, the funerary "Pyramid" which graced the monument to the heart of Duke Henri de Longueville is remarkable for its imposing stature. A high obelisk sculpted with the attributes of the arts and of high office, housed in the church of the Célestines, it stood on a high pedestal decorated with reliefs depicting the victories of the duke at the side of Henri IV. Four statues of the cardinal virtues lean against it. Strength, helmeted with the Nemean lionskin and holding the mace of Hercules, is a robust armoured matron, whose sinuous bend at the hips comes from a marked *contrapposto*.

Pierre PUGET
1620-1694

319 Milon of Croton

Provence, 1670-1683

Marble group. H 2.70 m; W 1.40 m; D 0.98 m

Commissioned by Louis XIV.

Parc de Versailles. MR 2075

A native of Marseille, Pierre Puget was taught the
dynamic force of Baroque art when in Rome and
especially in Genoa. In 1670 Colbert commissioned
from him three major works for Versailles, the
Milon of Croton, Alexander and Diogenes, and
Perseus and Andromeda. Puget sought a lyricism
and vigour that was to alter ideas about French
sculpture. Of the three great marbles housed in
the Louvre, the statue of *Milon* showing a man
with his hand trapped in the cleft of a tree he was
splitting being savaged by a lion, is a display of
intense torment. This dying hero, vanquished by
his own ebbing strength, caused the Queen to
exclaim in 1683: "the poor man, what suffering!"

François GIRARDON
1628-1715

319 Louis XIV on Horseback

Paris, 1685-1692

Equestrian statuette, bronze.

H 1.02 m; W 0.97 m; D 0.50 m

**Collection of the French Crown, Seized during
the Revolution.**

Entered the Louvre in 1821. MR 3239

Of all the great equestrian monuments raised
to the glory of Louis XIV in the towns of
France - Paris, Lyon, Dijon, Rennes and
Montpellier - not one escaped destruction. But the
fame of these works which exalted royal power
encouraged sculptors to make small-scale copies.
This one, signed by Girardon, reproduces the
gigantic bronze, cast in one piece, by Jean-
Balthazar Keller in 1692, after Girardon's model,
and under the supervision of Robert de Cotte, the
architect. Erected in 1699 in the *Place Vendôme,*
the new urban space conceived by Louvois in
Paris, the equestrian statue was intended as a sign

of the sovereign's power, shown here as a Roman Emperor in the classical style.

Jean ARNOULD ou REGNAUD
known in 1685-1687

320 The "Magnificent Buildings of Versailles"

Paris, 1686

Medallion, bronze. ∅ 0.775 m. From the
Place des Victoires, Paris. Acq. 1980. RF 3466

The *Maréchal* de La Feuillade, Gascon warlord and courtier at Versailles, undertook an ambitious project in honour of Louis XIV: the creation of a royal square, the *Place des Victoires,* in the heart of Paris. The architecture, by Jules Hardouin-Mansart, was completed by a statue of the king standing, cast in gilt bronze by the sculptor Desjardins. The Louvre possesses fragments which escaped destruction during the Revolution; the four reliefs and the two medallions from the pedestal. In addition, there are eight bronze medallions executed to decorate lamp-posts in the square. The ensemble illustrated the glorious events of the reign and the peace of Nimègue (1679). This one shows the building of Versailles, presented by a nubile nymph reclining in the foreground, in front of the château and the aqueduct. The painter Pierre Mignard did the drawing for the medallion which was made by Arnould and cast by Le Nègre.

Antoine COYSEVOX
1640-1720

³²¹ The Prince of Condé

Paris, 1688

Bust, bronze. H 0.75 m; W 0.70 m; D 0.32 m

Collection of the Prince de Conti.

Seized during the Revolution.

MR 3343

Under Louis XIV, the French bust sculpted in marble or bronze, expressed both the psychological depth of the person depicted and the importance of his functions. While Girardon worked within calm and reasoned frameworks, Coysevox aimed to capture the nervous tension of his model, along with a certain realist grandeur. The bust of Condé, prince of the blood and victor at the battle of Rocroy against the Spanish, depicts a man of compelling ugliness, with the thin, arrogant profile of a hawk. He is glorified by his classical breast-plate, picked out with griffons and with epaulettes in the form of a lion's muzzle. Although this portrait was done posthumously, destined for the Palace of the prince of Conti, it resembles a terracotta bust made by Coysevox during Condé's lifetime.

Antoine COYSEVOX
1640-1720

³²² Fame Riding Pegasus

Paris, 1699-1702

Marble group. H 3.26 m; W 2.91 m; D 1.28 m

Commissioned by Louis XIV for the horse-pond in Marly. Entered the Louvre in 1986.

MR 1824

The ornamental sculpture for the Park of Marly was the grand project at the end of Louis XIV's reign. The marble groups which gave rhythm to the lakes and waterfalls and the statues decorating

17th Century France **Sculpture**

the groves were all dispersed, first under the Regency, after 1715, then during the Revolution. Today, more than twenty pieces are in the Louvre and others can be seen in the Tuileries Gardens. The most celebrated monumental groups were *Fame* and *Mercury*, each astride a winged horse. Originally they dominated the horse-pond at Marly; under the Regency they were transported to the entrance of the Tuileries leading into the *Place de la Concorde*. They were replaced by replicas when the originals were moved into the Louvre. Typical of official rhetoric glorifying the king in the peaceful aftermath of war, these dynamic groups rearing above a trophy of arms are caught in mid-movement, and mark an early Baroque inflection in court art.

18th century France

Rococo, a Baroque art of contrasts, reached its peak at the beginning of Louis XV's reign. At the Royal Academy, admission pieces took on a dramatic and violent tone. At Court, the *Horses of Marly* by Coustou testify to an intense dynamism. In portrait, sculpture and small statuettes for connoisseurs the accent was rather on the charming and seductive. Around 1750 a reaction set in, signalled by a return to nature and to the Antique. Bouchardon, Pigalle and, at times, Falconet, gave new expression to the familiar classical themes. But they had to cater to the intellectual or wordly tastes of art lovers who became increasingly significant.

An authentic Neoclassical style took root around 1770. The cult of the great appeared with the series of statues commissioned by the royal administration for the future *Muséum*. Houdon, Pajou, Clodion, and Julien sought a simplicity of volume which was often enlivened by a deep sensuality. Much in favour at this time were statuettes and portraits expressing the sentiments and individuality glorified by contemporary philosophers. Caffieri and Houdon were leaders in this art of portrait sculpture.

Jean THIERRY
1669-1739

323 Leda and the Swan

Paris, 1717

Group, marble. H 0.81 m

Collection of the Academy. Entered the Louvre in 1854.
MR 2100

When Thierry was received into the Royal Academy, the painter Coypel provided him with a subject for his admission piece, which was submitted in 1717: Leda, Queen of Sparta, adored by Zeus who meets her on the riverbank in the form of a swan. This elegant and voluptuous theme is treated with the fluidity characteristic of the Rococo. Later, Thierry worked at the Court of Spain, where he introduced the spirit of Versailles infused by a new Baroque vitality.

Guillaume COUSTOU
1677-1746

324 **Horse Restrained by a Groom**
known as the **Horse of Marly**

Paris, 1739-1745

Marble group. H 3.55 m; W 2.84 m; D 1.15 m

Commissioned by Louis XV for the horse-pond at Marly.

Entered the Louvre in 1894. MR 1803

The winged steeds by Coysevox **322** were removed from the park of the *Château de Marly* during the Regency (1719). Twenty years later, Louis XV decided to furnish the empty pedestals with groups commissioned from Coysevox's nephew, Guillaume Coustou. Abandoning the constraints of official iconography, the royal administration ordered wild, rearing horses to be sculpted, held by naked men whose faces or feathered hats evoke parts of the world. They are homages to an untamed nature, and recall the classical Dioscuri. Horses and grooms offer an image of vigour, effort and the struggle between man and animal. This dynamism sought by a sculptor who wrote of "manes standing on end" and the "light and floating" tail, galvanizes groups that are still Baroque, but naturalistic too, since live models were used. Their fame, which earnt them their place, from 1795, at the entrance to the Champs-Élysées, on an order from the painter David, has remained constant.

Edme BOUCHARDON
1698-1762

**325 Cupid Making a Bow from the
Mace of Hercules**

Paris, 1739-1750

Marble statue. H 1.73 m; W 0.75 m; D 0.75 m

Commissioned by Louis XV. Entered the Louvre

before 1824. MR 1761

Defending classical art in face of the Baroque,
Bouchardon was a tireless draughtsman, finding
inspiration from the Antique and the study of the
human body. Moulds of the body and preparatory
drawings led, after long delays, to this marble
statue; the sketch was exhibited at the 1739 Salon,
and the marble sculpted from 1747-1750. A long
spiral shapes the body of the sardonic adolescent
who has stolen the weapons of Mars and Hercules
to fashion for himself a bow out of the mace. The
Versailles court was shocked, however, by the
naturalness of the body which seemed too real.

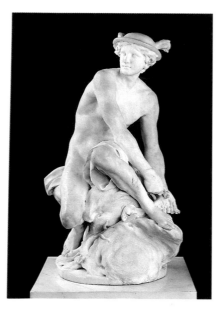

Jean-Baptiste PIGALLE
1714-1785

326 Mercury Attaching his Wings

Paris, 1744

Statuette, marble. H 0.59 m; W 0.35 m; D 0.30 m

Collection of the Royal Academy. Entered

the Louvre around 1848-1850.

MR 1957

This is a youthful work by a sculptor who was to
become the most significant figure in his field

under Louis XV. The *Mercury* was a long time in the making; the sketch may have been made at Lyons in 1739, when Pigalle returned from Rome where he had studied at the French Academy. The model and its pendant, *Venus giving a Message,* were shown at the Salon of 1742. In 1744, Pigalle was asked by the Academicians to execute the sculpture in marble as his admission piece into the company. Although the work has an official aspect to it - later still it was reproduced in a larger scale for a gift by the king to Frederick II of Prussia - the freedom in Mercury's turning movement is striking. Guided by a knowledge of the *Belvedere Torso* or a composition by Jordaens, he worked with a true understanding of anatomy and with a light, subtle sense of movement.

Etienne-Maurice FALCONET
1716-1791

327 Bather

Paris, 1757

Statuette, marble. H 0.82 m; W 0.26 m; D 0.28 m

Collection of Mme Du Barry. Seized during
the Revolution. MR 1846

A *protégé* of Madame de Pompadour, Falconet was torn between his desire to execute an ambitious, moralistic sculpture, and the requirements of a court which favoured decorative elegance. This nymph extending her foot towards the water is a refined work. The elongated and graceful feminine figure, with sloping shoulders and a small bust is a constant feature of Falconet's art. He introduced a scarcely perceptible reserve into this candid face with lowered eyelids, thus avoiding any risk of vulgarity. The work was shown in the 1757 Salon, and it defined the style of a sculptor which became widely known thanks to Sèvres porcelain figurines.

Jean-Antoine HOUDON
1741-1828

328 Louise Brongniart,
Aged Five Years

Paris, 1777

Bust, terracotta. H 0.35 m; W 0.242 m; D 0.24 m

Acq. 1898. RF 1197

Houdon is famous chiefly for his portraits; official marble busts such as *Madame Victoire,* more intimate terracottas, plasters and bronzes, as well as large marble statues like those of Washington and Voltaire. Portraitist of men of letters and philosophers (Voltaire, Rousseau, Diderot, Buffon) he also depicted the aristocracy and the early heroes of American Independence (Franklin, Washington). But it was in the close observation of his own family and friends that he captured his most tender, alive expressions. With the busts of his wife and of their daughters Sabine, Anne-Ange and Claudine, and the children of Brongniart the architect, the Louvre has fine examples of his realistic sculpture, full of a youthful freshness.

Pierre JULIEN
1732-1804

329 Dying Gladiator

Paris, 1779

Marble statuette. H 0.607 m; W 0.485 m; D 0.42 m

Collection of the Royal Academy. Entered the Louvre in 1855. MR 2006

The admission piece for the Academy, a masterpiece in marble which the artist had to produce to join the company, had to be dramatic in content during the 18th century. After the energetic, Baroque works of men like Adam or Slodtz, Julien, who was already a mature man, presented a resolutely Neoclassical piece. He had copied numerous classical statues, and his work is a densely composed recollection of the *Dying Gladiator* on the Capitol. Silent and heroic, this death is Stoic. The exaltation of virtue and the serene balance of the work are the components of this new classical feeling.

detail

Claude MICHEL
known as CLODION
1738-1814

330 Nymphs Bathing with Leda and
the Swan

Paris, around 1782

Relief, stone. H 1.03 m; W 3.23 m; D 0.27 m

Hôtel de Besenval, Paris.

Acq. 1986. RF 4103

18th century collectors, who appreciated Clodion for his light touch and sensitive modelling, cast him in the role of the great Neoclassical decorator. There are numerous exuberant terracottas by him, and a few austere marbles. The reliefs and vases which decorated the bathroom of Besenval, general of the Swiss Guard - more of a courtier than a warrior - are the remains of a major Neoclassical interior conceived by Brongniart the architect. Clodion manages to give a poetic atmosphere to the amusing scenes of astonished bathers. The liveliness in the modelling and the concise, rapid treatment of the foliage links the work to the Hellenistic art then being rediscovered.

Jean-Jacques CAFFIERI
1725-1792

331 Canon Alexandre-Gui Pingré,
the Astronomer (1711-1796)

Paris, 1788

Bust, terracotta. H 0.675 m; W 0.515 m; D 0.346 m

Observatory, Paris.

Entered the Louvre in 1909. RF 1496

Houdon's rival in the art of portraiture, Caffieri,
managed to convey the dry wit of the Canon,
without disguising his pendulous cheeks, short, fat
nose, thick sensual lips and double chin. Yet this
was an entirely official work, depicting a famous
astronomer and freemason, Canon of Sainte-
Geneviève, and was exhibited in the 1789 Salon.

Jean-Antoine HOUDON
1741-1828

332 Diana the Huntress

Paris, 1790

Statue, bronze. H 2.005 m; W 0.795 m; D 0.935 m

Acq. 1829. CC 204

Houdon's studies in France, and then at the
French Academy in Rome, led him to value the
Antique and respect human anatomy. His *Diana,*
the plaster model for which dates from 1776, the
marble from 1780, and this bronze cast executed
by the artist himself in 1790, is a synthesis between
an elegance of contour, a decided naturalism (the

detail in her nakedness was considered shocking),
and a quest for suppleness and balance which
harks back to a simplified form of Mannerism.

Augustin PAJOU
1730-1809

333 Psyche Abandoned

Paris, 1790

Marble statue. H 1.77 m; W 0.86 m; D 0.86 m

Commissioned by Louis XVI. Entered the Louvre in 1829. MR Sup 62

Official sculptor to Louis XV at the close of his
reign, then to Louis XVI and a survivor of the
Revolution, Augustin Pajou tried his hand at every
genre, portraits, architectural decoration and
monumental sculpture. The Royal administration
commissioned this *Psyche* from him in 1783,
designed as a pendant to Cupid **325** by Bouchardon.
The original plaster cast, shown at the 1785 Salon,
created a *succès de scandale* for its frank portrayal of
naked beauty in all its naturalness and sensuality,
far removed from the classical ideal. But the
treatment in marble, executed under the
Revolution, puts a greater accent on the
Neoclassical decoration of the furnishings.

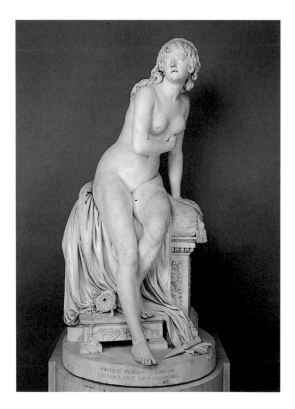

France in the first half of the 19th century

The Neoclassical style dominated French official art under Napoleon. Chaudet's silver sculpture *Peace,* and the statue of *Napoleon* by Ramey display a grand monumental vigour which is strong and austere. But the portraits and sketches by Chinard, and the sculpture Cupid **335** by Chaudet make way for something lighter and more fluid.

The Classical tradition was continued under the Restoration with Pradier, Bosio, Jaley and Le Moyne Saint-Paul. But they assimilated the Romantic revolution as well. Pradier, whom Victor Hugo compared to Phidias, infused passion into his group of satyrs, as does Jehan Duseigneur in his *Orlando Furioso* **339**. The animal sculptor Barye pursued his image of a wild and savage nature with great verve. There are two figures in particular who embody the contradictions of this period, torn between naturalism and the Antique, between feeling and expression: Rude, the eclectic sculptor of the *"Marseillaise"* on the *Arc de Triomphe,* and David d'Angers, who celebrated great men and grand causes.

Joseph CHINARD
1756-1813

334 Young Harpist

Sketch, clay.
H 0.28 m; W 0.25 m; D 0.12 m
Acq. 1910. RF 1503

The sculptor Chinard from Lyons was chiefly famous for his busts, portraits and medallions of revolutionary, and later imperial figures, such as the busts of Madame de Verninac in marble and the young woman in terracotta in the Louvre. But he was also a remarkable modeller, and a showcase displays maquettes and sketches of great freedom of execution. Some of them, such as the monument to Desaix, are official commissions while others, like the one shown here, are more spontaneous expressions of elegant sentiment.

France, first half of the 19th Century   **Sculpture**

Antoine-Denis CHAUDET
1763-1810

335 Cupid

Paris, 1802-1807

Marble statue. H 0.805 m; W 0.44 m; D 0.84 m

Collection of the French Crown. Entered

the Louvre before 1851. LL 56

The Neoclassical revival culminated in the celebration of heroism and of Republican, and Imperial virtues, alongside a graceful relaxation of tension. Chaudet embodied the first sentiment in his silver *Peace,* the bust of Napoleon and the group *Oedipus and Phorbas*. This Cupid, on the other hand, is more graceful. Holding a butterfly by its wings, he is perhaps tormenting a human soul, as the reliefs on the plinth, illustrating the pleasures and pains of love, would suggest. The philosophical allusion is a rich one; however, the sculptor who made this model in 1802 but died before he could execute it in marble was chiefly concerned with the dynamic lines of a young body.

François-Joseph BOSIO
1768-1845

336 Henri IV as a Child

Paris, 1822-1824

Statue in silver. H 1.25 m; W 0.46 m; D 0.40 m

Commissioned by Charles X. CC 37

Bosio came from Monaco, and having worked for Napoleon became "first Sculptor to the King" under Louis XVIII when the bronze quadriga which surmounts the *Arc du Carrousel* was inaugurated. As Official Sculptor - his *Louis XIV on Horseback* is in the Place des Victoires in Paris, and his *Nymph Salmacis* in the Louvre - he was commissioned to sculpt this retrospective statue of Henri IV as a youth. With this historical setting in the age of the troubadours, he plays his part in the dynastic propaganda of the Restored Monarchy reviewing its glorious past. Following this example, statues of famous children became an ingenuous, expressive genre.

The plaster model was shown in the Salon of 1822, and numerous copies were made of the statue in marble and bronze. But this version, cast in silver by Odiot the metalworker, and wrought by Soyer, was the most prestigious example reserved for the king.

James PRADIER
1790-1852

337 The Three Graces

Paris, 1831

Marble group. H 1.72 m; W 1.02 m
State Commission, 1831. LP 5

Originally from Geneva, Pradier managed to establish himself in the Parisian milieu. He received official commissions under the Restoration (the monument to the royal heir, the Duke of Berry) and under Louis-Philippe. He collaborated in the great political projects of the July Monarchy, decorating the *Assemblée Nationale,* the *Arc de Triomphe,* the *Place de la Concorde,* Napoleon's tomb, and the historical galleries in the

Museum at Versailles. His art is based on a Classicism which is sometimes austere, and sometimes tinged with sensuality as in this group of *Graces*. Exhibited in the Salon of 1831, this reminder of the classical *Borghese Graces* and of Raphael's painting is warmed by a langour and a tenderness which Pradier was later to intensify, under the influence of Romanticism, into a more passionate sensuality as seen in his group, *Satyr and Bacchante*.

François RUDE
1784-1855

338 Young Neapolitan Fisherboy Playing with a Tortoise

Paris, 1831-1833

Marble statue. H 0.82 m; W 0.88 m; D 0.48 m

Collection of the French Crown. LP 63

François Rude, the native of Dijon who created the famous *Marseillaise,* offers here a genre scene in which the classical style is overturned by a new freedom. A young Neapolitan fisherman, identified by his bonnet, his net and the scapular around his neck, plays with a tortoise, holding it back with a reed. He is naked, like the mythological heroes of the Neoclassicists. But in his striving for naturalness, this life-loving sculptor emphasized movement and above all the expression of joy in the boy's face, lit up by a candid laugh which uncovers his teeth. Rude made a preliminary study of the subject while in Italy in 1829; it was executed in plaster in 1831 and in marble in 1833. The sculpture inaugurated a romantic taste for popular Italian subjects as illustrated by Carpeaux.

Jean-Bernard, known as Jehan
DUSEIGNEUR
1808-1866

339 Orlando Furioso

Paris, 1831-1867

Statue in bronze. H 1.30 m; **W** 1.40 m

Luxembourg gardens. Entered the Louvre in 1900.

RF 2993

Nothing less than a Romantic manifesto in the 1831 Salon, Orlando Furioso was cast in bronze in 1867. In the rebellious attitude of Ariosto's hero, wrestling to get free from his bindings, the sculptor, who admired Victor Hugo, sought to break away from the classical formalities of Neoclassicism. Théophile Gautier who heaped lavish praise on this "chivalrous Orlando foaming at the mouth, with his savage rolling eye and knitted brow" was a perfect spokesman for this rejection of academicism in favour of lyrical and even passionate expression.

Antoine-Louis BARYE
1796-1875

340 **Lion Fighting a Serpent**

Paris, 1832-1835

Group in bronze. H 1.35 m; W 1.78 m; D 0.96 m

Commissioned by Louis-Philippe. From the Tuileries Gardens.

Entered the Louvre in 1911.

LP 1184. RF 1516

Fascinated by animal sculpture and professor of zoological drawing at the *Muséum,* Barye, who was an assiduous visitor at the *Zoological Gardens*, studied, drew and sometimes dissected and made casts from wild animals. Using these studies he would then execute statues and statuettes which were calm and accurate or furiously Romantic in vein. A lover of the big cats, birds of prey, and snakes, he was familiar with the merciless struggles of nature. Starting with a precise knowledge of the muscles under the pelt, he depicted the ferocious expression of the king of the animals, vanquisher of its enemies, in homage to King Louis-Philippe who came to power in July 1830, at the astrological conjunction of lion and hydra.

Pierre-Jean DAVID D'ANGERS
1788-1856

341 **Child with a Bunch of Grapes**

1837-1845

Marble statue. H 1.31 m; W 0.55 m; D 0.485 m

Collection Robert David d'Angers. Jean Gigoux Bequest,

1896. RF 1118

This sculpture has an autobiographical origin: during a walk, the sculptor's young son Robert tried to pick a bunch of grapes and narrowly missed being bitten by a viper, thanks to his father's intervention. David d'Angers, who was shaken by the incident and who liked to philosophize and draw morals, represented it as childhood unaware of future menace. Here, however, the snake is missing, although it appeared on the plaster model in the *Musée d'Angers*. David renders the tender plumpness of the childish body with its protuberant tummy and thick hair. It is a surprisingly emotive work from a sculptor who specialized in grand causes and was the most inspired portraitist of his time; his bust of Lamartine and several medallions by him can be seen in the Louvre.

France, first half of the 19th Century **Sculpture**

Italy

Pre-Romanesque art, represented by the pulpit from the abbey of Pomposa, and Romanesque art are scarce in the Louvre. But as far as the 13th century goes, certain works from Pisa *(Virgin of the Annunciation),* Florence (monumental statues from the Duomo in Florence), Naples (the *Cardinal Virtues* from a tomb) convey an idea of an art in which classical traces, Roman stylization and Gothic naturalism are reconciled. In the 14th century the Pisan *Annunciation* in wood possesses a monumental grandeur. The art of the Quattrocento, the period of Humanist harmony, is represented in its most idealized Florentine form, in such works as the so-called *Beautiful Florentine* or *Scipion Rattier* which were the best known works in the 19th century. Their success is eclipsed today by the great Florentine renovators Donatello and Verrochio, represented by major works, as well as Mino da Fiesole, Agostino da Duccio, Desiderio da Settignano and Della Robbia. But the jaggedness (in Mantegazza) or the delicacy (in Amadeo and GC Romano) of Lombard art, Ferraran anguish *(Dead Christ),* Sienese strength (Della Quercia, F di Giorgio Martini) and enigmatic langour (in the *Female Bust* by Laurana), are also represented.

For the general public the 16th century belongs to Michelangelo's *(Slaves* **347***)*. But the art of the portrait, especially in Venice with Vittoria, and the Classical revival in the North (Mosca) were accompanied by the birth of Mannerism, a movement which evolved out of Michelangelo's grand style, in which spirals and elongated forms reflect the anxieties of the period (Cellini, Pierino da Vinci, the *Mercury* by Giambologna).

Until recently, however, the Louvre remained oblivious to the Italian Baroque. Three pieces by Bernini, and by his son - who revived monumental sculpture - were already in France during his lifetime *(Richelieu, Urban VIII,* and the *Christ child).* Since then only a few sketches have been added to the collection. Collections of 18th century Baroque work began only recently (Mazzuoli, Corradini).

The Italian collection closes with two Neoclassical masterpieces by Canova.

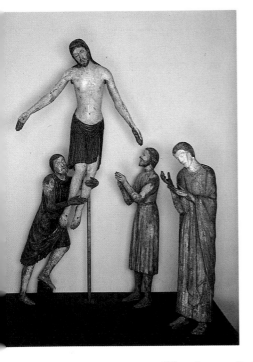

342 Descent from the Cross

Umbria or Latium, mid-13th century

Group, polychrome wood (poplar, walnut, willow).

Christ: H 1.83 m; W 1.23 m; D 0.43 m

Acq. 1968. RF 2966-2969

The theme of the Descent from the Cross was illustrated in France ₂₉₂, Spain and Italy by a certain number of groups showing Christ brought down from the Cross by Nicodemus and Joseph of Arimathea, mourned by the Virgin (absent here) and St. John. Linked to the group in Tivoli cathedral, the work shown still exhibits the stylized, geometrical folds in Christ's loincloth, of the Romanesque tradition. But the three-dimensional figures and the balance of masses look forward to a more naturalistic spirit.

Attributed to Jacopo DELLA
QUERCIA
Around 1371/74-1438

343 Virgin and Child

Bologna(?) c. 1430-1435(?)

Statue. Polychrome, wood. H 1.78 m

Acq. 1896. RF 1112

The Sienese sculptor Jacopo Della Quercia single-handedly introduced a grandiose expressiveness into sculpture. Master of the relief at the Fonte Gaja in Siena and in the San Petronio portal in Bologna, he strove less for individuality than for volume. Away from the emerging conflicts between Gothic and Renaissance, he pursued his research into form devoid of sentimentality and extraneous ornament. The *Virgin* in the Louvre, like that on the tympanum in San Petronio, has a compact density and harmony, enlivened by flowing draperies which enhance the melancholic expressiveness of the work.

Donato di Nicolo Bardi known as
DONATELLO
1386-1466

344 Virgin and Child

Florence(?) around 1400

Relief, polychrome terracotta. H 1.02 m;

W 0.74 m; D 0.12 m

Acq. 1880. RF 353

Donatello was the veritable embodiment of Renaissance discovery and invention with the monumental grandeur of his statues, equestrian works included, expressive portraiture, perspectival depth in reliefs, and incisive vigour of his bronze chiselling. The Virgin and Child reliefs by Donatello are often expressions of the tragic, in which the premonition of the Passion outweighs the tenderness of the subject. Here the profile of the Virgin with her long neck and of the Child who turns away from her, stand out from a background drapery which works with the chair in the foreground to produce an illusion of depth,

MINO DA FIESOLE

345 Dietisalvi Neroni

Florence, 1464

Marble bust. H 0.57 m; W 0.52 m; D 0.345 m

Gift of Gustave Dreyfus, 1919. RF 1669

Specializing in grand funerary monuments (the Louvre houses a fragment of one for Paul II in the Vatican), and in the Florentine tabernacle, Mino is famous chiefly for his busts. This one, of the Florentine humanist Dietisalvi Neroni, adviser to Piero de Medici, revives the Roman style of portraiture. Dressed in a kind of toga with angular folds gathered in a knot at the shoulder, his head is slightly turned in an imperious movement. The signs of age - he was 60 - the low forehead and the stooped neck of the model are a clear indication of the quest for truthfulness in this uncompromising art.

Italy **Sculpture**

Agostino d'Antonio di DUCCIO
1418-1481

346 Virgin and Child Surrounded by Angels

Florence, third quarter of the 15th century

Relief in marble. H 0.81 m; W 0.77 m

Acq. 1903. RF 1352

Often called the *Madone d'Auvillers*, after the name of the village in Picardy where it was kept during the 19th century, this relief still bears the arms and diamantine ring which identify Piero de Medici (1416-1469) as the original owner. Agostino's style is readily identifiable as author of the reliefs in the Malatesta Temple in Rimini. The convoluted drawing of folds and hair, the linear elegance of contours, the sybilline faces with their heavy eyelids, the subtle counterpoint set up between the large smooth mandorla and the elaborate draperies - all these elements combine in an intellectual exploration of ideal form.

Michelangiolo Buonarroti known as
MICHELANGELO
1475-1564

347 Slaves

Rome, 1513-1515

Unfinished statues in marble. H 2.09 m

Châteaux d'Ecouen, then *Richelieu*. Seized during
the Revolution. Entered the Louvre in 1794.

MR 1589

Because of the sheer force of his genius, Michelangelo is probably the most famous of all sculptors, and his two *Slaves* in the Louvre are the best known works in the Department of Sculpture. Their convoluted history represents one of Michelangelo's greatest struggles. Conceived in 1505 as part of the first project for the colossal funerary monument to Julius II, the sculptures were executed for the second project (1513). They were later set aside after the death of the pope, when economic factors altered plans for the tomb. Julius II, who had dreamed of lying in an isolated mausoleum in St. Peter's in Rome, was granted only a monumental vault in San Pietro in Vincoli, which houses the famous *Moses,* contemporary with the *Slaves*. Given by Michelangelo to the Florentine exile Roberto Strozzi, who offered them in turn as homage to the king of France, the *Slaves* reached France during the sculptor's lifetime, and were housed successively in the

château of the Connétable de Montmorency at *Ecouen* and afterwards at the *Château Richelieu*. Whether they represent the subjugated provinces, the arts reduced to slavery by the death of the pope; whether, more simply, they join in the eternal triumph of the pontiff, or symbolize passions subdued, or, in Platonic vein, the human soul dragged down by the grossness of the human body, the *Slaves* were never finished. The same is true of the other four in Florence which were executed later, around 1531-1532. "Unfinished" work is common in Michelangelo's output, as much because of the vagaries of his career as because of his unflagging quest for the absolute; but since he offered them as a gift, the master clearly considered these as works in their own right, finished or not. Perhaps this was because the marks left in the marble by his tools (stonemason's picks and points, files, gradines and rock drill) stand eloquently for the struggle with matter which is the nature of sculpture.

Benevenuto CELLINI
1500-1571

348 The Nymph of Fontainebleau

Paris, 1542-1543
High-relief, bronze. H 2.05 m; W 4.09 m
Château d'Anet. Seized under the Revolution.
Entered the Louvre in 1797.
MR 1706

In 1540, the silversmith Cellini moved to the court of François I where he made the famous salt-cellar, now in the Vienna Museum. Wishing to try his hand at monumental statuary, he cast a gigantic bronze tympanum for the golden gate at the *Château* of Fontainebleau. The tympanum is held up by two satyrs and flanked by two spandrels decorated with Victories. The bronze was cast in Cellini's Parisian foundry and workshop, chiselled by French sculptors - among them Pierre Bontemps - and placed in the porch of the *Château d'Anet,* the home of Diane de Poitiers, Henri II's favourite.

Even though the elongated female nude was modelled from nature - the capricious Catherine, then the shy, wild Jeanne - it is typical of a decorative antinaturalism which idealizes form and adapts it to its surround. The smooth skin and sinuous line of the naked water-nymph of Fontainebleau stands out against a background of wild animals, dogs and fawns drinking at the spring, overseen by a great stag evoking the forest setting.

Pierino da VINCI
Around 1531-1554

349 Young River God

Pisa, around 1548

Marble group. H 1.35 m; W 0.48 m

Schlichting Bequest. 1915. RF 1623

This young river god who holds a vase with water running from it, held up by three children, was intended for the collector Luca Martini who gave it to the Duchess of Tuscany, Eleanor of Toledo. She in turn offered it to her brother who placed it in his Neapolitan garden. Pierino was marked by fate, in Vasari's opinion, for a short life, and was related to the famous Leonardo. In this work he is searching for a personal style wavering between classical echoes and his fascination with Michelangelo. He conveys the suppleness of the young body with restrained virtuosity and a pleasure tinged with melancholy. The rhythm and curves of this hedonistic piece make it a precursor of the Mannerist movement.

Gian Lorenzo BERNINI
1598-1680

**350 Angel Carrying the Crown of
Thorns**

Rome, around 1667

Model, terracotta. H 33 cm; W 13 cm; D 19 cm

Acq. 1934. RF 2312

Bernini dominated the triumphant period of
Roman Baroque. As stage-manager of pontifical
extravaganzas, he breathed dynamic energy into all
his creations, and achieved an ambitious synthesis
of all the arts - architecture, painting and
sculpture. Commissioned in 1667 to decorate the
Ponte San Angelo which straddles the Tiber
opposite the Hadrian mausoleum, he conceived a
triumphal way, flanked by colossal statues of
angels holding the instruments of the Passion. The
model for the angel holding the crown of thorns
displays all the vitality of Bernini's modelling
- rapid, expressive and contorted. To convey
anguish, Bernini fashioned the flowing, flame-like
draperies into a spiral which leads the eye up to
the expressive but schematized face of the angel.
Bernini himself later carved the great marbles
depicting this angel and the one who carries the
INRI titulus. These were thought so excellent that
they were housed in Sant'Andrea delle Fratte,
while the statues installed on the bridge were
carved by pupils following his models.

Italy **Sculpture**

Antonio CANOVA
1757-1822

351 Eros and Psyche

Rome, 1793

Marble group. H 1.55 m; W 1.68 m; D 1.01 m

Château de Villier. Entered the Louvre

before 1824. MR 1777

Canova revived classical art in Italy; schooled in
Venice and active in Rome, he was, in his time,
the dominating figure in European art. A master

at marble, he sculpted great tombs, Napoleon in the Classical style, heroic Roman gods and delicate nymphs. This depiction of Eros reviving Psyche, who was put to sleep forever by inhaling a magic perfume, is as much an allusion to the legend of Psyche, the immortal soul of Platonic myth, as it is a hymn to love. Avoiding academicism, Canova constructs a pyramid out of the entwined bodies, animated by the delicate arrangement of limbs undulating in the light. The transparency of the white marble adds poetry to a group that was the fruit of long deliberation (the model dates from 1787), and then copied by Canova himself for Prince Youssoupoff.

Germanic Countries

With the exception of the fine 12th century *Christ on the Cross* from Bavaria, the Germanic sculpture collection in the Louvre dates essentially from the 15th and 16th centuries and reflects the evolution of style from International Gothic through to the Renaissance.

At the beginning of the 15th century the so-called "Soft Style" *(Weicher Stil)*, characterized by smoothness and refinement was at its height; the Salzburg *Virgin and Child* is a good example of it. At the same time more acerbic tendencies were present, in which Rhineland mysticism expressed, in angular lines, the torment of the late Middle-Ages. The enigmatic "Master of the Rimini Altarpiece", whose large pietà in alabaster is in the Louvre, exemplifies the subtle mixture of delicacy and harshness. Late Gothic *(Spätgotic)* was the name given to the stylistic renewal which mingled realist tendencies with an imaginative lyricism that swelled and contracted forms at will. The Louvre possesses examples of this style from several regions: *The Virgin of Issenheim* **352** from the Upper Rhine; the *Deacon* attributed to the Master of the Kefermarkt altarpiece from Austria; works by the great sculptor Riemenschneider from Franconia; and finally, from Swabia, the *Praying Christ in the Garden*, the *Group of Prelates* from the workshop of Daniel Mauch and the famous *Magdalene* **354** by Gregor Erhart.

352 Virgin and Child

*Upper Rhine, end of the
15th century*

Statue, limewood.

H 1.72 m; W 0.76 m; D 0.495 m

Acq. 1924. RF 1833

Probably from the famous Antonite Convent in Issenheim near Colmar, this great sculpture is one of the most famous examples of Germanic "late Gothic". With limewood, which is a soft wood, the sculptors who adopted this energetic and sometimes mystical style were able to apply their technical virtuosity to rendering ample draperies with sharp angles and deep hollows; sometimes they billow out in arabesques - as here, on the right leg - to break lower down, here on the crescent moon which alludes to the Woman of the Apocalypse. The arched, sinuous silhouette of the Virgin, enveloped in her voluminous cloak, is one of a group of works from the Basel workshops which were scattered between Freiburg-in-Brisgau and Freiburg in Switzerland.

Tilman RIEMENSCHNEIDER
c. 1460-1531

353 Virgin of the Annunciation

Würzburg, end of the 15th century

Statue, marble with polychrome highlights.

H 0.53 m; W 0.40 m; D 0.19 m

Acq. 1904. RF 1384

Riemenschneider was the great master of Würzburg. He was both an artist and a public figure in his town, head of a workshop which counted numerous artisans and apprentices, and was known throughout Franconia, Thuringen and Saxony. This *Virgin*, which comes from the church of St. Peter in Erfurt, Thuringen, is typical of his lyrical, sensitive art in which South German late Gothic reached its apogee. All the salient features of the style are there: the tender, delicately idealized expression, the slim stature adopted for the female figure, the refinement expressed through her delicate fingers, the slight wave in the hair and the fluid opulence of the cascading draperies enclosing the silhouette of a very young girl.

Gregor ERHART
d. 1540

354 St. Mary Magdalene

Augsburg, beginning of the 16th century
Statue, polychrome limewood.
H 1.77 m; W 0.44 m; D 0.43 m
Acq. 1902. RF 1338

This statue, which used to be known as *La belle Allemande*, depicts the repentant Magdalene as an ascetic, clad only in her own hair, who was assumed into heaven by the angels. The Assumption of the redeemed sinner was a favourite theme in 15th century Italy and Germany, one which Dürer helped to popularize through his etchings. Erhart himself was probably inspired by a print.

Gregor Erhart introduced a truthfulness to the human form into a tradition still marked by the linear sophistication displayed in the long locks of hair, with a rounded and serene feminine type which still conforms to the Gothic ideal. The body is pivoted in a slight *contrapposto*. The saint who gives herself up after renouncing the world is delineated with a grace that may owe something to contact with the Renaissance.

Germanic countries **Sculpture**

Attributed to Dietrich SCHRO
Known from 1545-1568

355 **Ottheinrich**
Count and Elector Palatine
(1502-1559)

Mainz, around 1556-1559

Statuette, alabaster.

H 0.155 m; W 0.155 m; D 0.16 m

Gift of C Sauvageot. 1856. DA 204

This precious image of the patron and collector Ottheinrich conveys something of the power and character of the man who built the Renaissance wing of the castle at Heidelberg to house the Palatine Library which he created.

Low Countries

The Low Countries were dominated by a Gothic art of two opposing tendencies; anecdotal and picturesque as in the altarpieces which are the best known and the most represented, or bold and angular in isolated statues. Works from the Southern Low Countries in the 15th and 16th centuries are the most abundant, often identified by an engraver's point, with a mallet indicating Brussels, a hand indicating Antwerp, and three stakes indicating Mechelen. At the same time, certain works give us an idea of work in the Northern Low Countries - the *Virgin and Child* attributed to Jan Nude, the relief of the *Nativity* and the imposing *St. Leonard* attributed to the Master of Elsloo. A more decorative Renaissance style succeeded this period, illustrated by the *Calvary* relief by Willem Van den Broek, and the gravestone by Jean de Coronmeus.

Northern Mannerism is represented only in the spiralling group by Achiaan De Vries [358], but the arrival of the Baroque, brought back from Italy by travelling sculptors like Duquesnoy, Delcour, and Quellien, is well documented by the large busts of the *Witsen* and by a suite of little terracotta models.

356 Calvary Virgin

Brabant, end of the 15th century

Statue, oak.

H 1.63 m; W 0.57 m; D 0.38 m

Probably from the rood-screen of the collegiate church of Sainte-Gertrude de Nivelles.

Acq. 1890. RF 822

The wooden Calvary, composed of Christ on the cross, at the foot of which stand the Virgin and St. John, often surmount glory beams or rood-screens at the entrance to the choir in churches. Here the Virgin is in tears, her face half-hidden by a fringed veil; she crumples a handkerchief in her right hand. This expression of grief is comparable to the tragic, but restrained expression on altarpieces painted by Flemish "Primitives". The considerable pathos is increased by the Virgin's static pose, and the steeply falling drapery with its folds breaking in sharp angles, but devoid of any gratuitous or decorative effect. There is complete coherence between expression, form and volume.

357 Altar-piece of the Passion (detail)

Antwerp, beginning of the 16th century

Gilt and polychrome wood.

H 2.03 m; W 2.15 m; D 0.265 m

Church of Coligny (Marne).

Acq. 1922. RF 1769

At the end of the 15th and in the 16th centuries, sculpted altarpieces were produced in abundance at Antwerp. The workshops branded the image of a hand on to their products as a seal of quality.

Exported abroad, the altarpieces were made up of small juxtaposed compartments, set in a case with painted shutters, here missing. The central Crucifixion, surrounded by a depiction of six sacraments, surmounts the Adoration of the Shepherds and of the Magi. The side compartments depict the Carrying of the Cross and the Descent from the Cross, which in turn surmounted other episodes from the Passion on the archivolts. The composition is deliberately dense and uses figures in different scales; the decorative elegance of the clothing and the adherence to the architectural formulas of flamboyant Gothic are also typical of the rich and picturesque effects of art from Antwerp.

Adriaan DE VRIES
1546-1626

358 Mercury and Psyche

Prague, 1593
Group in bronze. H 2.15 m; W 0.92 m; D 0.72 m
Collection of the French Crown.
Entered the Louvre around 1877.
MR 3270

At the end of 16th century and at the beginning of the 17th, the court of Emperor Rudolph II at Prague enjoyed a period of feverish artistic creativity thanks to the presence of some of the most famous European Mannerists. The Dutchman Adriaan De Vries, who trained in Florence under Giambologna, executed two pendant groups for Prague Castle, *Psyche carried by Cupids* and this one, *Psyche borne by Mercury to Olympus* where she rejoined Eros. Seized as booty by the Swedish troops in 1648, the first of these is now in Stockholm while the second, a diplomatic gift, entered the ministerial collections before embellishing the royal parks of Versailles and then Marly. The grand Mannerist spiral animates the group which owes its serpentine line and sense of space to the creations of Giambologna.

The Netherlands **Sculpture**

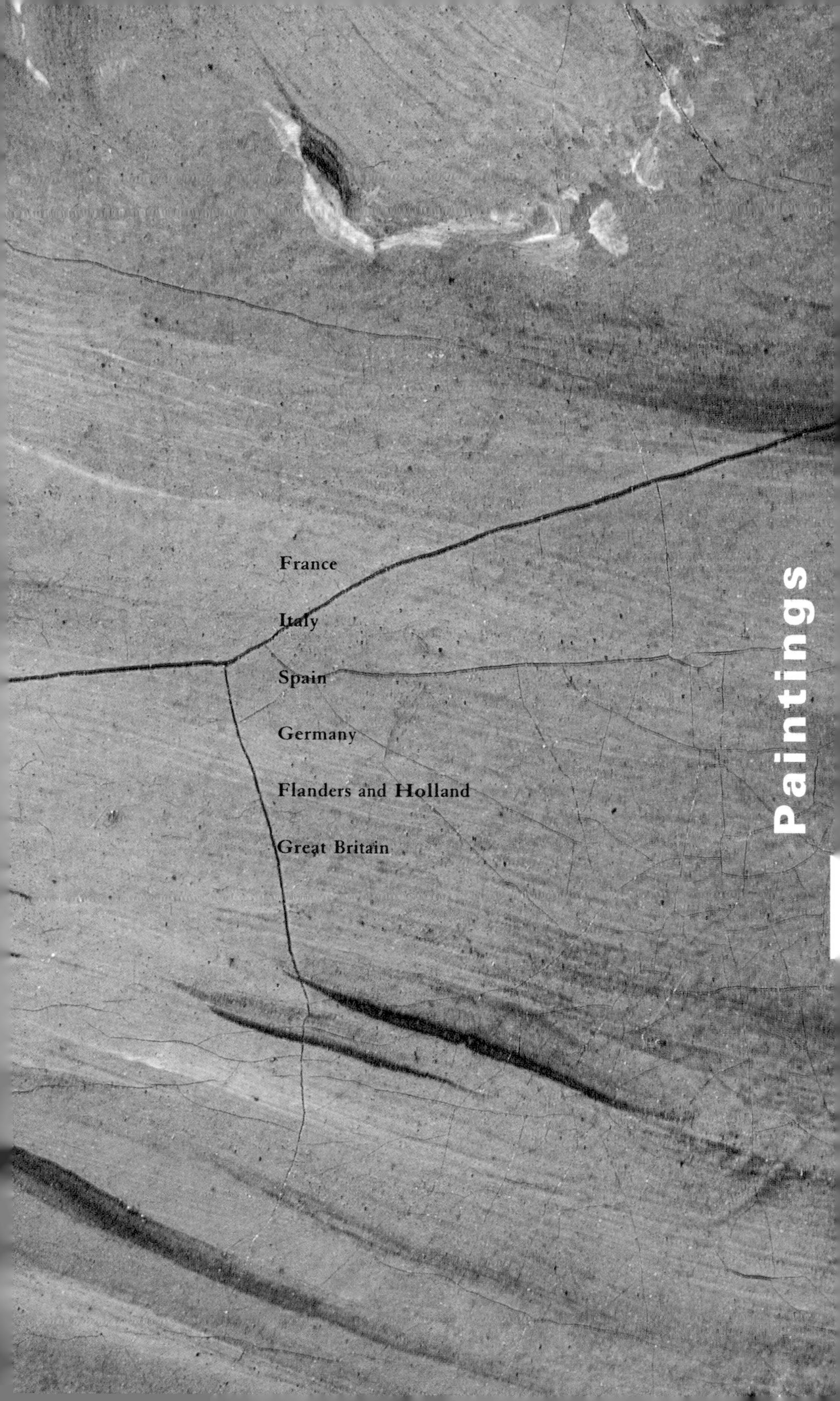

France

Italy

Spain

Germany

Flanders and Holland

Great Britain

Paintings

Introduction

There are over 6000 European paintings inside the Louvre, dating from the late 13th century to the mid-19th century. Despite the predominance of French paintings - almost two thirds of the collection - and some major gaps in foreign schools, the Louvre collections are unique for their uncompromising eclecticism. This was precisely the intention from around 1750, when the idea first emerged of giving the French nation the chance to see the Crown paintings which were scattered throughout royal residences or relegated to storage. The Comte d'Angiviller, administrative Director of Arts under Louis XVI, devoted much time to establishing the museum in the *Grande Galerie* of the Louvre. He also filled gaps in the royal collections which traditionally favoured the French, Italian and Flemish schools - linked by history and geography - and acquired other works, Dutch for the most part. The Spanish school, which was barely represented, acquired its first jewel, *The Young Beggar* **136** by Murillo. A few German masterpieces entering the royal collections during the 17th century completed the European panorama. Under the French Revolution, Louis XVI's project finally became a reality and the museum was opened to the public in 1793. The massive arrival of new paintings, the result of national requisitions and the spoils of war under the Convention and Empire, increased the diversity of the collection. Most of the works requisitioned from abroad were later returned, and French collections were divided out among the museums of France. But the experience impressed curators of the Louvre with the desire to reflect all the artistic developments of Europe and at the same time retain an exhaustive repository of French painting. The evolution of taste, the long-lasting fascination with Spain, and then with the Early Masters and English painting, not to mention the development of the discipline of art history, were all to contribute to the continuing comprehensive nature of the Department of Paintings, which as early as 1794, was organized into national schools for the benefit of visitors.

While the Louvre's collection of French paintings remains unsurpassed, interest in the origins of French art trailed behind later periods in the Louvre. The inclusion of French easel painting from its 14th century origins to the early 17th century is relatively recent. The *Portrait of François I* by Jean Clouet is an exception having been in the royal collection from the time it was painted. The makings of what now is the greatest collection of works of the French early masters or "Primitives" and the School of Fontainebleau began no earlier than the 19th century. The French school gained prominence with the Sun King, Louis XIV. He was an inveterate collector. Turning against his father whose patronage was sparse, he became the first king to develop a royal collection, proclaiming Classicism as its aesthetic, with three artists, Poussin, Claude Gelée and Le Brun favoured above all others. The king was well aware of Poussin's genius, which served as a model for the Academy that henceforth dominated artistic life. He acquired thirty-one of the thirty-eight Poussins now in the Louvre, no less than ten paintings by Claude Gellée, and virtually all the work of Le Brun. Buying up the remaining contents of official painters' studios, the work of Lebrun (followed by Mignard) became the property of the monarchy, on their deaths. Add to this the work of other contemporaries such as Perrier, Bourdon and Stella, and we can see how much French Classicism owes to Louis XIV. Louis XVI was to finish the work he began. Under his reign, Le Sueur entered the royal collection with his two great cycles (for the Chartreuse in Paris, and the Hôtel Lambert), which set the pattern for the subtle and refined "Parisian Attic" paintings of the mid-17th century. Revolutionary requisitions, which brought most of the Champaignes to the Louvre, virtually completed this classical collection which was, even early on, unparalleled, and increased only with chance acquisitions. The other

France **Paintings**

side to 17th century painting, the painting of reality, was revealed much later, during the mid-19th century, with a pioneering bequest to the Louvre by Dr La Caze who was fascinated by Le Nain. The complex path from Le Nain to La Tour, via paintings of still life, has been traced by historians. A series of works marked by the acquisition in 1988 of *Saint Thomas* (a French national subscription), illustrate the varied registers of La Tour, a painter whose passage from clear Caravaggiesque works, to his mysterious night scenes has at last been traced.

Unlike his contemporaries, Louis XV was no collector. There is not one Watteau or Fragonard at Versailles. Commissions by the administrative Director of Arts, the Marquis de Marigny, from Chardin to Vernet *(Views of the French Ports)*, history paintings ordered by the Gobelins and the decoration of royal residences (Boucher, Carle Van Loo) barely compensated for the uncommon indifference of the king. Acquisitions by the Marquise de Pompadour, the dictator of Rococo taste, were private and were dispersed at auction on the death of their heir, as were the collections of the most active patrons of the time. Despite its wealth of work by old Academicians (Watteau's *Pilgrimage to Cythera* **379**, Chardin's *The Skate* **382** etc.), the 18th century owes its wide representation in the Louvre to a providential gift by the greatest French collector, La Caze. His bequest in 1869 brought most of the Rococo masterpieces to the Louvre, principally a wonderful series of eight paintings by Watteau, the *Pierrot* **380** amongst them, thirteen Chardins and nine Fragonards.

The reign of Louis XVI, who showed little fondness for the art of his time, was marked by ambitious commissions from the administrative Director of Arts, the Comte d'Angiviller, in an effort to revive history painting. The Louvre still possesses the most remarkable of the great Salon compositions, beginning with the *Oath of the Horatii* **387** and David's *Brutus*.

After a brief break during the Revolution, this commission policy resumed under the Empire. The huge history paintings of the Napoleonic legend are perfect examples, *Bonaparte visiting the Plague Striken at Jaffa* by Gros and *The Consecration of the Emperor Napoleon* **391** and these rooms of the Louvre are invaluable for a proper understanding of that period.

The Restoration brought the establishment, in 1818, of the *Musée du Luxembourg,* the first museum of contemporary art, where most of the great classical paintings were displayed before entering the Louvre. Works by artists such as Girodet, Guérin, Gérard, Prud'hon, were bought regularly by Vivant Denon and the Comte de Forbin until 1830. The *Raft of the Medusa* by Géricault was acquired, not without problems, in 1825 by the Musées Français, proof that, at least until the middle of the century, new tendencies could be followed and that there was room for the boldest painters, Delacroix above all. The task of completing this series of history paintings with portraits fell to contemporaries. Three large bequests early this century helped to make up for the deficiencies of a buying policy which had become increasingly obessessed by academic painting, and had overlooked Courbet, Millet and Daumier; Thomy Thiéry (1902) introduced the Barbizon school, Moreau-Nélaton (1927) his Corots, and Chauchard (1909) brought Millet's *Angélus.* Courbet's *Studio* was not acquired until 1920, by public subscription. However, the two latter paintings now belong to the *Musée d'Orsay* where, with a few exceptions, works of artists born after 1820 are exhibited.

359 Portrait of Jean le Bon
(1319-1364), King of France
from 1350

c. 1350

Wood panel. H 0.60 m; W 0.445 m

Extended loan from the French National Library,

1925. RF 2490

The second king of the house of Valois had
a difficult reign marked by the defeat of Poitiers,
captivity in London, and the revolt of Etienne
Marcel and the Jacquerie. His portrait has a
special place in the history of easel painting.
Believed to be one of the oldest works of the
French school, it is also the first individual profile
portrait known in Europe.
It may reflect an earlier lost prototype by one
of the great Siennese masters working in Avignon,
Simone Martini or Matteo Giovannetti.

Henri BELLECHOSE
*Painter to the Duke of Burgundy
from 1415 to 1440/44*

360 The St. Denis Altar-piece

1416

Wood transferred to canvas. H 1.62; W 2.11 m

From the *Charteuse de Champmol.*

Gift of Frédéric Reiset, 1863. MI 674

To the left of the Trinity, St. Denis, apostle to the
Gauls, is taking the last communion from the
hand of Christ; to the right, he undergoes
decapitation as a martyr, with his two acolytes
Rustique and Eleuthère. The picture was painted
for the *Chartreuse de Champmol* in 1415-1416 by

the last representative of the "Franco-Flemish" school which flourished between 1380 and 1420 at the court of the Dukes of Burgundy at Dijon. Against a brilliant gold background, the scenes combine realism with the graceful stylization of international Gothic.

Jean FOUQUET
c. 1420 - 1477/1481

361 **Portrait of Charles VII**
(1403-1461), King of France
from 1422

c. 1445-1450
Wood panel. H 0.86 m; **W 0.71 m**
Acq. 1838, INV 9106

The inscription on the original frame of the painting records the fact that Charles VII, *le très victorieux roy de France,* liberated France from occupation by the English. This is one of the earliest remaining works by Jean Fouquet, the great painter of 15th century France, who invented a new type of official portrait with this lifesize, three-quarter-view bust. While the confined framing is still Gothic, the picture breaks definitively with tradition in the new depth given to the king's body.

Enguerrand QUARTON
Originally from the diocese of Laon.
Active in Provence
between 1444 and 1466

362 The Villeneuve-lès-Avignon Pietà

c. 1455

Wood panel. H 1.63 m; L. 2.185 m

Gift of the *Société des Amis du Louvre*, 1905.

RF 1569

Nothing was known about this picture other than its provenance from Villeneuve-lès-Avignon. It has now been attributed to the most illustrious member of the 15th century school of Provence, author of the no less celebrated *Coronation of the Virgin* (Museum of Villeneuve-lès-Avignon). Around the stiff body of Christ, the praying donor and St. John, the Virgin and Magdalen have an austerity and monumentality about them which belongs to the French sculptural tradition, interpreted by Quarton into the clearly delineated, heavily-shaded, stark forms of the school of Avignon.

Jean HEY, known as the
MASTER OF MOULINS
Working between 1480 and 1500
for the Bourbons
and the French Court

363 **Presumed Portrait of Madeleine
de Bourgogne, Lady of Laage, presented
by St. Mary Magdalen**

c. 1490
Wood panel. H 0.56 m; X 0.40 m
Acq. 1904. RF 1521

Last remnant of a lost diptych or triptych, this
panel shows St. Mary Magdalen and a donor
wearing a "tinder box" broach, a symbol of the
house of Burgundy. She is presumed to be
Madeleine de Bourgogne, bastard daughter of
Philippe the Good, who after her marriage resided
at the court of the Dukes of Bourbon at Moulins.
This would have been the most likely spot for her
to have been painted by this great late 15th
century artist. He was known as the "Master of
Moulins" from the triptych in Moulins cathedral,
and is now thought to have been a painter of
Flemish origin, Jean Hey.

364 **Diana the Huntress**

School of Fontainebleau
Mid-16th century
Canvas. H 1.91 m; W 1.32 m
Acq. 1840. INV 445

Of unknown authorship, the *Diana the Huntress* is
the archetype of the Bellifontain ideal flourishing
in 16th century France, under the influence of
Italian masters summoned by François I to the
Château of Fontainebleau from 1530 (Rosso,
Primatice). Some have seen this as a metaphorical
portrait of Diane de Poitiers (1499-1566), mistress
of Henri II, during the flourishing period around
1500, when the Château d'Anet was being built. It
testifies to a taste for mythological nudes, in which
drawing and a Mannerist-style elongated and
contorted body are predominant.

France **Paintings**

François CLOUET
d. 1572

365 **Portrait of Pierre Quthe**
(1519-after 1588, apothecary)

1562

Wood panel. H 0.91 m; W 0.70 m

Gift of the *Société des Amis du Louvre*, 1908

RF 1719

François Clouet painted his friend Pierre Quthe in 1562, at 43 years of age, as the Latin inscription indicates, and it is one of the few works signed by the artist. Clouet concentrates on the psychological study of the man, but does not forget his social position, placing a herbal at his side, which refers to the medicinal plants the apothecary grew in his Paris garden. The austere elegance of the pose suggests a knowledge of the Italian Mannerists, and the controlled light and meticulous technique point to the Flemish masters. It was at the junction of these two influences that François Clouet, in the footsteps of his father Jean, developed the new ingredients of French portraiture.

17th century

VALENTIN DE BOULOGNE
1594-1632

366 Concert

c. 1628-1630(?)

Canvas. H 1.75 m; W. 2.16 m

Coll. Louis XV, INV 8252

The concert subject and use of light and shade (*chiaroscuro*) are taken from Caravaggio, and this French artist was one of his most faithful followers in Rome. However, the master's brutal realism is filtered by the pupil's greater solemnity and elegance, and there is a subtler use of colour.

Lubin BAUGIN
c. 1612-1663

367 **Still Life with Wafer Biscuits**

c. 1630-1635
Wood panel. H 0.41; W 0.52 m
Acq. 1954. RF 1954-23

Four still lives signed *Baugin,* two of which are in
the Louvre, offer the basis of what is known of
the best 17th century French still life painter who
has now been identified with the religious painter,
Lubin Baugin. Only the subject itself derives from
Flemish art. The simplicity and geometric
arrangement of the composition reflect a current
in French art under Louis XIII which is sober and
austere and has occasionally been linked with
Protestant ideas or Jansenism.

Simon VOUET
1590-1649

368 **Allegory of Wealth**

c. 1640
Canvas. H 1.70 m; W 1.24 m
Collection of Louis XIII. INV 8500

Vouet painted this clever allegory for
a royal chateau, possibly the *Château-
Neuf* of Saint-Germain-en-Laye,
whence come the Louvre's *Charity*
and *Virtue.* The subject, related to
temptation and a rejection of worldly goods, is
resumed under its traditional title, *Wealth.* With
generous forms of the figures, the subtle arabesque
of drapery, and brilliant colour, the picture is at
the highpoint of a lyrical and decorative style
which Vouet developed after abandoning the
Caravaggiesque style he learnt in Rome, and,
when Louis XIII summoned him back to France in
1627, he imposed this new manner on the French
school.

Georges de LA TOUR
1593-1652

369 **Christ with St. Joseph in the Carpenter's Shop**

c. 1640

Canvas. H 1.37 m; W 1.02 m

Gift of Percy Moore Turner, 1948. RF 1948-27

Provincial painters in France continued working in a Caravaggiesque style up until the middle of the 17th century. Born in Lunéville, La Tour was appointed *"peintre ordinaire"* to Louis XIII in 1639, and gave his own very personal and pseudo-archaic gloss to the style in a series of "night scenes" with religious themes, his mysticism expressing itself in a simplified use of strongly directed light. In this picture, with its tightly-packed forms, the candle flame lights a dramatic and humble setting in which St. Joseph passes on his worldly knowledge to the young Jesus, with a painful premonition in his eyes of the tortures of the Cross.

Louis (or Antoine?) LE NAIN
c. 1600/1610-1648

370 **The Peasant Family**

Canvas. H 1.13 m; W 1.59 m

Acq. with Arthur Pernolet bequest, 1915, RF 2081

It is still not known precisely which of the three Le Nain brothers (most probably Louis or Antoine) was the author of a series of paintings with peasant subjects. The series is prominent among Western art of the genre, for its exceptional quality and solemnity, its muted colours and the austere dignity of the figures, fixed in their attentive, stilled poses. This scene, the largest of the series, has the universality of a classical text. Wine and bread are given a emphasis that is redolent with symbolism.

Nicolas POUSSIN
1594-1665

371 The Carrying off of the Sabines

c. 1637-1638

Canvas. H 1.59 m; W 2.06 m

Painted for the Cardinal Omodei.

Coll. of Louis XIV. INV 7290

Established in Rome in 1624, making only one trip to Paris in 1640-1642, Poussin posed as a master of the Classical ideal, founded upon an erudite knowledge of the art and literature of the ancients. He concentrated on rigorous compositions in the easel painting format for a avid circle of collectors (in this case, the Cardinal Omodei). This picture is a powerful illustration of the word *phrygien*, that "vehement, furious, very severe form of expression" which Poussin thought befitted "the horrors of war". On the left we see Romulus, founder of Rome, overseeing the abduction of Sabine women during a festival, in order to marry off his new citizens.

Claude GELLÉE, known as
Claude LE LORRAIN
c. 1602-1682

**372 The Disembarkation of Cleopatra
at Tarsus**

1642

Canvas. H 1.19 m; W 1.68 m

Coll. of Louix XIV. INV 4716

In an imaginary architecture
suggestive of ancient splendours,
Cleopatra disembarks at Tarsus intending to seduce
Mark Anthony and, in so doing, submit him to the
will of the Egyptians (41 BC). The moral portent of
the picture is made explicit by a pendant on the
subject of *The Consecration of David by Samuel*
(Louvre), which contrasts the destiny of a humble
boy crowned king, with the queen's ambition.
Ancient history was not, however, much more than
a pretext for this landscape painter from the
Lorraine who moved to Rome; he uses it to animate
a sun-drenched sea port, which is a perfect synthesis
of the Bolognesian classical ideal and the luminosity
of the Italianizing Dutch school.

Eustache LE SUEUR
1616-1655

373 Clio, Euterpe and Talia

c. 1652

Wood panel. H 1.30 m; W 1.30 m

Painted for the hôtel Lambert in Paris

Coll. of Louis XVI. INV. 8057

No real idea of 17th century painting can be had
without reference to the great ensembles which
once decorated the walls of newly built Parisian
hôtels particuliers. Although dismantled in 1776, the
decorations Le Sueur painted for the hôtel
Lambert on the *Ile Saint-Louis* are one of the most
complete ensembles to survive (13 paintings in the
Louvre). This panel shows the Muses of History,
Music and Comedy, which formed a Concert of

nine Muses with four more panels, in the alcove of
the bedroom of Mme Lambert de Thorigny.

Nicolas POUSSIN
1594-1665

374 **Summer on Ruth and Booz**

c. 1660-1664

Canvas. H 1.18 m; W 1.60m

Painted for the Duc de Richelieu.

Coll. of Louis XIV. INV 7304

Summer is one of *The Four Seasons* painted for the
Duc de Richelieu between 1660 and 1664.
Together they represent a major achievement in
the historical landscape genre. The theme of the
Seasons is linked with a Biblical story, symbolising
the ages of man, or major steps in the history of
the world. The summer harvest in which Ruth
and Booz meet recalls Christ's union with the
Church and thus the Christian era. But Poussin's
message to us, on the eve of his death, consists
above all of a timeless meditation on relations
between man and nature, in this case productive,
and in *The Deluge,* hostile.

Philippe de CHAMPAIGNE
1602-1674

375 The Ex-Voto of 1662

1662

H 1.65 m; W 2.29 m

Given by the artist to the *Abbaye de Port-Royal* in Paris. Seized during French Revolution. INV 1138

The *Ex-Voto* was painted as an act of thanksgiving for the miraculous healing of the artist's daughter, Catherine, a nun in the Jansenist convent of Port-Royal in Paris. She recovered from a serious illness after prayers held in the form of a novena by the community. Champaigne has depicted the moment when the Mother Superior, Agnes Arnauld, abbess of Port-Royal, who is praying with the sick nun, has a revelation of her imminent healing. This double portrait stands out from the enormous religious output of this Brussels painter after, he moved to France in 1621, for its austere, grandiloquent vision, well served by an impeccable Flemish technique.

Charles LE BRUN
1619-1690

376 Alexander in Babylon

1661-1665

Canvas. H 4.50 m; W 7.07 m

Collection of Louis XIV. INV 2898

Finished in 1665, this was the first of four huge canvasses painted between 1661 and 1673 on the history of Alexander by Louis XIV's principal Director of Arts. Standing on a chariot pulled by an elephant, Alexander makes his triumphal entry into a magnificent Babylon, as the myth describes (the event occurred in 331 BC). With their skilful allusion to military glory and the virtues of monarchy, the four paintings which had no specific destination were a pretext for Le Brun to give expression to an epic vein of which he was

the most brilliant exponent in France, before he painted the Galerie des Glaces at Versailles.

18th Century

Hyacinthe RIGAUD
1659-1743

377 Portrait of Louis XIV

(1638-1715), king of France
from 1643

1701

Canvas. H 2.77 m; W 1.84 m

Coll. of Louis XIV. INV 7492

Intended as a gift to Philip V, grandson of Louis XIV and King of Spain from 1700, this portrait of the Sun King was considered so fine at the Court of Versailles that it remained in France. Thriving on his royal commissions, Rigaud caught the majestic and grandiloquent tone of a monarch who became a symbol of absolute power. At sixty-three years of age, Louis XIV is shown in ceremonial robes with the instruments of his investiture: the ermine-lined mantle emblazoned with fleur-de-lys, white stockings and slippers, the sword "Joyeuse" and his crown. The sceptre and hand of justice belonged, however, to Henri IV. The head was painted from life, while costume and background were composed in the studio.

Nicolas de LARGILLIÈRE
1656-1746

378 Family Portrait

Canvas. H 1.49 m; W 2.00 m

Gift of Dr Louis La Caze, 1869. MI 1085

An artistic battle of almost thirty years duration
ended around 1700, with the victory of the
"Rubensians" who favoured colour, over
the "Poussinists", the defenders of drawing.
Established in Paris in 1682, Largillière along with
Charles de la Fosse, put into practice the colour
theories of Roger de Piles. In this portrait painter's
mature work, the copper gleam of the landscape,
the tonal harmony and the reflections on the
costumes are evidence of his debt to Van Dyke
and Titian. The conscious influence is
accompanied by a new conception of the portrait
which is not so hieratic, with poses which are
more relaxed and integrated into the setting.
These qualities are typical of French art under
the Regency.

Jean-Antoine WATTEAU
1684-1721

379 The Pilgrimage to Cythera

1717

Canvas. H 1.29 m; W 1.94 m

Collection of the Academy. INV 8525

Genre painting came back into favour when the
Academy admitted Watteau to its ranks in 1717
on the presentation of this work, the subject of
which was so novel that the term *fête galante* was
coined to describe it. Drawing its inspiration from
the theatre, the picture shows lovers in party
dress - some wearing the pilgrim's hooded
cape - coming to seek love on the island of
Cythera, under the statue of its goddess, Venus. In
an iridescent landscape which owes much to
Venetian painting, allegory is caught up in the

swirl of couples in a reverie; a new and less
didactic interpretation of Titan's elegiac mode.

Jean-Antoine WATTEAU
1684-1721

380 Pierrot also known as **Gilles**

c. 1718-1719

Canvas. H 1.84 m; W 1.49 m

Gift of Dr Louis La Caze, 1869. MI 1121

One of the few things we can be sure about, in this
famous but enigmatic work, is the fact that Gilles
is a Pierrot. Watteau may have painted it as a sign
for the café run by the former actor, Belloni, who
made his name as a Pierrot. The model, a friend
or another actor, is unknown. Standing with his
arms dangling at his sides, with a dreamy, naïve
look on his face, the moonstruck Pierrot stands

out monumentally and idiosyncratically against a leafy Italianate background. At the foot of the mound, reminiscent of a fairground stage, four half-hidden figures - the Doctor on his donkey, Léandre, Isabelle and the Capitaine - contribute to the singularity of the composition and the poetic drama.

François LEMOYNE
1688-1737

381 Hercules and Omphale

1724
Canvas. H 1.84 m; W 1.49 m
Gift of Dr Louis La Caze, 1869. MI 1086

Lemoyne was the most important of the history painters working during Louis XV's youth. Like his contemporary Watteau, he was to die young, after the ambitious decoration of the ceiling of Hercules at Versailles, which earned him the title of First Painter to the King in 1736. His knowledge of Venetian painting, completed by a trip to Italy in 1723 where he painted *Hercules and Omphale,* encouraged his use of a lighter palette and richer brushwork, appropriate to a celebration of the female nude, which after his example became the favorite theme of the generation of Boucher and Carle Van Loo.

Jean-Siméon CHARDIN
1699-1779

382 The Skate

Before 1728
Canvas. H 1.14 m; W 1.46 m
Collection of the Academy. INV 3197

Despite a rigid hierarchy of genres in which still-life held a very humble position, from his youth Chardin earned a reputation as a great artist, with a technical "magic" which excited Diderot's

admiration. The Academy was quick to recognize him. Contrary to custom, Chardin was made an associate and full member on the same day in 1728 because both *The Skate,* which was kept as an admission work, and *The Buffet,* surpassed the finest Flemish examples of the genre (Jan Fyt for example). A magnificent piece of painting, the work in its rigorous construction looks forward to the small and more austere still lifes of his maturity (such as *The Tobacco Shop, The Brioche,* and *The Silver Goblet*).

François BOUCHER
1703-1770

383 Morning Coffee

1739
Canvas. H 0.815 m; W 0.655 m
Gift of Dr Achille Malécot, 1895. RF 926

For a brief period, between 1739 and 1746, this painter of amorous mythical scenes extended his repertoire to contemporary genre scenes, influenced by 17th century Dutch masters and more directly by Jean-François de Troy. This picture describes in detail, with a dazzlingly fresh, graceful style, a scene of daily life in a Parisian family - like that of the painter himself, who was at that time father of two small sons - devoting themselves to the new craze for coffee. The painter of happiness has captured, with a gentler eye than Chardin's, a certain *art de vivre* which is vivid to us still.

Jean-Baptiste PERRONNEAU
1715-1783

384 **Portrait of Madame
de Sorquainville**

1749

Canvas. H 1.01 m; W 0.81 m

Gift of D David-Weill, 1937. RF 1937-8

The elegance of the costume and refined pose of
the sitter recall the work of Nattier. However,
what remains impressed upon us is its
psychological insight which is typical of a current
which developed in France during the mid–18th
century with Maurice Quentin de la Tour and
Perronneau, who were more interested in the
sitter's character than in flattery. The artist has
borrowed from his favorite technique of pastel,
painting in chalky tones and with thinly–layered
feathery brushwork which leaves some areas barely
finished.

Jean-Honoré FRAGONARD
1732-1806

385 **The Bathers**

Canvas. H 0.64 m; W 0.80 m

Gift of Dr Louis La Caze, 1869. MI 1055

The female nude was a constant preoccupation of French Rococo painters. Unlike his master Boucher, Fragonard needed no mythological text as an excuse for painting this gathering of blonde and Rubensian beauties, when he returned from Italy in 1761. Bodies, drapery and a lush natural setting are intermingled in the torrent of thick rapid brushstrokes. These give the picture the dynamic force of a sketch, a quality serving as a springboard for the most unconventional artist of his time.

Jean-Baptiste GREUZE
1725-1805

386 **The Punished Son**

1778
Canvas. H 1.30 m; W 1.63 m
Acq. 1820. INV 5039

Together with its pendant *The Paternal Curse,* this picture illustrates two scenes in a family drama painted by Greuze in 1777 and 1778. Here we see the son returning and lamenting over the death of his father, which he provoked by leaving for the army. All the resources of great history painting, by Poussin in particular, were used by this artist at the service of a new genre combining contemporary dress with a love of pathos. Greuze's effusive, patriarchal and "pastoral" moral didacticism, described a new bourgeois art in which the ideals of the age of Reason triumphed.

France **Paintings**

Louis DAVID

1748-1825

387 The Oath of the Horatii

1784

Canvas. H 3.30 m; W 4.25 m

Commissioned by Louis XVI. INV 3692

The three brothers, the Horatii, chosen by Rome
to defy the champions of the town of Alba called
the Curiaces, are taking an oath that they will win
or die and are receiving swords from their father.
Like Corneille in his tragedy *Horace,* David
contrasts the stoic resolution of the warriors,
underlined by strict geometry and strident colour,
with the gentle line of the women which expresses
their suffering. Painted in 1784 and shown
in Paris the following year, this painting earned
David a European reputation as uncontested leader
of the Neoclassical movement.

Hubert ROBERT
1733-1808

388 The Pont du Gard

1787
Canvas. H 2.42 m; W 2.42
Commissioned by Louis XVI. INV 7650

The fashion for archeology in the 18th century met a new interest in the national heritage when the Direction des Bâtiments commissioned Robert to paint for Louis XVI's appartments, at Fontainebleau, four decorative paintings on the subject of antiquities in France. The famous aqueduct of Agrippa, built in 19 BC to take water from the river Gard to Nîmes, figured in a prominent place. A follower of Pannini and Piranèse, this indefatigable painter of ruins, who deserved the success he achieved on his return from Rome in 1765, captures the picturesque details of the site without detracting from the harmonious colour scheme and dynamic force of his composition.

19th Century

Antoine-Jean GROS
1772-1835

389 Napoleon Bonaparte Visiting the Plague Stricken at Jaffa (March 11, 1799)

1804
Canvas. H 5.23 m; W 7.15 m
Commissioned in 1804. INV 5064

Anticipating the huge canvasses that Gros, a pupil of David, devoted to the Napoleonic epic, this picture celebrates General Bonaparte's courage and humanity, visiting the sick without fear of contagion, during the Syrian campaign. The novelty of the theme - a contemporary rather than classical hero - is matched by Gros's development of a style which from 1804 contained all the elements of Romantic painting. We see this here in the strikingly naturalistic bodies, the sense of colour, and in the cultural fascination with the Orient.

Pierre-Paul PRUD'HON
1758-1823

390 **The Empress Josephine**
(1763-1814)

1805

Canvas. H 2.44 m; W 1.79 m

Collection of Napoleon III. Entered the Louvre

in 1879. RF 270

A popular painter during the French Empire, much favoured by Joséphine and later by Marie-Louise, Prud'hon was fond of shrouding his figures in mist in the manner of Leonardo da Vinci and Correggio. This adds to the melancholic charm of his portraits, set in the open air in the English style. Born in Martinique and widow of the General de Beauharnais, Joséphine Tascher de la Pagerie married Bonaparte in 1796. When she did not provide the Emperor with an heir she was abandoned in 1809. Prud'hon depicted her in the grounds of her château at Malmaison in 1805, a year after Napoleon's consecration.

Louis DAVID
1748-1825

391 **The Consecration of the Emperor Napoleon and the Coronation of Empress Josephine**
(December 2, 1804)

1806-1807

Canvas. H 6.21 m; W 9.79 m

Commissioned by Napoleon I. INV 3699

Appointed official painter to the Emperor in December 1804, David was given the task of

commemorating the Coronation festivities
in four huge canvasses, only two of which were
executed (the *Distribution of the Eagles* is at
Versailles). This ceremony took place in the
cathedral of Notre-Dame in Paris. David chose to
show the episode following the actual consecration:
Napoleon crowning Josephine while Pope Pius VII
gives him his blessing. The action is only a small
part of a composition conceived as an enormous
group portrait containing over a hundred figures.

Anne-Louis GIRODET de
ROUSSY-TRIOSON
1767-1824

392 The Entombment of Atala

1808

Canvas. H 2.07 m; W 2.67 m

Acq. 1819. INV 4958

With the help of Father Aubry, the Indian
Chactas is burying Atala, a young Christian girl

who was to take the veil, and who preferred to
poison herself rather than succumb to carnal love.
Girodet's unusual talent, given to cavernous gloom
and spectral forms, was well suited to illustrating
Chateaubriand, who had his novel *Atala* published
in 1801 on his return from America. There is a
similar contained melancholy, a similar belief in
wild but beneficent nature and both men were
ideal exponents of the pre-Romantic sensibility.

Théodore GÉRICAULT
1791-1824

393 The Raft of the Medusa

1819

Canvas. H 4.91 m; W 7.16 m

Acq. 1824. INV 488

Géricault was highly moved by the real-life drama
of 149 shipwrecked sailors from the frigate
"Medusa", abandoned for twelve days on a raft off
the Senegalese coast. To illustrate it he chose the
moment on July 17, 1816 when the 15 survivors

were overcome with despair as the *Argus,* the ship that eventually was to rescue them, sailed off. This was the first time a contemporary news item had been made the subject for a painting on a large scale. The dark subject, matched by the colouring and the macabre though realistic depiction of the corpses, make what was a controversial exhibit of the 1819 Salon, the first epic example of Romanticism.

Eugène DELACROIX
1798-1863

394 The Massacre at Chios

1824

Canvas. H 4.19 m; W 3.54 m

Acq. 1824. INV 3823

The Romantics, Byron especially, keenly espoused the cause of the Greeks under Turkish oppression. The young Delacroix, whose *Dante and Virgil crossing the Styx* had caused a stir at the 1823 Salon, exhibited the following year this cruel episode from the Greek War of Independence, illustrating the savage repression of an uprising on the island of Chios in 1822. Provoking bitter critical divisions, it is a veritable manifesto of Romanticism. Though by no means unimportant, the lavish colours and exotic costumes are secondary to the contemporary subject matter which has political implications (the liberation of the people) and aesthetic undertones (the liberation of form).

France **Paintings**

Eugène DELACROIX
1798-1863

395 Liberty Leading the People
(July 28, 1830)
1830

Canvas. H 2.60; W 3.25 m

Acq. 1831. RF 129

Delacroix was not actively involved in the three
days of July 1830, known as the *Trois Glorieuses,*
which saw out the autocracy of Charles X and
brought in Louis-Philippe's parlementary
monarchy. But liberal and romantic as he was,
he was keen to celebrate the 28 July, when
Parisians took up arms in the vain hope of
restoring the Republic. The allegorical figure of
Liberty waves the tricolour flag and storms the
corpse-ridden barricades with a young combatant
at her side. Realism and epic vision work together.
Reviled by conservatives, the work was bought by

Louis-Philippe at the 1831 Salon. Soon after, it was hidden for fear of inciting public unrest.

Jean-Auguste-Dominique INGRES
1780-1867

396 Louis-François Bertin
(1766-1841)

1832

Canvas. H 1.16 m; W 0.95 m

Acq. 1897. RF 1071

Founder of the *Journal des Débats,* Ingres turned "Monsieur Bertin" into the perfect spokesman of the triumphant bourgeoisie of 1830, who supported his newspaper. The secret of his success lies in the sitter's forthright and commanding pose which Ingres hit upon after much searching, while his model was conversing with a friend: "'Come tomorrow", he told me, "Your portrait's done"'. Finished in under a month, this strikingly vivid portrait which is meticulously painted caused a public outcry at the 1833 Salon, and earned the admiration of the poet and critic Baudelaire. Ingres was, in his eyes, "the only man in France who can really paint portraits".

France **Paintings**

Théodore CHASSÉRIAU
1819-1856

397 Esther at her Toilette

1841

Canvas. H 0.455 m; W 0.355 m

Gift of Baron Arthur Chassériau, 1934. RF 3900

By the time he painted *Esther*, this precocious 22-year-old pupil of Ingres, had already exhibited in five Salons and had visited Italy. Keen to repeat the experience of *Suzanna in the Bath* (Louvre) which had earned him recognition in the 1839 Salon, Chassériau used the Old Testament as a pretext for painting the lavish colour and sensuality of an imaginary Orient. Learning from Ingres' drawing and hieratic models, and from Delacroix's vibrant use of colour, he combined both their approaches with subtlety, adding a charm all his own with, among other things, the languid melancholy of his figures.

Jean-Auguste-Dominique
INGRES
1780-1867

398 The Turkish Bath

1862

Canvas on panel. H 1.10 m; W 1.10 m

Gift of the *Société des Amis du Louvre,* with

Maurice Fenaille, 1911. RF 1934

Completed when he was 82, this composition was the result of many studies **477** which Ingres made from 1807 onwards of female bathers, a theme linking the female nude with Turkish exoticism. His illustrations of the harem might well have been inspired by the *Letters of Lady Montagu* (1764) which he read forty years earlier. The serpentile contours of the bodies and his repeated use of the same model add a note of abstraction to the sensuality of this accumulation of voluptuous flesh, a pure fantasy of an exotic, perfumed Orient which had entranced Europeans for over a century.

Camille COROT
1796-1875

399 The Church of Marissel near Beauvais

1866

Canvas. H 0.55 m; W 0.42 m

Gift of Etienne Moreau-Nélaton, 1906

RF 1642

Familiar with the Beauvais countryside from visits to his painter friend Badin whom he met in Italy, Corot shows the village of Marissel, on the banks of the Thérain, with a fortified church on the hill, which is still standing. Painted before the motif in nine morning sittings during the spring of 1866, the artist's intention was to combine the effects of perspective (the line of trees) with those of light (water reflections). The work owes a lot to the Dutch masters. Corot knew unwavering success during his lifetime. This picture, exhibited in the 1867 Salon, was admired by Queen Victoria and bought for the then substantial sum of 4000 francs by a tailor called Richard.

Italy

Disregarded by Classicists, the "Primitives" or early Italian masters before Leonardo and Raphael were not rediscovered until the end of the 18th century. This was, paradoxically, due to the Neoclassical movement. Under Emperor Napoleon's orders, Vivant Denon, Director of Museums, went to Italy and requisitioned altarpieces by masters ranging from Cimabue to Fra Angelico which went into the Louvre after 1815. But the French vogue for Italian Primitives dates from Napoleon III's acquisition of the Campana collection. Leaving a number to go to the *Musée du Petit Palais* at Avignon, around a hundred pictures entered the Louvre including Uccello's *Battle* 407 and Cosimo Tura's *Pietà* 410. This formed the kernel of the collection, which was subsequently expanded with occasional acquisitions, ranging from Mantegna's *Saint Sebastian* to Piero della Francesca's *Portrait of Malatesta* 406.

The Italian Renaissance, one of the Louvre's

greatest treasures, owes its presence almost entirely to two kings: François I and Louis XIV. The former, a patron of the arts, protector of Leonardo da Vinci and founder of Fontainebleau, housed the most famous works of his time under one roof; among them, the *Mona Lisa* **414** and the *Virgin of the Rocks* **412** by Leonardo, the great *Holy Family* by Raphael and *Charity* **413** by Andrea del Sarto. Louis XIV wisely purchased existing collections belonging to the Cardinal Mazarin and to the banker Jabach, which included works by Correggio, Raphael, Titian and Jules Romain. The Renaissance was thus broadly represented when the Louvre was created in 1793.

The museum kept only a fraction, though significant one, of the immense gains from Napoleonic campaigns, including Veronese's *Wedding Feast at Cana* **423**. Isabella d'Este's collection in the *Château de Richelieu* was seized during the Revolution. The collection, admirable as it is, betrays its origins. Mannerism, and late Mannerist art in particular, is not well represented; it was a period when even Renaissance art had to show evidence of a certain classical approach. Taken with art in the "Grand Manner", Louis XIV was as interested in the great Italian painters as he was in the great French of his century. His acquisition of Mazarin's and Jabach's collections, which came in turn from those of Charles I of England and the Dukes of Mantua, brought Caravaggio and the Bolognese school into the royal collection and their impact was long-lasting. His efforts were completed a century later by the minister, d'Angiviller, who made purchases for Louis XVI with a view to making the future museum more comprehensive.

With the Romantic perpetuation of the idyll of Venice, 19th century interest centred mainly on the 18th century Venetian school. However, 18th century Italian painting is poorly represented, despite an important collection of works by Pannini and the cycle of *Venetian festivals* **430** by Guardi, which was seized during the Revolution. This collection has expanded since the last war

Italy **Paintings**

and, aside from a few paintings by Tiepolo, includes works by Piazzetta, Pellegrini, Sebastiano Ricci, Pietro Longhi, Canaletto and Crespi.

13th-15th centuries

Cenni de Pepe, known as CIMABUE
c. 1240-after 1302

400 **Maestà. The Madonna and Child in Majesty Surrounded by Angels**

c. 1270 (?)

Wood panel. H 4.27 m; W 2.80 m

Church of San Francesco, Pisa.

Entered Louvre in 1813. INV 254

Drawing on Byzantine iconography, the *Maestà,* an enthroned Virgin on a gold background, was a major theme for the Tuscan masters, who developed a new pictorial language between the late 13th and the early 14th centuries. First among them, Cimabue painted his monumental *pala* for San Francesco at Pisa sometime around 1270, which probably precedes another *Maestà* by him, along with two by Giotto and Duccio in the Uffizi in Florence. Cimabue substitutes delicate modelling of skin tones and drapery for the linear formalism of the Byzantines.

GIOTTO di Bondone
c. 1267-1337

401 St. Francis of Assisi Receiving the Stigmata

Wood panel H 3.13 m; W 1.63 m
Church of San Francesco, Pisa. Entered
the Louvre in 1813.
INV 309

Italy **Paintings**

This altar-piece illustrates four episodes in the life of the holy founder of the mendicant order of the Franciscans (1182-1226). With some variants, the compositions are drawn from frescoes executed around 1290(?) by the young Giotto in the upper Basilica of Assisi. Signed along the lower edge of the frame, the Louvre panel is a decisive element in the attribution of the Assisi cycle to Giotto, which was once contested. He was the first painter in the history of Western art to set figures within a coherent space and give them structural consistency.

Simone MARTINI
c. 1284 - d. 1344

402 The Carrying of the Cross

Wood panel. H 0.30 m; W 0.20 m
Acq. 1834. INV 670 bis

The Carrying of the Cross is one of six panels of a portable polyptych which has now been dismantled (other panels are in Antwerp and Berlin-Dalheim). It is thought to have been painted by this Siennese master, a short while before his supposed arrival in 1336, at the ecclesiastical court of Avignon. The tightly packed and agitated figures give drama to the scene. Its most salient features, however, are the clear narrative line, jewel-like colours, stamped gold and a linear elegance, all of which mark the art of the most brilliant representative of Gothic painting in Italy.

Guido di Pietro, known as
FRA ANGELICO
Known from 1417 - d. 1455

403 The Coronation of the Virgin

Before 1435
Wood panel. H 2.09 m; W 2.06 m
Church of San Domenico, Fiesole.
Entered the Louvre in 1812. INV 314

A masterpiece of serene piety and harmonious colouring, the *Coronation of the Virgin* was painted for the church of the Dominican convent of Fiesole. The predella depicts the Entombment of Christ and six episodes from the life of St. Dominic who founded the order to which the painter belonged. Clever use of perspective and a skilful placing of figures in space demonstrate that despite his Medieval sensibility Fra Angelico was one of the first to make use of the architectonic

discoveries of Brunelleschi and Masaccio which ushered in the Florentine Renaissance.

Antonio Puccio, known as PISANELLO
Before 1395 - d. 1455(?)

404 Portrait of Ginevra d'Este

c. 1436-1438(?)
Wood panel. H 0.43 m; W 0.30 m
Acq. 1893. RF 766

The sitter, who is wearing a sprig of juniper *(ginevra)* and the Este family emblem on her robe - a two-handled vase - , has been identified as the princess Ginevra d'Este, first wife of

Sigismondo Malatesta, who had her poisoned in
1440. Painted around 1436-1438(?), this portrait
is one of the first known examples of an
independent profile portrait in Italy, a type much
favoured by Pisanello both in painting and
medallions. Her barely modelled face joins details
of her dress in a delicate web of arabesque lines.
This refinement is typical of the International
Gothic style and is enhanced by the flowering
branches behind.

Stefano di Giovanni, known as
SASSETTA
1392(?)-1450

405 **The Madonna and Child Surrounded
by Six Angels,
St. Anthony of Padua, St. John
the Evangelist**

c. 1437-1444

Wood panel. H 2.07 m; W 1.18 m

H. 1.95 m; W 0.57; H 1.95 m; W 0.57 m

Altar-piece of San Francesco, Borgo San Sepolcro.

Acq. 1956. RF 1956-11

These three panels belong to the main side of a
now dismantled, immense polyptych which was
the most ambitious of its time, and was executed
for the main altar of the Church of San Francesco
in Borgo San Sepolcro. Two elements on the
predella, illustrating the legend of the blessed
Ranieri Rasini, who died in this Tuscan town in

1304, are also conserved in the Louvre. The use of a gold ground indicates a respect for the Medieval tradition, which characterizes 15th century Siennese art. Sassetta, its most brilliant exponant, linked this to an infinitely tender, mystical quality

PIERO DELLA FRANCESCA
c. 1422 - d. 1492

406 **Portrait of Sigismondo Malatesta**
(1417-1468)

c. 1450

Wood panel. H 0.44 m; W 0.34 m

Acq. 1978. RF 1978-1

This portrait of the celebrated *condottiere* and patron of Rimini was doubtless painted shortly before the fresco of the *Tempio Malatetanio* dated 1451, where Piero gives him the same profile but shows him full length and kneeling by his patron saint, Sigismond. The formula of the profile bust, borrowed from the Gothic courtly tradition, is given a strict rendition here. Piero brought to it two new elements: the powerful solid volume of the bust and the fleshtones enlivening the face, the former deriving from Tuscan art, the latter from the Flemish, and combined them for the first time in an Italian painting.

Paolo di Dono, known as UCCELLO
1397-1475

407 **The Battle of San Romano**
The Counterattack of Michelotto da Cotignola

c. 1455

Wood panel. H 1.82 m; W 3.17 mm

Campana Collection. Entered in 1863. MI 469

The victory by the Florentines over the Venetians at San Romano, in 1432, is the theme of three panels painted by Uccello for the palace of Cosimo

Italy **Paintings**

de Medici at Florence (other episodes are in the
Uffizi and National Gallery, London). The
rhythm of lances and legs conveys a sense of
commotion in the army which is described in a
compact mass, with the artist making great use of
masterly foreshortening. This exercise in pure
geometry is enlivened by lavish costumes, which
indicate that while Uccello took the theoretical
experiments of the Florentine Renaissance to an
extreme, he did not entirely abandon the florid
forms of the Gothic tradition.

Andrea MANTEGNA
1431-1506

408 Calvary

c. 1456-1460
Wood panel. H 0.76 m; W 0.96 m
Church of San Zeno, Verona.
Entered the Louvre in 1798. INV 368

At Padua where he was trained, Mantegna made
two parallel discoveries: the art of antiquity and
perspective as introduced by Donatello and
Uccello. Before leaving for the court of Mantua in

1459, he produced his first masterpieces, including the altar-piece for the Church of San Zeno at Verona. *The Crucifixion* is the central panel of the predella which was dismantled in the early 19th century (the side panels are in the *Musée de Tours*). This tragic and stony vision of Golgotha displays a masterly command of space and a meticulous attention to archeological detail, which were the basis of Mantegna's bold Classicism.

ANTONELLO DA MESSINA
Known at Messina in 1456 - d. 1479

409 **Portrait of a Man** known as
Il Condottiere

1475
Wood panel. H 0.36 m; W 0.30 m Acq. 1865. MI 693

In a southern Italy open to Flemish influences, Antonello managed in a unique way to combine the fluid technique of Van Eyck with the theory of the Tuscans and Piero della Francesca. By the time he left Sicily for a brief period in Venice between 1475-1476, his style was assured and his visit had a decisive effect on Venetian painters. Among the masterpieces he produced, there were several portraits, including *Il Condottiere,* which is dated 1475 on the *cartellino*. In it, meticulous Flemish observation is allied to a sober monumentality.

COSIMO TURA
*Known in Ferrara from 1431
to 1495*

410 Pietà

c. 1480
Wood panel. H 1.32 m; W 2.68 m
Church of San Giorgio fuori le Mura, Ferrara.
Campana collection. Entered in 1863. MI 485

Founder of the school of Ferrara, Tura looked to the flourishing Paduan school and, with Mantegna's example, evolved an unusual style combining monumentality with linear incisiveness,

Italy **Paintings**

geometric rigour with a dry expressionism which may have been borrowed from Roger Van der Weyden. The anguished *Pietà* once formed the upper lunette of one of Tura's major works, the polyptych painted for the Roverella family in the church of San Giorgio fuori le Mura at Ferrara (dismantled, the central section is now in London).

Alessandro Filipepi, known as
BOTTICELLI
c. 1445 - d. 1510

411 **Venus and the Graces Offering Gifts to a Young Girl**

c. 1483
Fresco. H 2.11 m; W 2.83 m
Villa Lemmi. Acq. 1882. RF 321

This fresco and its pendant came from the Villa Lemmi near Florence which is thought to have belonged to the Tornabuoni family, that had links with the Medicis. They are generally dated to around 1483, between the two great Uffizi paintings, *Primavera* and *The Birth of Venus*. The earthly world, symbolized by the young girl, contrasts in its simplicity with the fluid rhythms of the celestial beauties, bearers of that classical ideal which Botticelli, adopting the refined humanism of Lorenzo the Magnificent, expresses with complex linear rhythms and soft colours.

Leonardo di ser Piero da Vinci, known as LEONARDO DA VINCI
1452-1519

412 Virgin of the Rocks

1483-1486
Transferred from wood to canvas.
H 1.99 m; W 1.22 m
Collection of François I. INV 777

A universal genius in the sciences as well as the arts, Leonardo's career took him from Florence to Milan and Rome, before following François I to Amboise in 1517. First of the masterpieces painted in the Sforza's court, the *Virgin of the Rocks* was destined for the Church of San Francesco Grande at Milan, then withdrawn after financial litigation (a second version is in London). It is suffused with a gentle *sfumato*, that indicates a new approach to space which is no longer purely geometric in construction and is conveyed by a tonal degradation expressing the enveloping atmosphere.

Italy **Paintings**

Domenico di Tomaso Bigordi, known as GHIRLANDAIO
1449-1494

413 The Visitation

1491
Wood panel. H 1.72 m; W 1.65 mm
Church of Santa Maria Maddelena dei Pazzi, Florence.
Entered the Louvre in 1812. INV 297

A contemporary of Botticelli, Ghirlandaio was

head of the main Florentine workshop of the late 15th century. Some of his major works were executed for the Tornabuoni family; the cycle of the *Life of the Virgin* in the choir of Santa Maria Novella, and soon after, the Louvre *pala* which was commissioned by Lorenzo Tornabuoni for the chapel of the church of Cestello in Florence (Santa Maria Maddelena dei Pazzi) and completed, according to Vasari, by the two brothers of the artist. The figures, which combine linear grace with monumentality, stand out against a classical arch which opens onto a view of Rome.

16th century

Leonardo di ser Piero da Vinci, known as
LEONARDO DA VINCI
1452-1519

414 The Mona Lisa

(1479 - d. before 1550)
also known as **La Gioconda**
1503-1506
Wood panel. H 0.77 m; W 0.53 m
Collection of François I. INV 779

If Vasari is correct, the portrait which Leonardo took to France, that was acquired by François I, was of the Mona Lisa, who in 1495 married Francesco di Bartolomeo di Zanoli del Giocondo. The title "La Gioconda" would thus derive from this notable Florentine's surname. But in Italian *giocónda* also means a light-hearted woman. With a lasting effect on Italian art, this portrait stood for an ideal. The smile that gives her life is, however, a feature of many of Leonardo's figures. Several scholars have concluded that the portrait was worked on over a long period, starting around 1505-1506 in Florence, and it was finished during the course of Leonardo's peregrinations in Milan or Rome.

Raffaello Santi, known as
RAPHAEL
1483-1520

415 **The Virgin and Child
with St. John the Baptist,** known as
La Belle Jardinière

1507
Wood. H 1.22 m; W 0.80 m
Collection of Louis XIV. INV 602

This "Belle Jardinière", which takes its nickname
from the pastoral background, is one of the most
famous of Raphael's Florentine-period Madonnas
(1504-1508). The period was an important one for
the young artist from Urbino, who abandoned his
master Perugino's manner for a classicism influenced
by his study of Leonardo, Michelangelo and Fra
Bartolomeo. With its gentle *sfumato* and pyramidal
composition the influence of Leonardo is particularly
apparent here, and the latter left Florence in 1506.
However, drawing remains Raphael's greatest
concern here and the serene atmosphere is quite
remote from the troubling complexities of Leonardo.

Leonardo di ser Piero da Vinci,
known as LEONARDO DA VINCI
1452-1519

416 The Virgin and Child with
St. Anne

c. 1510

Wood. H 1.68 m; W 1.30 m

Collection of Louis XIII. INV 776

Although quite rare, the depiction of the Virgin in
the lap of St. Anne goes back to Medieval times. It

was painted in Milan around 1510, and was the fruit of much deliberation, as drawings and cartoons indicate (the only surviving cartoon is in London). Leonardo never quite finished this panel, however, and kept it with him until he died. Painted in fine, translucent glazes with the underdrawing showing through in some areas, it represents a culmination of his research into aerial perspective, which Leonardo codified in his notes for the *Treatise on Painting*.

Vittore CARPACCIO
c. 1450/4 - d. 1525/6

417 The Sermon of St. Stephen at Jerusalem

Canvas. H 1.48 m; W 1.94 m

Acq. as an exchange with the Milan Brera

in 1812. INV 181

Carpaccio was the most brilliant exponent of the narrative style which developed in the frescoes of the *Scuole* in Venice from the second half of the 15th century. After the monumental cycle of the *History of St. Ursula* (Academia) and the frescoes which remain in place in the Scuola di San Giorgio degli Schiavoni, Carpaccio painted six *Scenes from the Life of St. Stephen* (Louvre, Brera, Milan, Stuttgart, Berlin-Dahlhem) between 1511 and 1520 for the Scuola dei Lanieri at San Stefano. This served as a pretext for a depiction of a resplendent Jerusalem, with Oriental costumes and exoticism giving an added richness to the classical ideal.

Raffaello Santi, known as
RAPHAEL
1483-1520

418 **Baltazar Castiglione**

(1478-1529)

c. 1514-1515

Canvas. H 0.82 m; W 0.67 m

Collection of Louis XIV. INV 611

Church patronage, which had attracted all the most celebrated masters to Rome from Giotto's time onwards, reached a peak with the election of Julius II and Leo X to the Holy See and their select artists Bramante, Michelangelo and Raphael (1508-1520). A valiant soldier and man of letters, Baltazar Castiglione was the quintessence of the Renaissance gentleman. His *Book of the Courtier,* published in 1528, reflects an ideal of aesthetic and spiritual perfection which is close to Raphael's achievements in painting. There could not be a better testimony of the friendship between these two men than this portrait, which combines a magnificent costume with deep psychological insight.

Andrea d'Agnolo di Francesco
known as ANDREA DEL SARTO
1486-1530

419 **Charity**

1518

Canvas. H 1.85 m; W 1.37 m

Collection of François I. INV 712

Andrea del Sarto added the finishting touches to Florentine classicism before the spread of Mannerism. Summoned to France by François I, he stayed there for less than a year (1518-1519). *Charity* is the only work known for certain to have been painted in France. In a perfect pyramidal composition with great depth, it depicts the theological virtue of *Charity* surrounded by her customary attributes - three children - and a complex mesh of symbolic objects, such as the burning jar, an open pomegranate and nuts.

Antonio Allegri, known as
CORREGGIO
1489(?)-1534

420 **Venus, Satyr and Cupid**

c. 1525

Canvas. H 1.88 m; W 1.25 m

Collection of Louis XIV. INV 42

Born in Correggio, the artist moved to nearby Palma in 1518, and in the cupolas of the churches there he developed a novel illusionism, enriching the science of perspective with luminous atmospheric effects. In the *Sleep of Venus,* painted for the Gonzagas at Mantua, possibly as a pendant to *The Education of Love* (London), Correggio bathes bodies in a uniformly glowing light, which joins the soft forms and fluid brushwork in a celebration of the delicate sensuality of this Venus in her abandonment, a symbol of carnal love, whose successors can be seen in the voluptuous mythological paintings of the 18th century.

Tiziano Vecellio, known as
TITIAN
1488/9-1576

421 The Entombment

c. 1525
Canvas. H 1.48 m; W 2.212 m
Collection of Louis XIV. INV 749

If the name of Venice is suggestive of the triumph of colour in painting, it is due to Titian. After an early period under the influence of Giorgione, who painted the *Concert Champêtre* in the Louvre, Titian reached maturity with a series of works in which classical rigour is allied to the effects of a "chromatic alchemy", which soon became paramount. The *Entombment* was painted for the Gonzagas at Mantua, and its composition was borrowed from Raphael. Titian heightens the drama with a warm-toned evening light which cuts across the figures, leaving the livid corpse of Christ half-hidden in shadow.

Giovanni Battista di Jacopo, known as ROSSO FIORENTINO
1496-1540

422 Pietà

c. 1530-1535
Canvas. H 1.27 m; W 1.63 m
Painted for the *connétable* Anne de Montmorency.
Chapel of the *Château d'Ecouen*.
Seized during the Revolution. INV 594

Italy **Paintings**

Rosso Fiorentino, thus known because of his red hair and Florentine birth, was summoned by François I to work on the Chateau of Fontainebleau in 1530. Of the numerous frescoes painted by this artist who was, along with Primaticcio, the leader of the School of Fontainebleau, all that remains are the frescoes in the *Galerie de François I*. Commissioned by Anne de Montmorency whose arms it bears, this picture is unlike this Mannerist master's usual ornamental inventions for its stern concentration on the drama, summed up in the pathos of the Virgin's gesture as the falters at the threshold of Christ's tomb.

Paolo Caliari, known as
VERONESE
1528-1588

423 The Wedding Feast at Cana

1562-1563

Canvas. H 6.66 m; W 9.90 m

San Giorgio Maggiore, Venice.

Entered the Louvre in 1798. INV 142

Called to Venice in 1553, this painter from Verona was an indefatigable worker, making use of his exceptional talent as a decorator, and a capacity to cover huge surfaces combining masterful stage sets, lavish contemporary costumes and resplendent colour. *The Wedding Feast at Cana* once decorated the refectory that Palladio built for the Benedictines on the island of San Giorgio Maggiore. The sacred story is transformed, taking a sovereign liberty with iconography, into the fashionable splendour of a Venetian wedding. If we are to believe a long-established tradition, all the Venetian masters are depicted here as musicians; Titian, Jacopo Bassano, Tintoretto and Veronese himself, who is dressed in white.

Jacopo Robusti, known as
TINTORETTO
1518-1594

424 Paradise

Canvas. H 1.43 m; W 3.63 m

Entered the Louvre in 1798. INV 570

After the fire which ravaged the Great Council
room in the Doges' Palace in 1577, a competition
was held to decorate the end wall with a huge
vision of *Paradise*. Veronese and Bassano won the
competition but were unable to take up the
commission, and Tintoretto took over, on
Veronese's death in 1588. More than the final
work, executed with his workshop, which is still
in situ, this preparatory sketch reveals the visionary
fervour of a man who was at his artistic peak,
painting the cycle of the Scuola di San Rocco at
that same time. His vibrant brushstroke, the
convulsive bodies, and circular rhythm of shadow-
filled clouds, express the turmoil that was
characteristic of Mannerism.

Federico BAROCCI
c. 1535 - d. 1612

425 The Circumcision

1590

Canvas. H 3.56 m; W 2.51 m

Entered the Louvre in 1798. MI 315

Though dated 1590, the work took a long time to
prepare with a series of drawings and sketches,
and it decorated the main altar of the church del
Nome di Gesù in Pesaro. The still life and the

Italy **Paintings**

403

two fine silhouettes of the shepherd and officiating priest lead the eye into the scene which is set towards the back of a deep space constructed in a perspective scheme typical of late Mannerism. The elongated bodies, strident colours of the drapery and pink and blue tones to the flesh colour are all stylistic elements of Mannerism.

Annibale CARRACCI
1560-1609

426 The Virgin Appearing to St. Luke
and St. Catherine

1592

Canvas. H 4.01 m; W 2.26 m

Entered the Louvre in 1797. INV 196

Painted for the cathedral of Reggio Emilia, the work dates from the painter's time in his native town of Bologna, three years before he left for Rome to lay down the foundations of classicism. It illustrates the preoccupations of the young Annibale who, along with Luigi and Augustino Carracci, founded a private academy in Bologna with the aim of enriching art with the study of nature and the great Renaissance masters. A synthesis of the art of Correggio and that of Titian, this monumental *pala* set both in a heavenly and an earthly register is testimony of the somewhat solemn eloquence of the triumphant Counter-Reformation.

17th century

Michelangelo Merisi, known as
CARAVAGGIO
c. 1571 - d. 1610

427 Death of the Virgin

1605-1606

Canvas. H 3.69 m; W 2.45 m

Collection of Louis XIV. INV 54

Painted for the church of Santa Maria della Scala
at Rome, the picture was turned down, for the
very reasons that made Caravaggio into the artist
who brought new life to religious painting : the
introduction of the humblest everyday details into
a divine setting. Shocked by this unorthodox
realistic portrayal of the Virgin, the clergy were
oblivious to the powerful effect of the human
message behind this corpse of a young woman
with swollen feet. Across the gloom of a barren
space, magnified by a large red drape, a stroke of
light gives depth to the figures. This expressive
use of *chiaroscuro* was Caravaggio's invention.

Guido RENI
1573-1642

428 Deianeira and the Centaur
Nessus

1620-1621

Canvas. H 2.39 m; W 1.93 m

Collection of Louis XIV. INV 537

After twelve successful years in Rome where he
deepened his knowledge of Raphael and antique
sculpture, Reni returned to Bologna where he
settled in 1614. His powerful and elegant
classicism came to the fore in four works on the
story of Hercules, painted between 1617 and 1621
for the Villa Favorita built by the Duke Ferdinand
Gonzaga near Mantua. The action, in which
Hercules is relegated to a minor role as a husband
ready to avenge Deianeira's abduction, is centred
on the foreground, a magnificent celebration of
bodies interwoven in a fluid rhythm of drapery
and gesture.

18th century

Giovanni Paolo PANNINI
1691-1765

429 Gallery of Views of Ancient
Rome

1758

Canvas. H 2.31 m; W 3.03 m

Gift of the Princesse Edmond de Polignac, 1944.

RF 1944-21

This picture, which has as its pendant a *Gallery of
Views of Modern Rome,* depicts an imaginary
museum made up of vestiges of ancient Rome. Its
architectural monuments are conjured up by
means of a gallery of paintings which is, in some
way, a repertory of Pannini's tireless studies of the
Roman past. Compelling for its perspectival
combinations and its cumulative effect, the
painting is eloquent testimony to the archeological
fervour in mid-18th century Europe which

followed upon the discoveries of the buried cities
of Herculaneum and Pompeii.

Francesco GUARDI
1712-1793

430 **The Doge on the Bucentaur**
at the Venice Lido
on Ascension day

Canvas. H 0.66 m; W 1.01 m

Seized during the Revolution. INV 20009

This picture belongs to a series of twelve paintings
(ten of which are in the Louvre and two others in
Grenoble and Brussels) illustrating Venetian
festivities on the occasion of the election of the
Doge Alviso IV Mocenigo in 1763. Painted around
ten years after the ceremonies, the paintings were
inspired by compositions engraved from Antonio
Caneletto, another master of the *Veduta* at Venice.
Here we see the Bucentaur taking off towards the
Lido, where each year the Doge celebrated
Venice's marriage with the Adriatic. For Guardi it
was the perfect occasion to paint a luminous and
vibrant city caught between sky and water, with a
lively brush and a novel sensitivity to atmospheric
effects.

Italy **Paintings**

Spain

With the exception of Murillo's *Young Beggar* 436 acquired under Louis XVI, the Louvre did not, at the outset, take any great interest in the Spanish school. The change came with Romanticism and the fashion for things Spanish, although the Napoleonic wars had already enabled collections to be amassed. Joseph Bonaparte and Maréchal Soult seized works from churches and convents, and the Musée Napoleon assembled the gains of war which Spain reclaimed when the Empire fell. The greatest promoter of Spanish painting was Louis-Philippe. Comprising hundreds of works by all the major masters, his collection was acquired by his emissary, the Baron Taylor, in Spain, and was exhibited in the Louvre from 1838-1848. The Spanish Gallery of Louis-Philippe, where Manet discovered Velasquez and Goya, had a profound effect on French art.

However, the collection was sold at auction in London in 1853 and dispersed. Much later the Louvre recovered El Greco's *Christ on the Cross* 433. The Maréchal Soult collection was also dispersed at that time, and the Louvre kept hold of a few masterpieces: Murillo's *Angel's Kitchen* and *The Birth of the Virgin* and Zurbaran's two *Scenes from the Life of St. Bonaventure* 434 and *St. Apollonia*. It was private collectors who helped to complete the Louvre's presentation of the *Golden Age* of Spanish painting. The most famous example is La Caze's gift of Ribera's *Club-footed Boy* 435. The curators took it upon themselves to acquire a series of Goya portraits, later marked by two notable examples, the *Marquesa de la Solana* 437, which was a gift, along with a tax succession, the *Marquesa de Santa Cruz*. This acquisition policy took on a pioneering role at the end of the century, with its inclusion of early masters, forming an ensemble from Martorell 431 to Huguet 432 which, outside of Spain, is virtually unsurpassed.

The Louvre has a Spanish collection which is small but representative. The Gothic artists of Catalonia and Castille, influenced by Italian and Flemish masters, are to be admired, along with the distinctive Mannerism of El Greco, expressive of the mystical aspirations of the Counter-Reformation; the greatest names of the *Golden Age* can be seen, with Goya at his peak in portraits in which even the colours are chosen for their psychological effect.

Bernardo MARTORELL
Known from 1427 - d. 1452

431 Judgement of St. George

c. 1430
Wood panel. H 1.07 m; W 0.53 m
Gift of the *Société des Amis du Louvre,* 1904
RF 1570

Spain **Paintings**

Catalonia was the centre of the International Gothic style in the Iberian peninsula, and had in Martorell the most original artist of the time. A masterpiece of the painter's early period, the St. Georges altar-piece (four panels of which are in the Louvre, and the central panel in Chicago) marks the artist's progression towards a certain narrative realism. The Judgement scene here illustrates this and, conforming to Jacques de Voragine's *Golden Legend,* it depicts a secret tribunal attending their president, Dacien, who is condemning the saint to death by decapitation after being paraded through the town for his militant faith.

Jaime HUGUET
c. 1415 - d. 1492

432 The Flagellation of Christ

c. 1450-1455
Wood panel. H 0.92 m; W 1.56 m
Chapel of St. Mark in the cathedral of
Barcelona. Acq. 1967 with help
of *Société des Amis du Louvre*. RF 1967-6

Close to the new developments along the Mediterranean in Italy and Provence, Huguet, who took over from Martorell in Barcelona, led Catalan Gothic art towards spatial unity and monumentality. Formerly, before the altar offered to the cathedral by the shoemakers (with the frame bearing their emblem, the ankle boot), this picture shows *The Flagellation of Christ*, set within a rigorous geometry. Arches open onto a luminous landscape, which takes the place of the traditional Medieval gold background.

Domenicos Theotocopoulos,
known as EL GRECO
1541-1614

433 Christ on the Cross adored
by Donors

c. 1585-1590
Canvas. H 2.60 m; W 1.781 m
Church of the Hieronymites de la Reina nuns,
Toledo. Spanish gallery of Louis-Philippe.
Acq. 1908. RF 1713

Born in Crete, hence his surname, El Greco moved to Toledo in 1577, bringing with him a visionary language developed in contact with the Mannerists in Italy. The Louvre *Christ on the Cross* is one of the finest and oldest known examples of a theme which recurs in his work. Contemporary with the *Burial of the Count of Orgaz* (Toledo), it belongs to his grandest period. His tormented style - thundery sky, elongated and twisted bodies, ecstatic faces - is tempered here by a rigorously symmetrical composition, with an austere colour scheme and a sculptural depth to Christ's body.

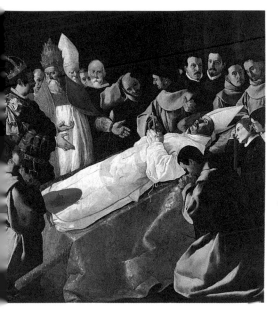

Francisco de ZURBARAN
1598-1664

434 St. Bonaventura on his Deathbed

1629

Canvas. H 2.45 m; W 2.20 m
Church of the Collège Saint-Bonaventura,
Sevilla. Acq. 1858 from the heirs of
Maréchal Soult. MI 205

In 1629, a few years after his move to Sevilla, Zurbaran supplied four canvasses (two are in the Louvre) to complete the cycle of St. Bonaventura begun by Herrera the Elder. Moral renovator of the Franciscan order, the saint died in 1274 at the Council of Lyon, which he had instigated, preaching of the church's mission and unification. Pope Gregory X, the King of Aragon and Franciscan monks are shown mourning the prelate. The fervent atmosphere, and simple composition, cut in two by the dazzling white of the saint's vestments, offer ample testimony to Zurbaran's skill, from a young age, in interpreting the monastic spirituality of the *Golden Age*.

Spain **Paintings**

Jusepe de RIBERA
1591-1652

435 The Club-Footed Boy

1642

Canvas. H 1.64 m; W 0.93 m

Gift of Dr Louis La Caze, 1869. MI 893

With his crutch carried like a useless weapon, and a begging note "Give me alms for the love of God", suggesting he is dumb, his deformed foot and gap-teeth, this young beggar apes the martial stance of a hidalgo, the cruel reverse-side to the *Golden Age*. Ribera subordinated realism to social satire. By 1642, he had attained his full stature as an artist. He had broken free from the Caravaggiesque shadows, at which he was a past master from his early period in Naples (1616), where he became official artist to the Spanish viceroys. And his bright paintings, with their Flemish influence, analyzed the hollow gestures of the "Court of Miracles" with an implacable acuity.

Bartolomé Esteban MURILLO
1618-1682

436 The Young Beggar

c. 1650

Canvas. H 1.34 m; W 1.00 m

Collection of Louis XVI. INV 933

Along with many religious works, Murillo has left us a striking image of childhood in this picture of a boy delousing himself. Caravaggiesque in inspiration, it is an uncompromising portrayal of a young and ragged Sevillano with dirty feet in a barren setting. But the real *tour de force* here lies in the slant of sunlight, boldly applied, with a concern for naturalism which attracted the attention of 19th century French painters like Edouard Manet, who were searching for new masters.

Francisco José de
GOYA Y LUCIENTES
1746–1828

437 The Marquesa de la Solana

(1757-1795)

Canvas. H 1.81 m; W 1.22 m

Gift of Carlos de Beistegui, 1942

Entred in 1953. RF 1942-23

Painter to the king, and protected by nobles, Goya was, from the 1780's onwards, the most fashionable portrait painter of Madrid society. "La Solana" (the countess of Carpio) was a friend of the Duchess of Alba, another famous model, and was a charitable, educated aristocrat who wrote plays and died prematurely in 1795 at the age of thirty-eight. Goya painted her in his usual society portrait manner: full length, against a neutral landscape, in an elegant, subtly-toned costume, adding a pink bow for the only luxury. The elegant brushwork does not detract from the psychological depth. The face is unusually grave, whether as a result of the model's illness or as a projection of the artist's mood. The picture is situated sometime after the attack of 1792-1793 which left him deaf.

Germany

The importance of this collection is unquestionable, despite the relatively limited number of works it contains. The 15th century is dominated by a collection of pictures of the school of Cologne which is unusual outside of Germany (Master of the Holy Family 438, of St Severinus, of the altar-piece of St. Bartholomew 439, and of the legend of St Ursula). The collection's strong point remains the Renaissance, with Dürer's *Self-portrait* 440, several Cranachs and Bruyn and above all the five portraits by Hans Holbein the Younger; Erasmus, Warham, the Archbishop of Canterbury, Kratzer (Henry VIII's astronomer) 442, Anne of Cleves (the king's fourth wife) and Sir Henry Wyatt (court councillor). These Holbeins have a notable origin; Louis XIV acquired them in 1671 from the Cologne banker and collector Eberhardt Jabach. Alongside the three great names, other artists testify to an artistic flowering in 16th century Germany, such as Hans Baldung Grien, Hans Sebald Beham (work acquired by Louis XIV from Mazarin's heirs), Mathias Gerung, Ulrich Apt, Hans Maler and Wolf Huber. For subsequent periods, examples are more scattered but no less significant; there are 17th century still-lifes (by Binoit, Flegel 443, and Gottfried von Wedig), portraits, mythological and religious paintings from the 18th century (Denner, Siebold, Dietrich, Platzer, Maulpertsch and Graff), Neoclassicism (Angelica Kauffmann, Anton Krafft), the Biedermeier period (Walmüller's portrait of a woman) and Romanticism (Friedrich 444).

MASTER OF THE HOLY FAMILY
Active in Cologne from 1470/80 to 1515

438 Altar-piece of the Seven Joys of Mary

c. 1480

Wood. H 1.27 m; W 1.82 m

Convent of the Maccabeans Cologne.

Acq. 1912, with contrib.

from children of Jean Dollfus. RF 2045

Germany **Paintings**

Divided into three scenes *(The Adoration of the Magi, The Presentation in the Temple, the Apparition of Christ to Mary),* this was the centre of an altar-piece painted almost certainly around 1480, which came from the Benedictine convent of the Maccabeans in Cologne. The two wings, each containing two scenes *(The Annunciation* and *The Nativity,* on the left, *The Ascension and* the *Assumption* on the right) are housed in the Germanisches Nationalmuseum at Nuremberg. The Master of the Holy Family, so named after his mature masterpiece in the Wallraf Richartz Museum in Cologne, took his inspiration for the *Presentation in the Temple* from a composition of the same subject by the great painter of the Cologne School during the first half of the 15th century, Stephan Lochner, but the colouring and taste for rich fabrics and gilt is proof of his own genius.

MASTER OF THE ALTAR-PIECE OF
ST. BARTHOLOMEW
Active in Cologne c. 1480-1510

439 The Descent from the Cross

c. 1501-1505

Wood panel. H 2.275 m and 1.525 m; W 2.10 m

Church of the Val-de-Grace.

Seized during French Revolution.

INV 1445

The origin of this imposing altar-piece is not known; all we can be sure of is its 16th century location in a Jesuit institution in Paris. St. Anthony's T-shaped cross and handbell decorating the *trompe-l'œil* frame indicate a possible connection with an Antonite community. Its author, very probably a Netherlander from Utrecht or Arnhem, so-named after his St. Bartholomew altar-piece from the Cologne Church of the Holy Dove (Munich, Alte Pinacothek), who settled in Cologne around 1480, transposes Van der Weyden's famous *Descent from the Cross* (Madrid, Prado), into a late Gothic mannerist-like style. His interpretation is powerful and full of pathos; within a *trompe-l'œil* painted box, characters, like actors in a Mystery play, are grouped in a complex interweaving of lines around Christ, who seems to protude into our space.

Albrecht DÜRER
1471-1528

440 Self-Portrait

1493

Parchment glued on to canvas. H 0.565 m; W 0.45 m

Acq. 1922. RF 2382

This is the only picture by Dürer in France, and his first self-portrait, preceeding that of 1498 (Madrid, Prado) and 1500 (Munich, alte Pinacothek), painted during his trip from Basel and Strasbourg before his return to Nuremberg. The painter shows himself as a serious young man of 22, holding a branch of eryngium (a type of thistle) in his right hand, the significance of which has prompted much discussion. Some see it as a symbol of conjugal fidelity, with the picture destined for his fiancée, Agnes Frey, whom he married in 1494. For others it is an allusion to Christ's Passion (more specifically to the crown of thorns), in connection with the inscription on the picture "Things happen to me as is written from on high", in a mood looking forward to the *Self-portrait* of 1500 in which Dürer appears as a "Salvator Mundi", surrounded by a God-given aura.

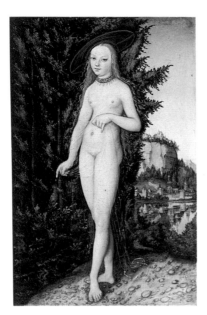

Lucas CRANACH THE ELDER
1472-1553

441 Venus Standing in a Landscape

1529

Wood panel. H 0.38 m; W 0.25 m

Entered the Louvre in 1806, from Germany.

INV 1180

Lucas Cranach was official painter to the prince electors of Saxony, painted Luther, and alongside Dürer and Holbein, was one of the three great painters of 16th century Germany. He excelled in mythological and allegorical painting, and devised a new iconographic image; a single woman in a landscape. The small Louvre painting, with its fine detail all by Cranach's own hand, shows a graceful Venus wearing a wide-rimmed hat, bejewelled necklace, and holding a transparent veil in front of her. The Gothic town in the background, reflected in the water, is evidence of his mastery of drawing and his deeply poetic sensitivity to landscape. The winged serpent holding a ring in its mouth is Cranach's seal and is skilfully merged into the stones on the ground.

Hans HOLBEIN THE YOUNGER
1497/8-1543

442 Nicolas Kratzer
(c. 1486 - after 1550)

1528

Wood panel. H 0.83 m; W 0.67 m
Collection of Louis XIV. Acq. from Eberhardt
Jabach in 1671. INV 1343

The sitter's name and date of the painting are indicated on the piece of paper on the left of the table. Kratzer was a compatriot who settled in England, like Holbein, and corresponded with Dürer. He became an important court figure as astronomer to Henry VIII. Holbein depicts him engaged in his principal task as "maker" of astronomical instruments. In one hand he holds a compass, and in the other a solar dial which he is constructing. This dial and two others of different shapes, which can be seen in the background, can also be found in the famous painting of the *Ambassadors* which Holbein painted in 1533 (National Gallery, London). In this portrait which, along with that of Warham, dates from 1527, during his first stay in London, Holbein displays his skills as an objective painter and his unparalleled craftsmanship in the painting of objects.

Germany **Paintings**

Georg FLEGEL
1566-1638

443 Still-Life with a Carafe of Wine and Small Fish

1637
Wood panel. H 0.19 m; W 0.15 m
Acq. 1981. RF 1981-21

Clearly influenced by Flemish artists who had settled in Germany, Georg Flegel, from Frankfurt, was one of the first German painters to give still-life a status of its own. Objects are skilfully arranged, linked to each other in an interplay of ovals and reflected colour. The keenly observed fish are a species that once lived in the river Main. A *trompe-l'œil* effect, the insects - a fly and drone bee - are shown lifesize on the bread and edge of the plate, as if they belonged not within the painting but to the world of the onlooker. They serve to remind us of the perishable nature of worldly goods, and this contrasts with the religious significance behind the bread, wine and fish, which traditionally refer to the communion meal that ensures the soul's eternal salvation.

Caspar David FRIEDRICH
1774-1840

444 **The Tree of Crows**

c. 1822

Canvas. H 0.59 m; 0.737 m

Acq. 1975. RF 1975-20

Far from being the simple depiction of a landscape, *The Tree of Crows* should be interpreted as a meditation on death, a major theme in German Romantic painting of which Friedrich was the uncontested leader. The barren tree which appears to be rooted in a tumulus dating from the time of the Huns, symbolises the vain aspiration of pagan heroes buried in such spots. The few leaves remaining on the tree, and the crows, similarly evoke death and adversity. A ray of hope remains however: the distant light symbolizing eternal life. In the background, scholars have identified the town of Arkona and the chalk cliffs of the island of Rügen in the Baltic sea, the region where the artist was born.

Flanders and Holland

In the Louvre collections, the Low Countries– Flanders and the Netherlands combined here for convenience's sake, given their geographical and linguistic proximity and shared history up to the end of the 16th century - are represented by no less than 1200 pictures dating from the 15th to the early 20th century (everything post-1850 has now been transferred to the Musée d'Orsay). This amounts to more than the entire collection of Italian paintings (around 1100) and to far more than the Spanish, German and English schools (amounting to a hundred or so works each), though is considerably less than the French school (between 3000 and 4000 paintings). This serves to indicate the relative importance of the Low Countries in the collections, the kernel of which was brilliantly put together by Louis XIV–the Brils, and, most notably, a large proportion of the work of Rubens and Van Dyck–and successfully enlarged by Louis XVI thanks to an early acquisition policy which brought in the best Dutch

masters (of the 17th century), including over 110
perfectly selected paintings (Ruisdael, Cuyp,
Wouwerman, Berchem, Ter Borch, Du Jardin,
Dou, the Veldes, Ostades, Metsu and, among the
Flemish, Rubens, Teniers, Jordaens etc.). Two
centuries of museum history with its ups and
downs (less than fifteen or so acquisitions under
Louis-Philippe and only eight between 1959 and
1979...) reflect vicissitudes of taste and history; but
the museum and its tireless donors (over 130
Flemish and Dutch masters were presented during
the Second Empire, not to mention the good Dr
La Caze who in 1869 presented Frans Hals'
The Gypsy Girl 440, Rembrandt's *Bathsheba* 462,
7 Rubens, and 19 Teniers, along with bequests
of 200 Dutch and Flemish paintings during the
Third Republic) have continued the task the kings
initiated so generously.

For this reason the collection is at once varied and
highly selective. To begin with it professes one of
the best Rubens collections in the world, rivalling
Munich and Vienna (because of the Medici Gallery
in particular), with 52 original works. Also
considerable are the series of Van Dykes (over
twenty works) and Rembrandt (a dozen certified
works, including the unequalled *Bathsheba* 462),
while the kernel of early 15th century masters
(Primitives) includes all the great names from Van
der Goes to Van Eyck, Weyden, Bouts, Memling,
Gerard David, Bosch, Geertgen tot Sint Jans, Joos
van Gent, Sittow etc.) and *The Madonna of
Chancellor Rolin* 445 is a masterpiece of universal
status. The 16th century is well represented and
endowed with fine works from Metsys (*The Banker
and his wife* 447) and Brueghel (*The Beggars* 450),
Hemessen and Floris, Lucas van Leyden, Van
Cleve, Gossaert and Mor, Dalem and Barendsz,
Sellaer, Jan van der Straet and Otto Veen, and
more recently the museum has opened its doors to
the troubled world of the Mannerists (Spranger,
Speeckaert, Wtewael, Cornelisz van Haarlem) who
join their predecessors, Bloemaert and Goltzius.

A golden age for painting, the 17th century is
even richer. In Flanders there is on the one hand

a lavish display of grand painting (mostly religious) following Rubens (Van Dyck, Jordaens, Van Mol, Crayer, van Oost, Gerard Seghers and Thulden) and on the other, the whole delightful company of minor "realist" masters (a triumphant gathering of 40 Teniers, 7 Francken, and Brouwer, Craesbeeck, Ryckaert and Vranck) as well as a superb series of still lifes (5 Fyt, 8 Snyders, and Van Bouck) and animal paintings (16 Pieter Boels). The collections of landscapes are no less remarkable (10 Brill, 10 Huysmans, and 5 Mompers) while Jan Breughel the Elder stands out for, among other things, *The Battle of Issus (Arbelles?)* and Daniel Seghers is notable for his crown of flowers surrounding Domenichino's *Triumph of Love,* again from Louis XIV.

Almost none of the Dutch of the great 17th century are missing, even though churches, marines and still lives are somewhat rare and a single work often serves to illustrate a particular tendency (such as Terbrugghen's *The Duet,* bought in 1954, to illustrate the Caravaggiesque tendency in Utrecht). The 4 Hals (including the *Gypsy girl* [460] and the *Buffoon with a lute*), the 10 Van Goeyn, the Ruisdaels (6 by Salomon and 6 by Jacob) are a significant acquisition. But also present are fine examples of great names which are now scarce: Bosschaert and Saenredam, Sweerts and Hoogstraen (his admirable *Pair of Slippers* was once thought to be by Pieter der Hooch and later by Vermeer), Venne *(The Truce of 1609)* and Potter, Claesz and De Heem, Steen and Pieter de Hooch, Hobbema and Van der Heyden. Vermeer has pride of place with his *Lacemaker* [467] and the *Astronomer*, which came to us in 1983, the last Vermeer to have come from a private collection.

Jan VAN EYCK
d. 1441

445 The Madonna of Chancellor
Rolin

c. 1435

Wood. H 0.66 m; W 0.62 m

Collegiate church of Notre-Dame, Autun.

Entered the Louvre in 1800. INV 1271

The Chancellor of Burgundy, Nicolas Rolin (1376-
1462) commissioned this picture of himself
kneeling in prayer before the Madonna, with Jesus
blessing him. He was a high dignitary in the court
of Philippe the Good (one of whose good deeds
was to have commissioned Van der Weyden to
paint the altar-piece of the Last *Judgement* for the
Beaune hospice). The urban landscape in the
background does not, despite its apparent
precision, depict a real town but is rather a
juxtaposition of several existing sites. All the
minutely rendered detail has a precise religious
significance. Van Eyck conferred an intense
spiritual value upon the infinitely small, with a
perfect, almost alchemical mastery of his
technique.

Roger VAN DER WEYDEN
1399/1400-1464

446 Braque Family Triptych

1450-1452

Wood. H 0.41 m; W 0.68 m (central panel);

H 0.41 m; W 0.34 m (wings)

Acq. 1913 RF 2063

The central panel shows Christ the Redeemer
between the Virgin Mary and St. John the

Evangelist, the left wing St. John the Baptist and the right, St. Mary Magdalen. The arms painted on the reverse side belong to Jehan Braque and his wife, Catherine de Braland from Tournai, suggesting that this portable triptych was painted either at their marriage in 1450-1451 or after Jehan Braque's death in 1452. In the latter case the skull and cross which can also be seen, accompanied by inscriptions reminding us of the vanity of life on earth, would have had a particular poignancy. At that period, Van der Weyden had just returned from Italy, and Fra Angelico's influence can be felt in the choice of a rigorous symmetry which is perfectly allied to the monumentality that is natural to this master.

Quentin METSYS
1465/6-1530

447 The Banker and his Wife

1514
Wood. H 0.705 m; W 0.670 m
Acq. 1806. INV 1444

Derived most probably from a lost work by Jan van Eyck dating from 1440, Metsys' picture is not a simple genre scene. A Latin inscription which figured on the frame during the 17th century, from Leviticus, "May the scales be fair and the weights be equal", would have explained the moral or even religious intention behind the work - the scales, which symbolize justice, also refer to the Last Judgement. The subject became very popular; the caricatural usurer, his hands greedily clasping the gold, was generally the only focus of attention. This work is very different, however, and has a serene gravity about it. Also worthy of note is a motif which Van Eyck favoured above all others: a mirror reflecting a man.

Jan GOSSAERT known as MABUSE
c. 1478-1532

448 Carondelet Diptych

1517

Curved wood

H 0.425 m; W 0.270 m (each panel)

Acq. 1847. INV 1442-3

interior   exterior

Jean Carondelet (1469-1545), dean of the Church of Besançon, councillor to Emperor Charles V and friend of Erasmus, is shown praying opposite the Madonna and Child. On the back of one wing a skull is painted in *trompe-l'œil*, in a niche, accompanied by a quote from St. Jerome inviting meditation on death. Carondelet's face is skilfully modelled and painted with a realism accentuated by the confining frame, and contrasts with the more timeless, idealised image of the Virgin. The finest element is the Vanity, which is terrifyingly real, gaining all its force from its formal intensity.

Frans FLORIS
1516-1570

449 The Sacrifice of Christ protecting Humanity

1562

Wood. H 1.65 m; W 2.30 m

Church of St. Sulpice. Seized during French Revolution.

INV 20746

In a magnificently fluid style using the elegant Mannerist forms which are the stamp of Floris (the leading painter of mid-16th century Antwerp, and true forerunner of Rubens in his use of transparent glazes), a complex religious metaphor is transcribed, the literal nature of which borders on boldness. Indicated in the foreground by St. John the Baptist in a fine red robe, Christ (crucified on a symbolic vine with great hen's wings) gathers together all the repentent sinners like the mother hen of the St. Luke and St. Matthew's Gospels - whence the fine realistic detail in the foreground - a sign of perfect and all-encompassing divine love. An extraordinary demon-bat hovers on the right above a pope and pharisees who, poor shepherds that they are, turn believers onto the wrong path. Opposite this on the left, is the heavenly Jesuralem indicated by Christ and his disciples. The whole work testifies to an interestingly personal faith (Floris and his wife are among those protected by God and his Holy Trinity), on the borderline between loyal Catholicism and the new Protestant Reform church.

Flanders and Holland **Paintings**

Pieter BRUEGHEL THE ELDER
c. 1525-1569

450 The Beggars

1568

Wood. H 0.165 m, 0.215 m

Gift of Paul Mantz, 1892. RF 730

The significance of this work - the only Brueghel
the Elder in the Louvre - remains obscure,
although it has given rise to many interpretations.
It may be an evocation of human suffering, a
political allusion to Spanish domination or a
satirical description of different classes of society.
The fox-tails attached to the cripples' clothing
have also given rise to much speculation. But even
without explanation, the work, which was painted
at the very end of the artist's career, is extremely
powerful despite its small size. Seen close up, the
absurd line-up is drawn together with a highly
skilled interplay of forms.

Cornelis VAN HAARLEM
1562-1638

451 The Baptism of Christ

1588

Canvas. H 1.70; W 2.06 m

Gift of the *Societé des Amis du Louvre*, 1983.

RF 1983-25

A work of his youth - the artist was only 26 in
1588 - *The Baptism of Christ* is one of the most
successful works by a Harlem Mannerist. Here the
new style is given its most eloquent expression. In

a typical inversion of hierarchy, the subject of the work, Christ's baptism, is relegated to the background, while the foreground is occupied by those waiting to be baptised, a veritable lexicon of academic nudes, *contrapposto* and expressive gesture. Fingers are stiff, muscles arched, and the painter is bold enough to show the bald naturalistic detail of the dirty sole of the foreground foot. The youthful, hotheaded brutality of this composition looks forward to Caravaggios' conquest of pictorial reality.

17th century Flanders

Peter Paul RUBENS
1577-1640

452 The Apotheosis of Henry IV
and the Proclamation of the Regency of Marie
de Médicis (May 14, 1610)

1622-1625
Canvas. H 3.94 m; W 7.27 m
Collection of Louis XIV. INV 1779

The end wall of the great Medici Gallery was
painted by Rubens between 1622 and 1625, for the

Palais du Luxembourg in Paris, at that time, residence of the queen, Marie de Médicis (wife of Henry IV and mother of Louis XIII). This imposing "machine", of over 7 meters wide, is the focal point and thematic centre of an immense decorative ensemble of 24 huge works painted in what was a record time for a single man. These 300 m² of painting give us a good measure of Rubens' singular genius. The whole cycle is an epic account of the great deeds and sublime destiny of a powerful and royal woman, celebrated in the midst of, as well as because of, her misfortunes, strengthened by adversity like a popular hero in 17th century literature. Here, in a lavish display of rich colour and solid and magnificent forms, the composition, skilfully organized in a system of huge, dynamic diagonals, balanced between two poles, draws attention to the dead king on the left, raised to heaven, a hero made divine, in a wonderful allegorical transposition of his tragic assassination (in 1610), while, to the right, the widowed queen, now regent, receives the divine mission to be governer of state, and is acclaimed by the great of the kingdom.

Antoon (Anthony) VAN DYCK
1599-1641

453 Venus asking Vulcan for Arms for Aeneas

c. 1627-1632

Canvas. H 2.20 m; W 1.45 m

Collection of Louis XIV. INV 1234

Here we have a great mythological subject to please cultivated 17th century minds, trained on the classics and Virgil in particular; but transposed by Van Dyck into the timeless realm of aesthetics. The beneficent influence of the Italian

Renaissance, examples of which Van Dyck had recently seen (Correggio, the painter of female flesh, Titian the sumptuous colourist) and the grand Baroque manner of Rubens, Van Dyck's master (ample, energetic forms) combine with the artist's subtle colours and febrile style in a composition that is as eloquent as it is refined (c.f. the contrast in skintone of the white goddess and dark Vulcan, the forger). It is deliberately situated out of time (there is no local colour or archaeological detail), devoid of any prosaic realism, and set within a suitably vertical format (the full-flung bodies seem to burst out of their space).

Antoon (Anthony) VAN DYCK
1599-1641

454 Charles I at the Hunt
(1600-1649), King of England

c. 1635

Canvas. H 2.66 m; W 2.07 m

Collection of Louis XVI. INV 1236

While not an official portrait in the usual sense (having been referred to by the painter, in a memoir written in French around 1638, as *le roi alla ciasse*), this is by far the most royal (most noble, thus the most successful) of portraits of the king, showing him as a paragon among educated men. He is distinguished and elegant, well bred and charming as befitted a twofold tradition, here effectively combined, of the courtier as an "honest

man" and as a "prince" among men; the
individual matching his persona. On the one hand
there are the servants, the cane standing for
government, clothes which are almost too
sumptuous for a hunt and the pround stance; on
the other, a masterly isolation of the main figure
silhouetted against a pale sky, and set subtly off-
centre, as is emphasised by the curve of branches.
His dignity is enhanced by muted colours applied
with a lively and caressing brushstroke. From the
Antique, via Titian, comes the culturally
"ennobling" detail of the horse scraping a
deferential hoof.

Peter Paul RUBENS
1577-1640

455 **The Village Fete**

c. 1635-1638

Wood. H 1.49 m; W 2.61 m

Collection of Louis XIV. INV 1797

Louis XIV could not have found a better or a more
representative example of the genius of
Rubens - the greatest painter of the century - when
he bought this monumental panel of the artist's
last years. With its sensual lyricism and vital
exhuberance - magnifying life in all its aspects
animal and human -, it conveys the sense of
frenetic pleasure and irresistible energy, that is
allied to and fed by an old tradition of Flemish
realism from Brueghel, though the moral tone is

absent here. The swarming mass of bodies (a tumult cleverly organized in a beautiful succession of waves) contrasts with the calm, deeply-felt immensity of the landscape.

Peter Paul RUBENS
1577-1640

456 Helena Fourment with a Carriage

c. 1639
Wood. H 1.95 m; W 1.32 m
Marlborough and Rothschild Collections.
Acq. 1977. RF 1977-13

With its notable provenance, this large and ravishing "state" portrait is one of the Louvre's finest post-war acquisitions. It is probably one of the last depictions of Rubens' second wife, Helena Fourment (married in 1630), who was a frequent model for the artist in his last years. She is accompanied by her young son Frans, born in 1663, and here about 6 or 7 years old. In a black costume of great distinction (but not of mourning!), adorned like a society lady, with the raised pompom hat then fashionable in the Low Countries, attached to a fine veil, she leaves her palatial residence to take her carriage (hence an alert piece of landscape painting on the left). It represents a summit of Rubens' invention; a picture that displays ease and skill, triumphantly Baroque in its spatial dynamism and superbly balanced relationship between forms, compelling for both its sentiment and painterliness, and a highpoint of the great tradition of humanistic and aristocratic portraiture that developed during the Renaissance.

Jacob JORDAENS
1593-1678

457 Jesus driving the Merchants from
the Temple

c. 1650

Canvas. H 2.88 m; W 4.36 m

Collection of Louis XV. INV 1402

This superb royal purchase of 1751 presupposed
the foundation of a museum in the Louvre, given
that such a work with its eminently evangelical
tone - Jesus purifying a sacred place of material
and pagan corruption - could hardly serve as a
palace decoration. The picture, sold by Natoire, an
artist protected by the King and a major figure in
18th century French Rococo, testifies to the
impressive vigour of the great rival and successor
to Rubens in Antwerp, who painted this huge
canvas around 1650. It is a masterfully organized
pictorial tumult, a triumphal chain of full,
dynamic forms, within well-constructed and
elaborate architecture. Its rich tones and clear light
combine knowledge and licence, a sculptural depth
and pure painting which is a pleasure to the eye.
It is at a highpoint of Baroque art.

Joachim WTEWAEL
1566-1638

458 Perseus and Andromeda

1611

Canvas. H 1.80 m; W 1.50 m

Gift of the *Société des Amis du Louvre,* 1982

RF 1982-51

Daughter of Cepheus (the king of Ethiopia) and of Cassiope, Andromeda was foolish enough to challenge the Nereids with her beauty. They chained her to a rock, at the mercy of a sea monster sent by Neptune. Perseus, mounted on Pegasus, rescued and took her for his wife.
The subject was popular with Mannerist painters. The Utrecht painter Wtewael interprets the story in an original way. It is really three pictures in one: the superb nude study, the rare detail of the blue-toned enchanted landscape, and finally, in the foreground, an astonishing still life of shells, a picture within a picture. *Andromeda* is an excellent example of this artist's subdued Mannerism, with the fresh elegance of the nude winning over the exacerbated style of his first period.

Ambrosius BOSSCHAERT
the Elder
1573-1621

459 Bouquet of Flowers in an Arch

c. 1620

Copper. H 0.23 m; W 0.17 m

Acq. with aid of *Société des Amis du Louvre,* 1984.

RF 1984-150

The charm of this small picture, which is nevertheless monumental in feel, lies in Bosschaert's power of invention. He was a protestant from Antwerp who emigrated to Holland. There are three aspects to this still life: the poignant contrast between the infinite horizon

Flanders and Holland **Paintings**

435

and the close precision of the flowers and transparent glass; an intellectual vision of a harmonious nature linking recognisable flowers that bloom in different seasons; and the moral, quasi-religious atmosphere suggested by half-eaten leaves and the worn stone of the niche, reminders of the vanity of things and the fragile nature of ephemeral reality. The little insect (a kind of wasp) on the right-hand border forms the painter's monogramme *AB*.

Frans HALS
1581/1585-1666

460 The Gypsy Girl

c. 1628-1630

Wood. H 0.58 m; W 0.52 m

Gift of Dr Louis La Caze, 1869. MI 926

The realistic subject of this picture, a courtesan with a provocatively open *décolleté* rather than a "gypsy", which at that period generally referred to a storyteller - links it to the clear painting of the Caravaggiesque painters of Utrecht. Hals' contribution resides in the bravura of his varied brushwork: supple and fluid across the face, the strokes become more animated, sharp and broken in the costume. The figure follows a line of "genre portraits" by Hals. One element giving added dynamism to the work is Hals' somewhat atypical treatment of the background, consisting of an area of cloudy sky or rocky landscape, traversed by an oblique strip giving it movement.

Harmensz REMBRANDT VAN RIJN
1606-1669

461 The Supper at Emmaüs

1648

Wood panel. H 0.68 m; W 0.65 m

Collection of Louis XVI. INV 1739

The well-known subject of Christ being
recognized, during a meal at Emmaüs, by two of
his disciples, was much loved by Rembrandt. The
interpretation he gave it in 1648 is full of solemn
grandeur. Traditional in its composition, which
draws on recollections of High Renaissance
masters (Leonardo da Vinci, Titian and Veronese),
the picture is striking for its iconographic
intensity. The figure of Christ, which is beautifully
displaced away from the central axis of the
composition, is poignantly realistic. His pale, gaunt
face is that of the vanquisher of death. This is
alluded to with the empty, overturned wineglass
and the lamb's head chopped in two, symbolising
the Passion of God made Man, as revealed in the
Last Supper. In one picture, Rembrandt renovates
a whole tradition of religious painting, giving it
depth and humanity.

Harmensz REMBRANDT VAN RIJN
1606-1669

462 Bathsheba

1654

Canvas. H 1.42 m; W 1.42 m

Gift of Dr Louis La Caze, 1869. MI 957

Rembrandt chose to paint the episode most often
illustrated by artists, in which King David catches
a glimpse of Bathsheba while she is bathing,
and claims her for a servant. A measure of
Rembrandt's genius lies in the liberties he takes
with traditional iconography. The king does not
appear in the painting, and is represented only
by the slightly crumpled letter of request in
Bathsheba's hand. The model is generally agreed

to be **Henrickje Stoffels**, the artist's mistress. Quite "Venetian" in feeling, with its warm tonalities and emphasis on the lifesize nude figure, *Bathsheba* is, aside from any influence, an outstanding example of painterly bravura, visible in the superbly constructed white cloth, richly-worked layers of paint and glowing highlights over deep red accents.

Pieter de HOOCH
1629-1684

463 **A Young Woman Drinking**

1658

Canvas. H 0.69 m; W 0.60 m

Gift of Mme Piatigorsky, née Rothschild.

RF 1974-29

Painted at Delft - despite the map of Amsterdam visible on the back wall - this is one of the most flawless works of Pieter de Hooch, from his best period, when he painted warmly-lit interiors in a carefully arranged perspective. Far from being an imitator of Vermeer, this picture shows him as a forerunner in the depiction of quiet interior subjects. The figures, which are intentionally static as the result of a desire to locate them in geometrical space, have a story to tell. It is a study of human behaviour with moralising allusions to dissolute pleasures (the figures are none other than a courtesan, a procuress and suitors) and to the vanity of sensual pleasures such as drinking and smoking. The picture of *Christ and the Adulteress,* visible on the right, has the power of a moral and religious admonishment.

Gabriel METSU
1629-1667

464 The Amsterdam
Vegetable Market

c. 1660

Canvas. H 0.70 m; W 0.845 m

Collection of Louis XIV. INV 1460

Its subject - a genre scene set outside, rather than indoors - and relatively large size, is somewhat unusual in Metsu's work. Alongside a canal, a humble market is in full swing and the protagonists - notably the housewife in the centre and young man in red at her side - are more occupied with the exchange of gallantries than goods. The lively colours of costumes and vegetables contrast with the softness and poetic calm of the urban landscape, while the perfectly rendered still-life elements in the foreground display the artists' admirable pictorial command. Notice on the right the confrontation between dog and cockerel, at the foot of which lies a piece of paper, apparently dropped by chance, upon which the artist's signature figures.

Gerard DOU
1613-1675

465 The Dropsical Woman

1663

Wood. H 0.860 m; W 0.678 m

Gift of Betrand Clauzel, 1798. INV 1213

With his gift of this picture to the Directoire, for the "Museum", the future General, Bertrand

Clauzel became the first donor to the Louvre. He obtained the picture from Charles Emmanuel IV of Savoy, King of Sardinia, a gift of distinction since it had been one of the glories of the royal gallery at Turin. The visit to the doctor is a choice subject of Dutch genre pictures. Gerard Dou gives it a masterly interpretation, putting his technique to good use, having a skilful and precise stroke which gives the scene a smooth, enamelled appearance. The picture was once protected by two wings, upon which were painted in *trompe-l'œil* a silver ewer (alluding to feminine illness) in an arched niche (also in the Louvre).

Jacob van RUISDAEL
c. 1628/9-1682

466 The Ray of Sunlight

Canvas. H 0.83 m; W 0.99 m
Collection of Louis XVI. INV 1820

Using elements drawn from reality - a windmill, the ruins of Brederode castle near Harlem, the hills of Guelders and the banks of the Rhine - Jacob van Ruisdael composed a particularly grandiose imaginary view. The almost architectural cloudscape, underlined by the effects of sunlight, plays an important part in the dynamic construction of the whole. While the reference to Rembrandt landscapes is striking, the pale tonalities in grey-blue and green are at the antithesis of that master's warm and somber manner. Most critics believe the figures are by Philips Wouwerman, in a collaboration that was very common at that period.

Jan VERMEER
1632-1675

467 The Lacemaker

Canvas on wood. H 0.24 m; W 0.21 m
Acq. 1870. MI 1448

When this painting was acquired, Vermeer had only just been rediscovered by the critic Gustave Thoré, alias Bürger. Another hundred and thirteen years elapsed until, quite recently, another equally famous Vermeer, *The Astronomer*, entered the Louvre.

The small size, tight composition and pale neutral ground all help to concentrate the spectator's attention on to the lacemaker's action. The foreground (the tapestry and the red and white threads) is treated in a less precise manner, as if exaggeratedly large. This technique was much used by this artist, who played with optical effects like an artist-photographer.

Great Britain

The British school is, relatively-speaking, a recent one. It did not really attain definition and independence before the 18th century, which was the great period for portraiture. Hence British painting was a latecomer to the Louvre. With the love of things English in France around 1900, a sustained interest developed, in which collectors (Groult for example) and dealers played a decisive role. It was the great 18th century portrait painters that the Louvre first acquired: Lawrence, Romney, Raeburn, and Reynolds, with one of his most famous works, *Master Hare* **469**. But not until after the last war - the other peak for the British collection - did the first Gainsborough enter the Louvre, the portrait of *Lady Aston*, a fine example of his mature work. Tastes changed and the accent moved from portraits to landscape. Bonington and Constable, founders of Romantic landscape painting, were already present in the 19th century. The famous *View of Salisbury,* acquired in 1952, is the best of the Constables, developing from the Dutch tradition of panoramic landscape. The most glaring gap in the museum was filled in 1967 with a picture by Turner **470** in his final period, in which forms dissolve into a subtle interplay of patches of colour.

A new priority has emerged in recent years: narrative painting. The Louvre has added to its collections artists only just being rediscovered, like the great Fuseli, whose *Lady Macbeth* is an exploration of horror and the sublime that was beloved of Burke, at the same period as David's *Oath of the Horatii*; the meditative Wright of Derby, whose *Lake Nemi* is much more than a view of the Roman countryside; and the elegant Zoffany, adept at the well-known genre of the "conversation piece", capturing a social elite in the act of being sociable. All the same, lacking a single Hogarth or Blake, the Louvre still has a long way to go to make up for its indifference to painting across the Channel.

Thomas GAINSBOROUGH
1727-1788

468 Conversation in a Park

c. 1746-1747

Canvas. H 0.73 m; W 0.68 m

Gift of Pierre Bordeaux-Groult, 1952. RF 1952-16

This stiff couple are presumed to be the artist himself with his wife Margaret. Dating from the year of his marriage (1746), the work has a special value as a marital souvenir. The young Gainsborough, who was barely twenty when he moved to London, combined his two favorite genres in this work: landscape, ennobled by a folly, and portraiture, with all the finesse of an engraving by Gravelot, whose pupil he had been. The bravura of the execution adds to the charm of a genre which flourished in 18th England; the "conversation piece", an intimate society portrait of the genre format.

Sir Joshua REYNOLDS
1723-1792

469 Master Hare

1788-1789

Canvas. H 0.77 m; W 0.63 m

Painted for the model's aunt, Lady Jones.

Verbal bequest by Baron Alphonse de Rothschild,

gift of his heirs, 1905. RF 1580

At the end of a long, ambitious and didactic career, Reynolds succumbs in this work to an English love of the family, childhood and mild sensibility. Reproduced almost immediately in an engraving entitled *Infancy,* this portrait of Francis George Hare (1786-1842), at two years of age, was painted for the sitter's aunt. Loyal to his convictions, Reynolds took care to ennoble the painting with a gesture which has a religious connection with St. John the Baptist, and an autumnal landscape, the rich colouring of which is a homage to Titian.

Joseph Mallord William
TURNER
1775-1851

470 **Landscape with a River and a Bay in the Background**

c. 1845

Canvas. H 0.93 m; W 1.23 m

Acq. 1967. RF 1967-2

Of all the British artists to revive European
landscape painting, Turner went furthest, pushing
the dissolution of forms in light to the edge of
abstraction. This painting belongs to a group of
unfinished works composed around 1845, when
the elderly artist reprinted his *Liber Studiorum,* a
kind of sample book of landscapes. One plate of
this anthology, inspired by Claude Gellée, the
Confluence of the Severn and the Wye (1810),
supplied the basis for this composition, a flaming
'chimaera', in which Romanticism finds expression
in a free technique, close in its diaphanous effects
to the medium of watercolour.

France

Italy

Spain

Germany

Flanders

Holland

Great Britain

Graphic Arts

Introduction

The Department of Graphic Arts, which conserves
all works on paper, is probably the least known in
the Louvre because of the fragile nature of the
exhibits and their sensitivity to light, which
prevents permanent exhibition.

The acquisition, in 1671, of the collection of the
Cologne banker, Eberhardt Jabach, represented a
desire, on the part of Louis XIV, to establish
institutions designed to last with the funds he
provided. The *Cabinet des Dessins,* situated from
the very beginning in the Louvre, grew very
rapidly, with collections of drawings from the
studios of First Painters to the King acquired at
their death such as those of Le Brun in 1690,
Mignard in 1695, and Coypel in 1722. By 1730,
there were 8593 items. The acquisition policy was
less determined in the 18th century. After allowing
the Crozat collection to be dispersed, a large
purchase (1031 drawings) was made on the sale, in
1775, of works assembled by Mariette, the greatest
collector of his time.

The upheavals of the French Revolution had their
repercussions on the collection. In 1790, there were
10,999 exhibits in storage. The number was
doubled on the requisition of collections belonging
to *émigrés,* including the Comte d'Orsay and the
Comte de Saint-Morys. The arrival of the
collection seized at Modena in 1797 and the
ensemble of drawings by Carlo Maratta and his
studio was a great addition to the Italian schools,
which were the object of constant attention
throughout the 19th century. In 1806, Dominique
Vivant-Denon, director of the Imperial Museum,
acquired in Florence albums of drawings
assembled by the Florentine art lover Filippo
Baldinucci, while in 1856 Reiset brought into the
Cabinet des Dessins the *Codex Vallardi* made
up of over three-hundred drawings by Pisanello
and his circle.

The growth of the department during the second
half of the 19th century began with a series of
prestigious gifts; from His de la Salle in 1851 and
1878, the Gatteaux bequest in 1881, the gifts and

bequest from Léon Bonnat (1912, 1919, 1923) and from Étienne Moreau-Nélaton (1907 and 1927). The Doistau (1919) and David-Weill (1947) bequests contributed to the growth of the miniature collection which began with works from the royal collections and from the Académie. The engravings and drawings which the Baron Edmond de Rothschild assembled throughout his life, and which was offered to the Louvre by his children in 1936, constitued a great collection. There are over 40,000 engravings, nearly 3,000 drawings and 500 illustrated books.

To this must be added 16,000 copper plates engraved in *Chalcographie*. This word, of Greek origin, originally referred to the art of copper engraving for printing on paper; dating from the same time as printing, this technique enabled images to be reproduced. After the French Revolution, *Chalcographie* also referred to the place where original plates were inked and passed through the press by expert engravers; an engraving studio is still used by the Louvre and prints are sold by the *Réunion des Musées Nationaux*. The collections of copper engravings extend over five centuries, from the Renaissance to the present, covering a wide range of fields.

After 1797 (year V), when the first exhibition of around 400 engravings in the Galerie d'Apollon was held, temporary exhibitions have been regular features. These permit systematic study of the collections and give rise to publications. They are intended to make the exceptional resource of over 100,000 works of every school, from the 15th to the end of the 19th century, more widely known. Some exhibitions concentrate on a particular technique such as etching, watercolour or artists' cartoons (those large preparatory drawings executed on the same scale as the final work); the Louvre has over 200 cartoons. Other French collections (Rennes, Montpellier, Dijon, and Bayonne) and foreign collections (Haarlem, the Vienna Albertina, New York, Chicago, Darmstadt and London) have also been the subject of exhibitions. 130 pastels from the 17th and 18th century are displayed in rotation in the rooms devoted to French Painting. 19th century pastels are on view at the Musée d'Orsay. A consulting room and documentation room provide access on request, and under certain conditions, to art lovers, researchers, and students.

The *Grande Salle* of the *Cabinet des Dessins*
This room, where original drawings can be examined, is open to the public by appointment. Since 1970 its setting has been a staircase, designed for Napoleon III's principle guest appartments. The ceiling is by Cabanel. The bas-reliefs are by Guillaume and the statues in the niches are the work of Franceschi.

detail

France

471 Narbonne *Parement* (altar frontal)

Royal workshop (Paris), c. 1375

Black ink on silk. H 0.775 m; W 2.860 m

Found in Narbonne by the painter Jules Boilly in the early 19th century Acq. 1852. MI 1121

This monochrome work on white silk *(samit)* is the oldest altar decoration known and was used in a chapel at Lent. It would have been hung above and behind the altar. Its precise origins are not known. The praying figures are King Charles V (1364-1380) and Queen Jeanne de Bourbon; the figure K (Karolus) on the border is evidence of royal patronage. The skilful handling of monochrome, the compositional clarity, linear elegance, the use of contrasts in the modelling and the expressive force of the figures have prompted the suggestion that the Master of the *Parement,* in the tradition of Parisian illumination, painted some of the miniatures in the *Très Belles Heures de Notre-Dame* (Paris, National Library) by Jean de Berry, begun around 1380.

Nicolas POUSSIN
1590-1665

472 Venus at the Fountain

Verso of a letter written by the painter A Bouzonnet-Stella, addressed to N Poussin
and dated August 17, 1657.

Pen and brown ink, brown and grey wash.

H 0.255 m; W 0.232 m

Gift of His de la Salle, 1878. RF 762

This was drawn by the most celebrated French artist of the 17th century, working chiefly in

France **Graphic Arts**

Rome. The subject has poetic and literary sources
in Classical Antiquity. Leaning on a font, Venus is
shown doing her hair with her right arm raised
over her head, and as an alternative, lowered in
contemplation of herself with a mirror. At her
feet, cherubs are chasing a hare. A statue of Pan
in the background recalls pastoral life, love and
inebriation. The drawing is in a shaky hand due
to Poussin's illness in old age; in it he moves away
from the rigorous compositions of his maturity
and the solemn and static arrangements of his
religious and philosophical subjects.

Robert NANTEUIL *1623-1678*
Gilles ROUSSELET *1610-1686*

473 Allegorical Portrait of Colbert

1667

Burin and etching on copper H 0.810 m;
W 0.740 m

Louvre Chalcography. INV 2141

This copper plate, engraved in 1667, is still used to make prints in the Louvre Chalcography workshop. The portrait of Colbert is by Nanteuil. Around it, allegorical figures of *Piety* and *Fidelity,* and children recalling the Arts and Sciences, were engraved by Rousselet after drawings by Le Brun, to illustrate some of the minister's qualities. Colbert was quick to understand that engraving, the only means of diffusing images at that time, enabled Louis XIV's achievements to be more generally known and preserved for posterity. To that end, he assembled engravers at the Gobelins, under the direction of S Leclerc, to work for the *Cabinet du Roy,* and thus laid the foundations of the Louvre Chalcography workshop.

Edme BOUCHARDON
1698-1762

474 Standing Female Nude

c. 1750-1760
Red chalk. H 0.770 m; W 0.450 m
Gift of legacee of the artist, 1808.
INV 24446

This sculptor's drawing from a posed model is a preparation for one of the four figures decorating the equestrian statue of Louis XV, commissioned in 1748 by the Ville de Paris to celebrate the armistice of Aix-la-Chapelle, and destined for what is now the Place de la Concorde, which was then being devised. The Louvre possesses around forty studies for these figures which were draped

France **Graphic Arts**

when sculpted. The nudes drawings show the artist's efforts to obtain the perfect movement, along with his realism, sense of line and form, and his clear vision of overlapping structures, seen in the play of shadows over the supporting block.

Jean-Siméon CHARDIN
1699-1770

475 Self-Portrait at the Easel

Pastel on blue paper over canvas strecher.
H 0.407 m; W 0.325 m
Acq. 1966. RF 31770

Chardin depicts himself tracing and colouring his

portrait on blue paper over canvas - the same portrait we are seeing. He is holding the pastel used to render the skin tone of his face and hand. Pastel is a form of coloured crayon made up of powdered pigments and diluted mediums. Its tactile qualities were appreciated by 18th century portrait painters like La Tour and Perronneau. Chardin, who is known for his still-lifes and genre scenes, used it for the portraits he executed, toward the end of his life, of his wife and particularly of himself; this is probably the last of his self-portraits.

Eugène DELACROIX
1798-1863

476 Moroccan Notebook

1832

Album with cardboard covers covered in dark
green paper, containing 56 sketches in lead
pencil or brown pen and ink, often highlighted
with watercolour and accompanied
by manuscript notes. H. 10.5 cm; W. 9.8 cm.
Acq. 1983. RF 39050

Delacroix had this notebook with him when he landed at Tangiers in 1832, with a mission led by the Comte de Mornay and sent by the king, Louis-Philippe, to the sultan of Morocco, Moulay Abd-er-Rahman. Four of the seven notebooks that he filled during this visit to North Africa, which lasted six months, have been preserved, and three are in the Louvre. Two contain a very personal mix of sketches and notes forming the unique "journal" of a travelling painter, anxious to preserve every one of his many discoveries. Among the considerable fund of albums in the *Cabinet des Dessins*, Delacroix's "Moroccan" notebooks are some of the most precious, lively expressions of an artist's immediate responses, and the memory of this period was to haunt him for the rest of his life.

France **Graphic Arts**

Jean-Auguste-Dominique
INGRES
1780-1867

477 Studies of Female Nudes

Charcoal and black crayon. H 0.620 m; W 0.450 m

Gift of the *Société des Amis du Louvre*

and M David-Weill, 1929. FR 12292

This collection of studies of unusual format is
related to the *Turkish Bath* 398. For Ingres,
drawing lay at the foundation of the work of the

artist, enabling preliminary studies to be made from life, and here we see his quest for a credible gesture for the woman kneeling to do her companion's hair. With the "discovered truth", (i.e. the gesture considered most appropriate to the figure and its role in the composition), the artist took up his pencil again and, playing with contours and modelling, sought a stylized image resulting from study of the model.

Jean-François MILLET
1814-1875

478 Fisherman

Black crayon

H 0.328 m; W 0.492 m

Gift of Isaac de Camondo, 1911

RF 4104

This scene of lobster fishing is set in the Cotentin, the area of Normandy where Millet was born. The Louvre has a fine collection of his drawings. The artist's monumental style, based on light effects achieved by black crayon, his favorite medium (one thinks of Seurat), attains an almost epic realism here. This work has been variously dated to his maturity (1857-1860) and to old age, around 1870-1871. His noble vision does not detract from the subversive strength of the contents; this night fishing scene is also the kind of direct depiction of reality (the fishermen are dropping their lobster pots) which made Millet a *social* painter.

Italy

Antonio POLLAIUOLO
1431/2-1498
479 Nude Warriors in Combat

c. 1470-1475
Burin. H 0.40 m; W 0.60 m

Collection Edmond de Rothschild, bequeathed 1935

INV 6813 LR

One of the greatest plates engraved during the
15th century, both for its size and breadth of
composition, the *Nude Warriors in Combat* is the
oldest Italian engraving bearing the artist's full
name: "OPUS, ANTONII, POLLAIOLI, FLORENTINI".
The subject of the frieze-like scene, which art
historians disagree on, is doubtless simply a pretext
for depicting nudes in action, possibly gladiators,
over a decorative blackcloth of olive trees, millet
and vines. Pollaiuolo also worked in enamel inlay;
here he adopts zigzag lines, long parallel cuts and
crosshatching to convey something of the style of
pen drawings of his time.

Andrea MANTEGNA
1431-1506

100 The Judgement of Solomon

c. 1490-1500
Tempera on canvas. H 0.465 m; W 0.370 m
Collection of the Dukes of Modena. Entered the
Louvre in 1797. INV 5608

Mantegna was official painter to the court of
Mantua as well as a sculptor and engraver, and
had a great influence on the art of northern Italy.
This monochrome painting, imitating a grey stone
bas-relief on violet-tinged marble, dates from
around 1490-1500. It exemplifies Mantegna's taste
for different materials, his passion for recreating
Antiquity and his rigorous use of perspective.
Incisive forms are symptomatic of the important
contribution of sculpture to his art. The traditional
attribution of this *grisaille* to Mantegna has been
contested. Many believe it is a workshop
production after an original drawing by the artist.

Antonio Allegri, known as
CORREGGIO
1489(?)-1534

481 Allegory of Vices

c. 1529-1530
Tempera on canvas. H 1.42 m; W 0.85 m
Collection of the French Crown. INV 5927

Although there is no record of the
commission of this allegory or the
Allegory of Virtues, both pictures
hung in the Studiolo of Isabella
d'Este at the Palazzo Ducale in
Mantua. The subject is disputed. It
may depict a mythological story
(Apollo and Marsyas) or an allegory
of Pleasures, Vices or Evil. The
technique of tempera which, by 1530,
had become something of an
anachronism, was probably chosen to harmonise

Italy **Graphic Arts**

with other works in the room by older artists (Mantegna, Costa and Perugino). The grouping of figures is an interpretation of the *Laocoon,* a Hellenistic sculpture found in Rome in 1506, in the sculptural manner of Giulio Romano, the great Mantuan painter of the period. But the softened line and flowing style, the delicate colouring, the fluid highlights and shadows are Correggio's own contribution to the Italian Renaissance.

Francesco PRIMATICCIO
1504-1570

482 The Antipodes

Pen and brown ink, brown wash, white
highlights. Sketch in black chalk
on buff paper. Squared in black chalk.
H 0.357 m; W 0.458 m
Collection Saint-Morys. Seized during
French Revolution. INV 8517

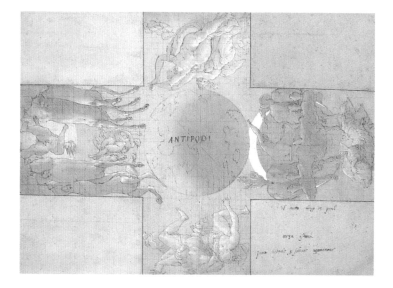

This was a preparatory drawing for a painting in the third compartment of the vault in the Galerie d'Ulysse at the Château de Fontainebleau, depicting the globe with Diana and Apollo and Juno descending from heaven in chariots to save Agamemnon. Commissioned by François I around 1541-1547, the decoration continued under succeeding reigns but was entirely destroyed between 1738-1739. It was one of the most important of the ensembles by Italian artists called to Fontainebleau by François I. The drawing has all the characteristics of this early "School of Fontainebleau": an original sense of space, exaggerated foreshortening, a taste for tapered lines which gives a floating rhythm to the work and a grace, full of artful devices. In its quest for the sublime by means of artifice, this art was well suited to evoking the extraordinary and transcendant aspects of fables, epics and myths.

Annibale CARRACCI
1560-1609

483 Polyphemus

Below right, study for right hand of Polyphemus. Pierre noire, touched with white, blue grey paper. H 0.521 m; W 0.385 m
Collection of the French Crown. *Cabinet du Roi.*
INV 7319

This sketch depicts the cyclops, Polyphemus, who was in love with Galatea, a marine goddess taken with Acis, and who was rejected by her. The alterations visible on the head of the giant show how the painter hesitated over the representation of a face with only one eye. This masterly study is a preparation for the fresco showing *Polyphemus and Galatea* at the Farnese gallery in Rome. Begun in 1597, this was the most ambitious undertaking of Annibale Carrachi's career, aided by his brother Agostino. It was very important for the development of decorative painting in the 17th century. The majority of preparatory drawings for the Farnese cycle, issuing directly from Annibale Caracci's studio, are conserved in the *Cabinet des Dessins*.

Andrea APPIANI
1754-1817

484 The Apotheosis of Napoleon

Black chalk white highlights

H 2.73 m; W 4.80 m

Acq. from artist's family, 1861. MI 754

The greatest work by Appiani, master of Lombardian Neoclassicism, was the decoration of the Milan royal palace in 1808, devoted to the greatness of the Empire. This cartoon is a preparation for the monumental fresco which decorated the vault of the Throne room. The required note of flattery is couched in allegorical abstractions, a language revived by the imitation of antiquity according to Winckelmann. Four Victories hold up the throne where the Emperor sits in majesty, amid the diverse attributes of immortality. Escaping the bombing of 1943 which destroyed its setting, the fresco is now housed in the Villa Carlotta at Tremezzo. The Louvre has a unique collection of over 200 examples of artists' cartoons.

Spain

Francisco José de
GOYA Y LUCIENTES
1746-1828

485 Es el Dia de su Santo

Brush and grey wash

H 0.235 m; W 0.146 m

Cosson bequest, 1926. RF 6912

In 1796, Goya was in Sanlúcar in Andalusia, with
the Duchess of Alba, before going on to Cadiz.

Here, he made many wash drawings in a small notebook, beginning with sketches of amorous subjects. Then come captions in another register: the ferocious burden of a visionary, masked figures and sorcerers, popular customs, depicted with a bitter irony. To hang someone on their saint's day is a well known idiomatic expression in Spain, probably deriving from rough familiar customs such as blanket tossing. The corrosive treatment of the scene subverts the simple fun - from whence comes its clear status as a *caricature:* Goya's vision borders on cruelty.

Germany

Albrecht DÜRER
1471-1528

486 Livonian Lady

1521

Pen, sepia ink and watercolour.
H 0.282 m; W 0.188 m
Collection Edmond de Rothschild,
bequeathed 1935. INV 19 DR

The series of three drawings showing women of Livonia is one of the jewels of the Edmond de Rothschild Collection. These watercolours served as models for the wood engravings by Jost Amman, illustrating the work entitled *Habitus praecipuorum populorum* edited by Hans Weigel at

Nuremberg in 1577. It is possible that the famous Nuremberg artist saw these Livonian costumes at Antwerp (a flourishing cosmopolitain town at that time), during his trip to the Netherlands (1520-1521). This richly dressed woman is a good illustration of Dürer's ethnographical interest, noting down carefully every odd or interesting sight he saw in his *Journal*.

Hans BALDUNG GRIEN
1484/5-1545

487 The Witches

1510

Monochrome print, two plates (grey and black).

H 0.378 m; W 0.258 m

Collection Edmond de Rothschild,

1 .. acquired 1935. INV 784 LR

This pupil of Dürer was interested in the camaieu printing technique, a wood engraving which imitated highlighted drawings on tinted paper. It was in Strasbourg, between 1509 and 1512, that Baldung was particularly preoccupied with the theme of witches and death. This nocturnal sabbath is one of his most well-known works and perhaps his first as an independent master at Strasbourg. The figures are shown on a large scale, and the composition is precise, with a geometric arrangement in a pyramidal group with diagonals fanning out from the centre and a system of hatching to create light effects.

Germany **Graphic Arts**

488 The Apocalypse of St. John

Netherlands, c. 1440

2nd edition. Wood engraving. H 0.262 m;

W 0.198 m

Collection Edmond de Rothschild,

bequeathed 1935. INV L 51 LR

The left-hand folio of the book of wood engravings, *The Apocalypse* of St. John (which predicts the fall of Rome and the New Jerusalem, representing the Kingdom of God), illustrates the *Opening of the Third and Fourth Seal*. The third horseman, Famine, riding a black horse carrying a scale; the fourth, emerging from the mouth of hell, is labelled Death or more precisely the Plague, astride a pale horse with a bowl from which flames emerge. The error in the colouring of the horses and inscriptions was corrected after the first three editions. This incunabular takes its inspiration from French and Anglo-Norman manuscripts as well as from the tapestry of the *Apocalypse* at Angers, made in the last quarter of the 14th century.

Flanders

Peter-Paul RUBENS
1577-1640

489 Young Woman Kneeling

c. 1630-1633

Black chalk, red chalk, white highlights.
H 0.508 m; W 0.458 m
Collection of Saint-Morys. Seized during
French Revolution. **INV 20194**

This young woman with her head on her hand reappears on the left of the *Garden of Love* in the Prado, Madrid. Generally dated to around 1630-1633, the *Garden of Love* depicts an elegant company preoccupied with gallantries and music. Rubens has abandoned the gods and heroes, which dominate his work between 1620 and 1628, in favour of the company of revellers. The skilfully-drawn sumptuous costume highlights the young woman's freshness. Some historians have identified this model as Hélène Fourment, whom Rubens married in 1630.

Holland

Harmensz REMBRANDT VAN RIJN
1606-1669

490 Two Studies of a Bird of
Paradise

Pen and sepia ink and wash, white highlights.
H 0.181 m; W 0.155 m
Gift of L Bonnat, 1919. INV RF 4687

Rembrandt's drawings reveal a vision which
combines a profound religious understanding with
an unprejudiced understanding of humanity.
Sometimes he concentrated on landscapes in his
native land, or the animals he could see in
Amsterdam. He was most interested in exotic
breeds which were a stimulus to his imagination.
Coming from New Guinea and Australia, these
birds of Paradise were appreciated for their
elegance and the colour of their plumage. One of
them was stuffed and appears in an inventory of
his belongings drawn up during his bankruptcy in
1656. This drawing is somewhat earlier, however,
and is generally thought to be dated between 1635
and 1640.

Isaac OLIVER
c. 1565(?)-1617

491 Robert Devereux, Second Earl
of Essex

c. 1605
Miniature in gouache on vellum. Oval.

H 5 cm; W 4 cm

Gift of C Sauvageot, 1856. INV Sauv 1068

Son of a Huguenot goldsmith from Rouen, Isaac
Oliver studied in London under Nicholas Hilliard,
the well-known Elizabethan miniaturist. Of an
extreme delicacy, the portrait stands out against a
blue background decorated with a Latin
inscription in gold "VAE SOLI" ("Cursed be the
lone man"). He wears the raised collar fashionable
during the early reign of James I, so this must be a
posthumous work. Robert Devereux was the eldest
son of Walter Devereux, First Earl of Essex, and
became a favourite of Queen Elizabeth from 1587.
Conspiring against her, he was executed in the
Tower of London in 1601.

Index of artists

ABAQUESNE Masséot **248**

AGOSTINO DI DUCCIO **346**

ALLEGRI Antonio,
known as CORREGGIO **420, 481**

ANDREA DEL SARTO **419**

ANGUIER François **317**

ANGUIER Michel p. 16

ANTONELLO DA MESSINA **409**

APPIANI Andrea **484**

ARNOULD or REGNAUD Jean **320**

AUGUSTE Robert-Joseph **279**

BALDUNG GRIEN Hans **487**

BALZAC Edme-Pierre **275**

BAPST Evrard **287**

BARROCCI Federico **425**

BARTOLINI Lorenzo p. 22

BARYE Antoine-Louis **340**

BAUGIN Lubin **367**

BELLANGÉ Hippolyte p. 23

BELLANO Bartolomeo **241**

BELLECHOSE Henri **360**

BERNINI Gian Lorenzo **350**

BIARD François p. 24

BIARD Pierre **314**

BIENNAIS Martin-Guillaume **285**

BONTEMPS Pierre **310**

BORDONI Francesco **315**

BOSIO François-Joseph **336**

BOSSCHAERT THE ELDER,
Ambrosius **459**

BOTTICELLI, Alessandro
Filipepi, known as **411**

BOUCHARDON Edme **325, 474**

BOUCHER François **277, 383**

BOULLE André-Charles **263**

BOULOGNE Jean **245**

BOULOGNE Valentin de **366**

BRAQUE Georges p. 29

BRUEGEL THE ELDER Pieter I **450**

BUONARROTI Michelangiolo,
known as MICHELANGELO **347**

CAFFIERI Jean-Jacques **331**

CALIARI Paolo,
known as VERONESE **423**

CANOVA Antonio **351**

CARAVAGGIO, Michelangelo
MERISI, known as **427**

CARPACCIO Vittore **417**

CARPEAUX Jean-Baptiste p. 26

CARRACCI Annibale **426, 483**

CELLINI Benvenuto **348**

CHAMPAIGNE Philippe de **375**

CHARDIN Jean-Siméon **382, 475**

CHASSERIAU Théodore **397**

CHAUDET Antoine-Denis **335**

CHINARD Joseph **334**

CIMABUE, Cenni di Pepo,
known as **400**

CLODION, Claude Michel,
known as **330**

CLOUET François **365**

COLOMBE Michel **305**

COROT Camille **399**

CORREGGIO, Antonio
ALLEGRI, known as **420, 481**

COUSINET Henri-Nicolas **267**

COUSTOU Guillaume I **324**

COYPEL Noël p. 19

COYSEVOX Antoine **321, 322**

CRANACH THE ELDER
Lucas **441**

CRESSENT Charles **269**

DAVID Louis **387, 391**

DAVID D'ANGERS Pierre-Jean **341**

DELACROIX Eugène
p. **25, 394, 395, 476**

DELLA FRANCESCA Piero **406**

DELLA QUERCIA Jacopo **343**

DEL SARTO, Andrea
d'Agnolo di Francesco **419**

DE NITTIS Giuseppe
p. 27

DE VRIES Adriaan **358**

DONATELLO, Donato di
Niccolo Bardi, known as **344**

DOU Gérard **465**

DUBAN Félix p. 25

DUBOIS Jacques **271**

DUCCIO Agostino
d'Antonio di **346**

DÜRER Albrecht **440, 486**

DUSEIGNEUR Jehan **339**

ERHART Gregor **354**

EVRARD D'ORLÉANS **299**

FALCONET Étienne-Maurice **327**

FLEGEL Georg **443**

FLORIS Frans **449**

FONTAINE Pierre p. 22, 23, 24

FOUQUET Jean **238, 361**

FRA ANGELICO,
Guido di Pietro, known as **403**

FRAGONARD Jean-Honoré **385**

FRAGONARD
Alexandre Evariste p. 21

FRANCQUEVILLE Pierre **315**

FRIEDRICH Caspar David **444**

FROMENT-MEURICE
François-Désiré **290**

GAINSBOROUGH Thomas **468**

GELLÉE Claude,
known as LE LORRAIN **372**

GERICAULT Théodore **393**

GERMAIN François-Thomas **273, 274**

GHIRLANDAIO, Domenico
di Tomaso Bigordi,
known as **413**

GIOTTO di Bondone **401**

GIRARDON François **319**

GIRODET DE ROUSSY-TRIOSON
Anne-Louis **392**

GOSSAERT Jan,
known as MABUSE **448**

GOUJON Jean p. 14, 15, **308**

GOVAERS or GOUERS
Daniel **266**

GOYA Y LUCIENTES
Francisco José de **437, 485**

GRECO, Domenicos
Theotocopoulos,
known as EL **433**

GREUZE Jean-Baptiste **386**

GROS Antoine-Jean **389**

GUARDI Francesco **430**

GUERIN Gilles p. 17

HALS Frans **460**

HEIM François p. 23

HEY Jean, known as
THE MASTER OF
MOULINS **363**

HOLBEIN Hans **442**

HOOCH Pieter de **463**

HOUDON Jean-Antoine **328, 332**

HUGUET Jaime **432**

INGRES, Jean-Auguste-
Dominique **396, 398, 477**

JACOB Georges **280, 283**

JACOB-DESMALTER
François-Honoré-Georges **284**

JORDAENS Jacob **457**

JULIEN Pierre **329**

LARGILLIERRE Nicolas de **378**

LA TOUR Georges de **369**

LE BRUN Charles p. 18, **376**

LELEU Jean-François **278**

LE LORRAIN, Claude
GELLÉE, known as **372**

LEMERCIER Jacques p. 16

LEMOYNE François **381**

LE NAIN Louis
(or Antoine?) **370**

LEONARDO DA VINCI **412, 414, 416**

LESCOT Pierre p. 14

LE SUEUR Eustache **373**

LE VAU Louis p. 18

LIMOUSIN Léonard **246, 247**

MABUSE Jan
GOSSAERT, known as **448**

MASTER OF THE HOLY
FAMILY **438**

MASTER OF MOULINS,
JEAN HEY, known as THE **363**

MASTER OF
SAINT-BARTHOLOMEW **439**

MASTER OF
SAINT-GERMAIN-DES-PRÉS **13**

MANTEGNA Andrea **408, 480**

MARTINI Simone **402**

MARTORELL Bernardo **431**

MENIERES Paul-Nicolas **287**

MERISI Michelangelo,
CARAVAGGIO known as **427**

MESSINA Antonello da **409**

METEZEAU Louis p. 15

METSU Gabriel **464**

METSYS Quentin **447**

MICHELANGELO, Michelangiolo
BUONARROTI, known as **347**

MILLET Jean-François **478**

MINO DA FIESOLE **345**

MISERONI Ottavio **255**

MURILLO Bartolomé Esteban **436**

NANTEUIL Robert **473**

NICOLA DA URBINO **243**

OLIVER Isaac **491**

OUIZILLE Charles **282**

PAJOU Augustin **333**

PALISSY Bernard **249**

PANNINI Giovanni Paolo **429**

PEI Ieoh Ming p. 30

PERCIER Charles p. 22, 23

PERRAULT Claude p. 18

PERRONNEAU Jean-Baptiste **384**

PIERINO DA VINCI **349**

PIERO DELLA FRANCESCA **406**

PIGALLE Jean-Baptiste **326**

PILON Germain **311, 313**

PISANELLO, Antonio
Puccio, known as **404**

POLLAIUOLO Antonio **479**

POUSSIN Nicolas **371, 374, 472**

PRADIER James **337**

PRIEUR Barthélémy **254, 312**

PRIMATICCIO Francesco **482**

PRUD'HON Pierre-Paul **390**

PUGET Pierre **318**

QUARTON Enguerrand **362**

RAPHAEL, Raffaello
Santi, known as **415, 418**

REMBRANDT
Harmensz van Rijn **461, 462, 490**

RENI Guido **428**

REYMOND Pierre **250**

REYNOLDS Joshua **469**

RIBERA Jusepe de **435**

RICCIO, Andrea Briosco,
known as **242**

RIEMENSCHNEIDER Tilman **363**

RIGAUD Hyacinthe **377**

ROBERT Hubert p. 20, 21 **388**

ROBUSTI Jacopo,
known as TINTORETTO **424**

ROMAIN Jules (after) **261**

ROMANNELLI
Giovanni Francesco p. 16

ROSSO FIORENTINO, Giovanni
Battista di Jacopo, known as **422**

ROUSSELET Gilles **473**

RUBENS
Peter Paul **452, 455, 456, 489**

RUDE François **338**

RUISDAEL Jacob van **466**

SARAZIN Jacques p. 16, **316**

SASSETTA, Stefano di
Giovanni, known as **405**

SCHRO Dietrich **355**

SIMART Pierre Charles p. 25

THIERRY Jean **323**

TINTORETTO, Jacopo ROBUSTI **424**

TISSIER Ange p. 26

TITIAN, Tiziano
VECELLIO, known as **421**

TURA Cosme (Cosimo) **410**

TURNER
Joseph Mallord William **470**

UCCELLO, Paolo di Dono,
known as **407**

VALENTIN DE BOULOGNE **366**

VAN DYCK Antoon
(Sir Anthony) **453, 454**

VAN EYCK Jan **445**

VAN DER WEYDEN Roger **446**

VAN HAARLEM Cornelis **451**

VAN ORLEY Bernard (after) **253**

VECELLIO Tiziano,
known as TITIAN **421**

VERMEER Jan **467**

VERONESE, Paolo
CALIARI, known as **423**

VINCI Leonardo da **412, 414, 416**

VINCI Pierino da **349**

VOUET Simon **257, 368**

WATTEAU Jean-Antoine **379, 380**

WEISWEILER Adam **281**

WTEWAEL Joachim **458**

ZURBARAN Francisco de **434**

Liste of authors

Daniel Alcouffe
Conservateur général, chargé du
département des Objets d'Art
pp. 212-213, 246-247, 252,
258, 268,
notes 251, 252, 255, 258, 259, 263-267,
269, 271, 273-275, 278-283

Pierre Amiet
Inspecteur général honoraire des
musées
pp. 34-67

François Baratte
Professeur à l'Université de
Paris-IV Sorbonne
pp. 183-209

Sophie Baratte
Conservateur au département des
Objets d'Art
notes 246, 247, 250

Lizzie Boubli
Conservateur au département des
Arts Graphiques
notes 471, 480

Geneviève Bresc-Bautier
Conservateur au département des
Sculptures
pp. 282-347

Annie Caubet
Conservateur général, chargé du
département des Antiquités
Orientales
pp. 67-77

Maguy Charritat
Documentaliste au département
des Antiquités Orientales
pp. 78-85

Dominique Cordellier
Conservateur au département des
Arts Graphiques
notes 481, 482

Anne Dion
Conservateur au département des
Objets d'Art
pp. 273, 276, 278
notes 284, 285, 287, 290

Jannic Durand
Conservateur au département des
Objets d'Art
pp. 213-216
notes 215-217, 222, 225-229, 237, 238

Pierre Ennes
Conservateur au département des
Objets d'Art
notes 239, 240, 243, 248, 249, 268,
270, 272, 276, 286, 288, 289

Jacques Foucart
Conservateur général au
département des Peintures
pp. 421-423
notes 449, 452-457

Elisabeth Foucart-Walter
Conservateur en chef au
département des Peintures
pp. 414-421
notes 445-448, 450, 451, 458-467

Danielle Gaborit-Chopin
Conservateur général au
département des Objets d'Art
pp. 218-219, 227
notes 214, 218-221, 223, 224, 230-236

Pierrette Jean-Richard
Documentaliste à la collection
Edmond de Rothschild
notes 479, 486-488, 491

Michel Laclotte
Président-Directeur de
l'Etablissement public du
Musée du Louvre
pp. 6-7

476

Amaury Lefébure
Conservateur en chef au
département des Objets d'Art
pp. 234-240
notes 241, 242, 244, 245, 253, 254,
256, 257, 260-262, 277

Jean-François Méjanes
Conservateur en chef au
département des Arts Graphiques
notes 472-475, 477

Régis Michel
Conservateur au département des
Arts Graphiques
notes 478, 484, 485

Alain Pasquier
Conservateur général, chargé du
département des Antiquités
Grecques, Etrusques et Romaines
pp. 146-183

Geneviève Pierrat
Conservateur au département des
Antiquités Egyptiennes
pp. 88-138

Marie-Hélène Rutschowscaya
Conservateur en chef au
département des Antiquités
Egyptiennes
pp. 139-143

Marie-Catherine Sahut
Conservateur en chef au
département des Peintures
pp. 350-414, 443-445

Arlette Sérullaz
Conservateur général au
département des Arts Graphiques
notes 476

Emmanuel Starcky
Conservateur du musée des
Beaux-Arts de Dijon
notes 489, 490

Hélène Toussaint
Chargée de mission à
l'Etablissement Public du Grand
Louvre
pp. 11-31

Françoise Viatte
Conservateur général, chargé du
département des Arts Graphiques
pp. 448-450
notes 483

The introductory pages
to each department are details
of the following works:

Goudea, prince of Lagash 11

Mastaba of Akhetep 83

Female head 141

Virgin and Child commissioned by Jeanne d'Evreux 233

Slave 315
by Francqueville and Bordoni

Portrait of Madame de Sorquainville 384
by Perroneau

Virgin and Child INV 2590
by a Venetian artist (Pisanello ?)
working in the mannerof
Gentile da Fabriano

Photographic crédits: Réunion des musées nationaux
(D. Arnaudet, M. Bellot, G. Blot, M. Chuzeville,
M. Coursaget, C. Jean, C. Rose, J. Schormans)
except for the following photos:
p. 31: © EPGL - Architecte I.M. Pei - RMN
n° 348: P. Willi

This book was printed by Mame Imprimeurs,
Tours (France) in August 1994

Premier dépôt légal : mars 1991
ISBN : 2-7118-2489-6 première édition, 1991
Dépôt légal : août 1994
ISBN : 2-7118-3009-8, 1993
GG 20 3009